What Blest
Genius?

What Blest *Genius?*

THE JUBILEE THAT MADE *SHAKESPEARE*

Andrew McConnell Stott

W. W. NORTON & COMPANY
Independent Publishers Since 1923
New York | London

For information about permission to reproduce selections from this book, write to
Permissions, W. W. Norton & Company, Inc., 500 Fifth Avenue, New York, NY 10110

For information about special discounts for bulk purchases, please contact
W. W. Norton Special Sales at specialsales@wwnorton.com or 800-233-4830

Manufacturing by Lake Book Manufacturing
Book design by JAM Design
Production manager: Beth Steidle

Library of Congress Cataloging-in-Publication Data

Names: Stott, Andrew McConnell, 1969– author.
Title: What blest genius? : the jubilee that made Shakespeare / Andrew McConnell Stott.
Description: First edition. | New York : W.W. Norton & Company, [2019] |
Includes bibliographical references and index.
Identifiers: LCCN 2018051189 | ISBN 9780393248654 (hardcover)
Subjects: LCSH: Shakespeare, William, 1564–1616—Anniversaries, etc. |
Garrick, David, 1717–1779.
Classification: LCC PR2923 .S76 2019 | DDC 822.3/3—dc23
LC record available at https://lccn.loc.gov/2018051189

W. W. Norton & Company, Inc., 500 Fifth Avenue, New York, N.Y. 10110
www.wwnorton.com

W. W. Norton & Company Ltd., 15 Carlisle Street, London W1D 3BS

1 2 3 4 5 6 7 8 9 0

FOR MUM AND DAD

Since 1824, the Warwickshire town of Stratford-upon-Avon has held a birthday celebration in honor of William Shakespeare, its most famous son. Music plays, banners are unfurled, and town criers from surrounding communities lead the celebrants in three hearty cheers as they parade through quaint and garlanded streets. In 2016, to mark the four hundredth anniversary of Shakespeare's death, the celebration doubled also as a funerary parade, as by custom, Shakespeare is said to have been born and died on the same date—April 23—which (coincidentally or otherwise) also happens to be St. George's Day, the national day of England. The 2016 celebration acknowledged this duality by beginning in funerary mode as hundreds of respectful devotees, including celebrities, schoolchildren, and dignitaries from around the world, paraded mournfully until the halfway point, when the mood was transformed by the arrival of a New Orleans jazz band who led them joyfully to the poet's graveside at Holy Trinity Church for the laying of wreaths.

The night before the parade, Holy Trinity was the site for a performance that it had first hosted 247 years earlier and never again since, a long poem in praise of Shakespeare set to musical accompaniment that had originally been delivered by the actor and theatre manager David Garrick. The "Dedication Ode," as it was known, was the centerpiece of the world's first literary festival, the Shakespeare Jubilee of 1769, and the subject of this book. Re-creating the ode was an especially fitting way to mark a milestone anniversary, as it provided Stratford with an opportunity to acknowledge the historical debt it owed to Garrick not only for the role he played in making the town a site of tourism and literary pilgrimage but in cementing forever its civic pride by ensuring Shakespeare's immortal fame.

AIR

I

Thou soft-flowing Avon, *by thy silver stream,*
Of things more than mortal, sweet Shakespear *would dream,*
The fairies by moonlight dance round his green bed,
For hallow'd the turf is which pillow'd his head.

II

The love-stricken maiden, the soft-sighing swain,
Here rove without danger, and sigh without pain,
The sweet bud of beauty, no blight shall here dread,
For hallow'd the turf is which pillow'd his head.

III

Here youth shall be fam'd, for their love, and their truth,
And chearful old age, feel the spirit of youth;
For the raptures of fancy here poets shall tread,
For hallow'd the turf is that pillow'd his head.

IV

Flow on, silver Avon, *in song ever flow,*
Be the swans on thy bosom still whiter than snow,
Ever full be thy stream, like his fame may it spread,
And the turf ever hallow'd which pillow'd his head.

Contents

Prologue

King George III was not mad about Shakespeare. "Was there ever such stuff as the great part of Shakespeare?" he complained to the novelist Frances Burney, listing all the characters and plays he objected to. "Only it's *Shakespeare*, and nobody dare abuse him . . . one should be stoned for saying so!"

Why would the king, a monarch with dominions spanning five continents, need to hide his opinion of a playwright? Yet at the time of this royal confession in 1785, Shakespeare had attained near godlike status, and harboring an opposing view ran the risk of seeming lunatic. Such veneration was still relatively new, the result of a period of intense cultural and artistic focus that had transformed Shakespeare from one writer among many to the "Blest Genius of the Isle." While this transformation occurred over several decades, one event stands out as the moment at which his ascension into national icon and literary deity was finally realized, the Shakespeare Jubilee of 1769.

Following Shakespeare's death in 1616, after two decades working in London as an actor, manager, shareholder, and playwright of the King's Men, his plays fell quickly from the repertoire. Were it not for the outbreak of the Civil War in 1642, they may never have survived at all. The war brought public entertainments to a halt, and with them a rich theatrical tradition that had been evolving since the Middle Ages. When the theatres reopened with the restoration of the monarchy in 1660, the new king, Charles II, gave the job of reviving the theatre to two of his loyal courtiers, Thomas Killigrew and Sir William D'Avenant, presenting each man with a royal patent to open a playhouse. With no new plays and few experienced actors, the task was a challenging one. Killigrew had the advantage, as thanks to a close friendship with the king he was allowed to style his troupe "the King's Company," and thus claim a direct lineage from Shakespeare's King's Men, along with the rights to perform its theatrical properties. While this included Shakespeare's work, the real prize was the enormously popular comedies of Shakespeare's contemporary Ben Jonson, as well as the tragicomedies of Francis Beaumont and John Fletcher, Jacobean writing partners still held in high esteem. By contrast, D'Avenant, a pug-faced poet with a wig as thick as a privet hedge, was granted the rights to only two plays from the old repertoire. After much grousing, he petitioned the Lord Chamberlain with a "proposition of reformeing some of the most ancient Playes," presenting him with a list that included "Tempest, Measures, for Measures, Much a doe about nothing, Rome and Juliet, Twelfe night, The Life of Kinge Henry the Eyght . . . Kinge Lear, the Tragedy of Mackbeth, [and] the Tragedy of Hamlet prince of Denmarke."

D'Avenant got what he asked for, but only on condition that he make the plays "fitt"—that is, adapt them for a culture that had essentially moved on. As Shakespeare's plays had first debuted when D'Avenant's audience's grandparents were children, it was clear that he would need to revise heavily. And this is what he did, changing endings and updating themes to suit the newness of the age, adding music and spectacle to exploit the technologies available in the new theatres, and introducing new characters and subplots, especially ones that emphasized another innovation—female actors in female roles. D'Avenant even conflated two plays to make one, all the while making sure to plane the knots and tubercles from Shakespeare's original language that sounded archaic and tortuous to the Restoration ear. The result was a resounding success, as epitomized by his 1664 production of *Macbeth*, which featured flying witches, songs, dances, and a happy ending accompanied by a semi-operatic score. This *Macbeth* was not a Shakespeare play so much as a Shakespeare-inspired entertainment, one that had the contradictory effect of elevating Shakespeare within the culture even as its popularity was based on how far it had moved away.

The thought would not have crossed D'Avenant's mind that Shakespeare's text was sacrosanct, an inviolate canon that couldn't be touched. It was instead a wellspring of concepts, characters, and situations to be plundered at will. This was the paradox that fueled Shakespeare's initial ascent to cultural icon: the more that theatre audiences came to know him through versions that had been altered, adapted, and heavily revised, the more his capital grew. By the advent of the eighteenth century, this was buoyed by the appearance of many cheap editions of his works, permitting a more private and contemplative relationship with the plays to emerge. More often than not, these came prefaced with a biographical sketch written by the poet Nicholas Rowe for his 1709 edition of the works and reprinted in almost every edition of Shakespeare for the next hundred years.

As is often noted, the verifiable facts of Shakespeare's life can be written on a postcard while still leaving room for a greeting: he was baptized, he married, he owned some property and wrote some plays. Into this void, Rowe threw unverified fragments and second-hand anecdotes to portray an Englishman of wit, sincerity, compassion, and good fellowship, "Sweet Willy," "the Bard of Avon," a raw talent tutored by nature and unhindered by the artificial prescripts of formal literary culture. This was the hero championed by groups like the Shakespeare Ladies Club, formed in the 1730s to oppose the influence of French and Italian dramatic models on the British stage, promoting instead an English drama that they felt represented "Decency and good Manners." By the 1740s, Shakespeare's status was such that a marble statue was erected to him in Westminster Abbey's Poets' Corner. Despite being praised by the *London Evening Post* for its presentation of the poet in "the Dress of his Time . . . natural, free and easy," it was a highly Georgian vision of the past, not so much a likeness as the apparition of genius within English literature's holiest spot.

Even as Shakespeare's reputation grew, there was some way left to go before he would reach his current status as the world's most famous writer. For that, we can thank the actor, dramatist, and theatre manager David Garrick, who, from his debut in 1741 to his retirement from the stage in 1776, was the most famous man in Britain after the king, not to mention a cultural broker so influential that the poet William Whitehead wrote of him that "a nation's taste depends on you / Perhaps a nation's virtue too."

Garrick built his career around the performance and promotion of Shakespeare, becoming so closely associated with him that the biographer James Granger has written that "it is hard to say whether Shakespeare owes more to Garrick, or Garrick to Shakespeare." Having taken over the management of Drury Lane in 1747, which, along with Covent Garden, was one of the most important theatres in the kingdom, Garrick immediately declared it *the house of William Shakespeare,*" and embarked on a project intended to bring artistic and intellectual gravity to the stage. But Garrick was no purist either, cutting, adapting, and remodeling the works of his idol as he thought fit.

Sometimes, like D'Avenant before him, he made entirely new entertainments from more unpopular plays—his *Catherine and Petruchio,* for example, was a successful and much loved version of *The Taming of the Shrew,* which in its unaltered form was considered wholly unwatchable by eighteenth-century audiences. Even when largely following a text, he was unafraid to make structural alterations. In 1756, he debuted a version of *King Lear* built on the foundations of an earlier adaptation that gave the play a happy ending by making Cordelia queen and allowing Lear "to pass away his Life in Quietness and Devotion," a version that was still standard when Queen Victoria came to the throne. For the critics of the day, this was a marked improvement. Garrick, claimed *The London Magazine,* had "assisted the deficiencies" of Shakespeare.

The Shakespeare Jubilee of 1769 was the conclusive moment of Garrick's relationship with Shakespeare, a literal coronation of his muse witnessed and legitimized by some of the most influential tastemakers in the nation. Garrick's friend James Boswell, the writer, lawyer, diarist, and future biographer of Samuel Johnson, was one of them. Describing it as "an elegant and truly classical celebration of the memory of Shakespeare," he and his fellow attendees (numbering in the thousands) enjoyed three days of songs, balls, and pageants set in the "hallow'd turf" of Shakespeare's hometown of Stratford-upon-Avon, culminating in Garrick's bravura reading of the *Dedication Ode,* a long, rambling poem scored by the Drury Lane orchestra and delivered before a statue of the Bard Garrick had gifted the town.

But while the Jubilee was a formal instantiation of Shakespeare as the creative genius par excellence, capping a century of his movement toward the center of the literary pantheon, it was a peculiar foundation on which to build an enduring hagiography. The Jubilee was a hodgepodge, a gallimaufry of inconsistencies and contradictory motivations that featured little of the work of its honoree. Not a single scene from Shakespeare was performed, let alone an entire play. Shakespeare was more like the Jubilee's "sponsor," presiding over a series of events and entertainments that by themselves had very little to do with him, the body of his work featuring only as echoes and fragments, or as song lyrics and quotations, and allegorized images painted on the backlit transparencies that illuminated the windows of the Town Hall. While Boswell reveled in the event, others found the Jubilee bizarre. The writer Horace Walpole blushed to hear of Garrick's "nonsense," while Samuel Johnson boycotted it entirely. For the actor-manager Samuel Foote, a constant thorn in Garrick's side, the Jubilee was nothing more than "avarice and vanity," such was Garrick's desire "to fleece the people and transmit his name down to posterity, hand in hand with Shakespeare." Personal and commercial ambitions were certainly never far from the surface. This included the mayor and aldermen of Stratford-upon-Avon, who hoped that the influx of visitors would boost their flagging economy, as well as Garrick, whose own sense of finitude as he neared the end of his acting career and managed his failing health played a big part in his plans.

There were political considerations too. By choosing to celebrate Shakespeare in the town of his birth, with its timber-framed houses, reedy riverbanks, and airy open fields, Garrick sought to deploy Shakespeare as a soothing and bucolic parent to the nation at a time when Britain was in turmoil, with riots and hunger commonplace and political institutions shaken by a strong populist movement led by a pugnacious and resilient leader named John Wilkes. Add to this a ruckus in the papers, a giant sea turtle, crooked waiters, the suspicions of the locals, dubious relics, extortionate prices, chaotic organization, a floating rotunda, death from exposure, and unceasing floods of rain, and the Jubilee of 1769 comes to seem like an abject folly. Yet a multitude attended, albeit for a variety of reasons, some coming out of reverence for Shakespeare's artistic achievement, others to be seen at what quickly became the most-talked-about society event of the year. Boswell, always such a candid and agreeable recorder of life, came to do both. His story adds useful context to the Jubilee, since in many ways he was the perfect audience for Garrick's spectacle, making the most of everything it had to offer.

Boswell experienced the Jubilee in the fullness of its contradictions, not as a singular or prescriptive event, but as a space of loose
and improvised connections providing the opportunity to braid
together separate strands of the worlds he occupied, including his
love of theatre, his talent for shameless self-promotion, and a chance
to engage in the pleasures of friendship, hedonism, and the erotic
possibilities of other people's bodies. An outspoken advocate for
Garrick's project, Boswell believed devoutly in the civilizing power
of communal artistic experiences and in the actor's responsibility to serve as an agent of intellectual ennoblement via his or her
role as the intermediary between audiences and great art. Whether
being playful or somber, he made the Jubilee entirely his own, "like
a Frenchman at an ordinary," he said, "who takes out of his pocket
a box of pepper and other spices, and seasons a dish his own way."

In many respects, the ability to season the dish and adapt Shakespeare to suit one's own palate is the lasting contribution of the Jubilee. For all its paradox and absurdities, Garrick's revel on the banks of

Garrick gazes adoringly at Shakespeare on a paper to be slipped in the
cover of a pocket watch, c. 1769. © *The Trustees of the British Museum*

the Avon established the terms under which Shakespeare has infused our culture through the succeeding centuries, as an enduring ghost, ever present yet insubstantial, the weightiest of cultural authorities understood as much by his name and the associations he invokes as by sustained engagement with his works. As such, the Jubilee is a defining moment in our cultural history, and one that goes to show how, through a confluence of intent, mishap, and grubby self-interest, the most glorious and enduring of myths was made.

1

On May 3, 1769, George Keate and Francis Wheler emerged from the vegetal shade of Covent Garden market and strode the twenty paces down to David

Garrick's house at 27 Southampton Street. Stiff with reverence for the object they bore before them, they made an unlikely pair. Keate, a camel-faced minor poet who in the course of many years abroad had become close friends with Voltaire, the genius of French literature, now enjoyed a leisurely life, thanks to a substantial portfolio of Whitechapel properties that afforded him the time to write delicate volumes of verse that he doted on like children. Wheler, by contrast, worked for a living, serving as the steward of the Court of Records for the Borough of Stratford in Warwickshire, the reward for which was a modest ten pounds a year.

Garrick greeted his guests with characteristic good grace, despite having only recently risen from what he described as "ye Bed of Death," fighting off a combined assault of fever, gout, jaundice, and stones. Illness lowered him often, the result of being born with only a single kidney, and even more so now that he had entered his fifties. It was following a bout of sickness that he had first made Keate's acquaintance while convalescing in Bath. Garrick's skin was yellow then and, shaking and puking between curative dips, he had found that Keate's drowsy, convivial manner and unusual face—he had no eyelashes or eyebrows—lifted his spirits. The two men had been on good terms ever since, which is why Wheler had asked Keate to come along. Being in the London home of the world's most famous actor was an unsettling experience for this provincial man, and he mirrored his host's cautious, recuperative movements in his own uncertain bearing. On the walls hung views of Garrick's Hampton villa with its classically inspired "Temple to Shakespeare," where Garrick, his wife, the Austrian dancer Eva Maria Veigel ("La Violette"), and their spaniel, Biddy, presided over a span of the Thames, fat and prosperous and fringed with lithe willows.

A box   Introductions over, Wheler presented Garrick with a "cassolette," an ornately carved box fashioned from wood the color of oxblood. On one side, the box showed the naked figure of Fame offering up a bust of William Shakespeare to be crowned with laurels by the three Graces, while behind them rose the sharp spire of Stratford-upon-Avon's Holy Trinity Church. The other side showed Garrick performing King Lear, mad and unbattened on the moor. Garrick turned it in his hands like a magical object. With its fine carving and silver feet in the form of dragons, it was a thing of beauty with a divine provenance he understood immediately, carved as it was from a mulberry tree planted by William Shakespeare himself.

The box contained more than the Warwickshire air, for inside was a sealed proclamation resolving that out of "love and regard to the memory of that incomparable poet, MR. WILLIAM SHAKESPEARE," and in honor of "the extraordinary accomplishments and merits of his most judicious admirer, and representative, DAVID GARRICK, Esq.," Garrick had been unanimously elected an honorary burgess of Stratford-upon-Avon by the Corporation, as the small town council was known. He had been given notice that the honor was coming but was delighted all the same. "The freedom of your town given to me unanimously, sent to me in such an elegant, and *inestimable* box," he wrote to the mayor and

An "inestimable box": The Mulberry cassolette presented
to Garrick by the Corporation of Stratford-upon-Avon.
© *The Trustees of the British Museum*

aldermen, "and delivered to me in so flattering a manner, merit my
warmest gratitude. It will be impossible for me ever to forget those
who have honoured me so much as to mention my unworthy name
with that of their immortal townsman."

Others saw darker motives. "I have long made it my Observa-
tion," wrote a correspondent to the London newspaper *Public Advertiser*, "that no Gifts are in general so pernicious as those composed
of WOOD. The most antient of these Gifts on Record was, I believe,
that of the Gods to Pandora, and next in Order of Time, the Trojan
Horse." The box certainly came with intent, for at the same moment
that Garrick was accepting the freedom of the town, the mayor and
his aldermen were preparing paragraphs to send to the London
papers that claimed that Garrick was considering holding an event
in their town, a festival he would call "Shakespeare's Jubilee." The
press did the rest. "We hear the Entertainments in general at the

Jubilee will be the most elegant and magnificent ever exhibited in the country," wrote the *Public Advertiser*, adding that the celebration was "to be kept up every seventh Year." Placed on the back foot and keen to get ahead of the news, Garrick decided to announce the plans himself from the stage at Drury Lane following his final performance of the season, a benefit for the Fund for Decayed Actors. "My eyes, till then, no sights like these will see," he told the audience on May 18, 1769,

Announcement of the Jubilee

> Unless we meet at Shakespeare's Jubilee!
> On Avon's *Banks, where flowers eternal blow!*
> Like its full stream our Gratitude shall flow!
> Then let us revel, show our fond regard,
> On that lov'd Spot, first breathed our *matchless* Bard;
> To Him all Honour, Gratitude is due,
> To Him we owe our all—To *him* and *You*.

"Jubilee" was a curious word to describe a gathering in honor of a playwright. With its origins in Jewish antiquity, the word had become closely associated with the Catholic Church following its adoption in the fourteenth century by Pope Boniface VIII to describe a year of solemnity and pilgrimages in which the faithful might earn a plenary indulgence and be granted remission from temporal sin. Garrick chose it to connote the extent of his devotion, as well as time apart from the usual run of life, but whether he truly meant to invoke the full extent of its religiosity was unclear. As a pilgrimage, no one knew exactly what it would entail—least of all David Garrick.

The last time Garrick had seen the mulberry tree he had been standing in its patulous shade in the garden of New Place, Stratford-upon-Avon's second largest house and the home William Shakespeare had purchased in May 1597 with the money he had made as a successful poet and playwright. When Garrick visited one fine afternoon in 1742, the tree was thriving, as was Garrick, who was fast on his way to becoming the most famous man in Britain.

The third of seven children, David Garrick had been born at the Angel Inn, Hereford, in 1717, before moving to the Midlands town of Lichfield, where his maternal grandfather was vicar choral. The family was of French *Apology for the life of David Garrick* descent, Huguenot Protestants from east of Bordeaux who had fled to Britain in 1685 following the revocation of the Edict of Nantes, anglicizing their surname from "Garrique." Garrick's father had become an army officer, albeit one who spent much of his career on half pay. Despite financial constraints, the Garricks approximated a genteel life, which meant that at the age of ten, David was sent to Dr. John Hunter's grammar school to receive a formal education. While too prankish and distracted to focus on his studies, it was here that he received his first opportunity to perform in a play, corralling his classmates at the age of eleven into a production of George Farquhar's *The Recruiting Officer.* Soon after, the want of money forced Garrick's father to take a commission in Gibraltar. David was also sent away, traveling to Lisbon, where he apprenticed for an uncle who worked in the wine trade.

This uncle, a somber bachelor who struggled to endure a lively twelve-year-old with a talent for mimicry, sent him home again. David returned to England to find that with his father away, his older brother, Peter, serving in the navy, and his mother and elder sister frequently ill, he had been promoted to the household's titular head. The first signs of a talent for management emerged as David took on this responsibility, writing long letters to his father full of financial news and family matters that reveled in their own importance. As he grew and became better known around the cathedral close and its small but accomplished social circle, his open countenance, winning manner, and confidence in his own abilities began to show themselves as assets capable of overcoming his indifferent scholarship and modest family. Aged eighteen, he left Dr. Hunter's school and went to study at the establishment of a young schoolmaster named Samuel Johnson, who had founded an academy three miles outside town. Johnson, an intense and lurching man of formidable erudition, was at odds with conventional schooling and wished to practice his own theories of education. Despite springing for an advertisement in *The Gentleman's Magazine,* Johnson's school attracted only three students, two of whom were David Garrick and Garrick's younger brother, George. The experiment was doomed from the start. Johnson was too volatile to be a teacher and could not mask his perpetual annoyance or forbear from swearing. His pupils afforded him little respect, and would stand at his bedroom door giggling as he made passionate protestations

"At Edial, near Litchfield in Staffordshire, Young Gentlemen are Boarded, & Taught the Latin & Greek Languages, by Samuel Johnson"

of love to his wife, Tetty, twenty years his senior, and, according to Garrick, "very fat, with a bosom of more than ordinary protuberance, with swelled cheeks of a florid red, produced by thick painting, and increased by the liberal use of cordials; flaring and fantastick in her dress, and affected both in her speech and her general behaviour."

Johnson closed his school within a year but retained a close relationship with his former pupil. In March 1737, having both outgrown Lichfield, they paired up to depart for new lives in London. Garrick's father intended him to study for the law, whereas Johnson dreamed of becoming a playwright and carried with him a half-finished tragedy called *Irene* that he hoped to see onstage. To save money, they shared a horse with one man riding ahead and tethering it up the road where the other would find it and ride himself for a while. Garrick, compact, energetic, and fevering to meet the world, had just turned twenty. Johnson, twenty-seven, loomed over him, a monstrous house of bones, "hideously striking to the eye," as his friend and biographer, James Boswell, would remember him, with "the scars of his scrophula . . . deeply visible."

London in 1737 had a population of almost six hundred thousand—a tenth of all Britons—making it the largest city in Europe, choked with traffic and noise and narrow streets of stercoraceous mud touched by the slightest slivers of sunlight. The city had begun to burst its seams as ancient gateways were demolished to allow for more wheeled traffic, and fields and farmland were eaten up by new estates. Development bolted west, bricking over the marshes to establish gracious squares and terraces, while the rest of the city grew denser as householders filled in their yards and pinfolds, replacing their pigs and cows with new rooms and buildings at the back of their houses. Within two weeks of Garrick and Johnson's arrival, Garrick's father died, thus freeing him from his obligation to pursue the law. Partnering instead with his brother Peter (returned from the sea), he resumed the wine trade, a business that held no more appeal than the law but at least required less study. The brothers set up in Durham Yard, a sagging quad of timbered warehouses backing onto river wharves and the Gordian mesh of masts and rigging from the barges, boats, and wherries that crowded the Thames, plying their trade as wholesalers selling wine by the barrel. Johnson found himself a garret above the Black Boy tavern in the Strand and continued to work on his play.

Garrick hated the wine trade, but through Peter's business contacts, he began to visit local inns and coffeehouses such as the Grecian and Tom's, watering holes that served the workers and patrons of the royal theatres of Covent Garden and Drury Lane, less than a mile away. These visits yielded little business, but they did provide the occasion to loiter around theatre folk. Garrick soon became friends with the actor and manager Henry Giffard, as well as John Arthur, a comedian and stage machinist with whom he built a catapult. In time, these friendships led to a wholesaling contract with the Bedford Coffee House, a reeky bolt-hole nestling beneath the arches of Covent Garden piazza, its walls papered over with playbills and booths filled with jammering theatre buffs. The Bedford, which "signalized, for many years, as the emporium of wit, the seat of criticism, and the standard of taste," was a harbor for many successful theatre people, as well as a significant number of unsuccessful ones, all in need of a drink and providing David with the perfect opportunity to immerse himself in their world.

Theatre in 1737

The London theatre scene of 1737 was enjoying a wild and creative moment, driven by the juggernauts of John Gay's *The Beggar's Opera* (1728), with its innovative mixture of high art and low places, and the colorful, frenetic harlequinades devised by John Rich, Covent Garden's pantomimical genius. Regular companies at Covent Garden, Drury Lane, Goodman's Fields, Lincoln's Inn, and the Haymarket competed for audiences with a medley of irregular venues that offered the spectrum of entertainments from rope dancers, jugglers, and acrobats, to dramas and spectacles, and operas by Handel and Bononcini. It was a city of curiosities and diversions, many of them borrowed from the theatrical cultures of Europe and performed by French and Italian singers and dancers who commanded enormous salaries and dictated fashion—"the English are the Frenchman's Apes," as a popular saying went.

Yet the swell of invention was about to end because, just weeks after Garrick's arrival, the government of Sir Robert Walpole passed legislation that would shape the theatres for more than a century.

Effect of the Licensing Act

The law, known as the Licensing Act, had been prompted by the increasing use of the stage as a platform for antigovernment mockery and invective, with the satirical beatings that First Minister Walpole and his fellow politicians incurred in plays such as Henry Fielding's *The Historical Register for the Year 1736*, producing such offense among government officials that they moved to silence them forever. Campaigning for his bill in the House of Commons, Walpole read aloud passages from a play called *A Vision of the Golden Rump*, so "larded" with "Scurrility and Treason," he claimed, that to perform it would mean endangering the moral fabric of the nation. Despite resistance—most notably from Lord Chesterfield, who called the proposed law "a dangerous wound to liberty"—the bill passed with the result that spoken drama was now banned throughout the country at all venues with the exception of those that had been expressly licensed by the Crown—in effect, the theatres of Covent Garden and Drury Lane, granted royal patent by Charles II at the end of the Civil War. In addition, all new plays and revisions to old ones had to be submitted for censorship to the office of the Lord Chamberlain fourteen days prior to production or face a fifty-pound fine. Censorship was sweeping but inconsistently applied. While some venues closed, others simply looked to exploit loopholes, such as advertising plays as "concerts," whereby the audience were charged to hear music but offered a play for free. Other theatres offered a play gratis but required that patrons purchase a pint of ale. That the authorities let this go unpunished confirmed that the law's real target was its political enemies rather than unlicensed performances more generally. One of the venues that escaped almost entirely unchanged was Goodman's Fields, owned by Garrick's new friend Henry Giffard. Coincidentally, it was Giffard who had supplied Robert Walpole with *A Vision of the Golden Rump*, a fact that led suspicious minds to speculate that Giffard had written the play to order, with no intention other than letting Walpole read it aloud to help secure the passage of his bill. Giffard's reward, so rumor had it, was immunity from prosecution.

The drudgery of the wine business was making Garrick depressed, but his friendship with Giffard provided an outlet that led to him dabbling in theatrical piecework, even writing his first play, *Lethe; or Esop in the Shades*, a comic afterpiece in which a series of unworthy stereotypes cross into the underworld and are judged for their sins. The play was performed at Drury Lane, but despite this breakthrough, Garrick remained firmly in the wine wholesaling business, cautious not to reveal too much to his brother, who disapproved strongly of such disreputable interests. Things became easier once Peter Garrick moved back to Lichfield to oversee business from the family home. Delivered from filial oversight, Garrick took an irrevocable step toward his calling by appearing onstage in an amateur production of *The Mock Doctor*. The seal broken, an impressed Giffard offered him a place in the professional ranks appearing in a series of summer productions in the East Anglian town of Ipswich. Garrick accepted. Ipswich was distant enough not to run the risk of meeting anyone he knew, but to be doubly certain he adopted the pseudonym "Mr. Lydall," hiding his features behind the blackface customary for his role as the African prince in *Oroo-*

"Mr. Lydall"
takes the stage

noko. Standing at the footlights, dressed in a short linen tunic and old feathered turban, his face smeared with burnt cork and fixed with goose dripping, Garrick peered out across the faces shifting white and orange in the candlelight and knew that this was where he belonged.

Back in London, Garrick accepted an offer from Giffard to appear at Goodman's Fields, making his debut there on October 19, 1741, playing Richard in a heavily adapted version of Shakespeare's *Richard III*. Listed on the bills as a "GENTLEMAN (*who never appear'd on any Stage*)," Garrick once again hoped that this performance would be sufficiently anonymous to avoid a family row. Located at the wrong end of town, east of the Minories and behind the Tower of London, from the street, Goodman's Fields had the look of a cooperage or a warehouse for municipal orphans. Its inauspicious appearance did nothing to shield Garrick from public attention as critics took note of his "easy and familiar, yet forcible style in speaking and acting." According to Garrick's first biographer, the actor-turned-bookseller Thomas Davies, while the public were at first uncertain what to make of him, their hesitation fell quickly away as scene after scene Garrick "gave evident proofs of consummate art, and perfect knowledge of character." "Their doubts," wrote Davies, "were turned into surprise and astonishment, from which they relieved themselves by loud and reiterated applause."

Garrick was a new and different actor who "came forth," it was said, "at once a complete master of his art." Word soon reached London's politer corners, emptying the theatres of Drury Lane and Covent Garden as "the splendour of St. James's and Grosvenor-square" packed the seven hundred seats of Goodman's Field to witness the sensation. Admirers included aristocrats and members of Parliament, among them the future prime minister William Pitt, who told him he was "ye best Actor ye English Stage had produc'd." Such voluble accolades made it difficult to keep his new career from his disapproving brother, so having settled his accounts and taken stock of what was left of his wine, Garrick braced himself and wrote to Peter. "My Mind," he said,

> (as You must know) has always been inclin'd to ye Stage, nay so strongly so that all my Illness and lowness of Spirits was owing to my want of resolution to tell You my thoughts when here, finding at last both my Inclination and Interest requir'd some New way of Life I have chose ye most agreeable to my Self and tho I know You will bee much displeas'd at Me yet I hope when You shall find that I may have ye genius of an Actor without ye Vices, You will think Less Severe of Me and not be ashamed to own me for a Brother.

The confession appalled Peter, who was furious that his brother had let his business fail and scandalized lest the low reputation of actors should cast a pall over their respectable family name. David tried to assuage his fears, conceding that while the stage "in ye General it deserves Yr Censure," some actors were received in the best company, and that "I have rec'd more Civilities & favours from Such Since my playing than I ever did in all my Life before." Furthermore, he assured him, he could earn as much as three hundred pounds a year.

Peter remained "utterly Averse," leaving his brother no choice but to forgo his approval and continue to pursue "what I am so greatly Inclin'd & What ye best Judges think I have ye Greatest Genius for." His next step was to accept a summer season at the Smock Alley theatre in Dublin alongside the actress Margaret Woffington, an excellent comedian with a talent for impersonation that rivaled Garrick's own. The actors began an affair, setting up house at 6 Bow Street when they returned to London to become members of the prestigious Drury Lane company. The relationship lasted only six months, with Woffington suggesting that Garrick was both a penny-pincher who saved money by reusing dried tea leaves, and a novice in bed—"he was," she said, alluding to two contrasting roles Garrick would play later in his career, "Sir John Brute all day, and Billy Fribble all night."

The house at Bow Street was home to a third resident whose effect on Garrick would be even more impactful—Charles Macklin, a broad-shouldered northern Irishman almost twenty years Garrick's senior. Macklin was a minor genius, having first drawn attention to himself as a schoolboy by memorizing the challenging role of Monimia, the heroine of Thomas Otway's tragedy *The Orphan*, and subsequently working his way up the theatrical ladder from appearing in booths at the London fairs to becoming the most influential member of the company at Drury Lane. As Garrick was making his debut at Goodman Fields, Macklin was himself stunning audiences with a radical interpretation of *The Merchant of Venice*'s Shylock, the Jewish moneylender traditionally performed as a clownish racial stereotype. Macklin, however, sought to plumb the complexity and contradictions of Shylock, a character who is systematically abused and dehumanized by Christian Venice even as it hypocritically turns to him to save it from its own improvidence. To prepare for this new interpretation, Macklin had taken the unprecedented step of researching the role, reading Josephus's *Antiquities of the Jews* and visiting the Royal Exchange to meet in person with Jewish merchants, taking care to emulate their mannerisms and accurately re-create their dress. The result was revelatory. Instead of being buffoonish, Macklin's Shylock was, in the words of his biographer, "subtle, selfish, fawning, irascible, and tyrannic," exhibiting a ferocity that opened up new interpretive possibilities, gave King George II nightmares, and garnered enthusiastic endorsement from famous men of letters. "This is the Jew," said the poet Alexander Pope, allegedly, "that Shakespeare drew."

Macklin's reforms were at the vanguard of a profession that was sorely in need of change. The era of Barton Booth, Robert Wilks, and Colley Cibber, giants of the *On styles of acting* stage who had dominated the theatre until the 1730s, had ended without establishing a clear line of succession. There were notable actors, such as the stately and corpulent James Quin, although his roles, complained the critic Richard Cumberland, could barely be distinguished one from the other, "save by costume and outbursts of fury." Quin's acting remained firmly in the stiff, neoclassical mode in which actors would transition from one pose to another within a repertoire of "attitudes," a language of gestures intended to reinforce the words by conveying emotions such as love or grief. Alternatively, they would interrupt the flow of action entirely in order to come to the front of the stage to deliver their "points," big scene-stealing speeches or moments of dramatic climax that allowed an actor to demonstrate the range and virtuosity of his voice in a way that was calculated "to intrap applause." It was awkward, artificial, and intended to appeal to the ear rather than the eye. "Declamation roared in most unnatural strain," recalled another of Garrick's earliest biographers, the dramatist Arthur Murphy, "rant was passion; whining was grief; vociferation was terror, and drawing accents were the voice of love." It was not for nothing that Quin, with his habit of "heaving up his words," was nicknamed "Bellower."

Macklin's assault on what he called "the fixed glare of tragic expression" began in the legs. He stood naturally when speaking, instead of taking a broad stance as if preparing to be tackled, and spoke as normally as possible while still being heard. Such innovations did not always win him admirers, as he discovered after being dismissed from Lincoln's Inn theatre for speaking "too familiarly on stage." Similarly, he did not follow the lead of his colleagues who would deliver their own lines in character and then look bored while they waited for their next turn to speak. Instead, he continued to act even when silent, inserting reactions and bits of naturalistic business into his performances that had a tendency to infuriate cast mates who were unprepared for it. One of these was James Quin, who grew so enraged at what he saw as Macklin's unnecessary fidgeting during a performance of Wycherley's *The Plain Dealer* that he flung a piece of apple in his face backstage between scenes. The result was a fight in which Quin was so badly beaten he was unable to go back on.

Macklin attacks

That Macklin would readily assault a man who was known himself to have killed two men in duels was a sign of how volatile he could be, a volatility that arose from his drinking, his uncertain social status, and the transient life he led moving back and forth across the Irish Sea. During a greenroom argument with the actor Thomas Hallam over the ownership of a wig, Macklin had bolted from his chair and in one fluid movement thrust a crab-tree walking stick, rapierlike, into Hallam's left eye. Blood ran from Hallam's face as he clapped his hand to his face and fell onto a settee.

"Lord," he said, "I believe my eyeball is shoved to the other side of my head," and calling over to the young brother of the composer Thomas Arne, then dressed as a Spanish girl for that night's play, he cried, "Whip up your clothes, you little bitch, and urine in my eye." The boy was too terrified to comply, so Hallam was taken to another room where Macklin urinated on his victim himself. Urine was thought to have antiseptic qualities, but in this case the remedy was entirely ineffective as Macklin's stick had entered Hallam's eye socket so sweetly that it had broken the thin layer of bone separating it from his brain. He died the following day. Indicted for murder, Macklin got off with the lesser charge of manslaughter and was punished by having his hand branded with a cold brand.

It is unsurprising that such an imposing man should make a big impression on Garrick, and the two were rarely apart as the younger actor absorbed all he could of his mentor's theories and meticulous habits of preparation. Under Macklin's tutelage, Garrick went to visit a bereaved friend, a man who had accidentally let his baby daughter slip from his arms and fall headfirst onto flagstones, killing her instantly. Driven to distraction by his mortal carelessness, the man would stand "playing in fancy with his child" in a ghoulish mime at the spot where the accident had occurred. After some dalliance, recalled Arthur Murphy, "he dropped it, and, bursting into a flood of tears, filled the house with shrieks of grief and bitter anguish. He then sat down, in a pensive mood, his eyes fixed on one object, at times looking slowly round him, as if to implore compassion." "There it was," said Garrick, "that I learned to imitate madness; I copied nature, and to that owed my success," channeling these observations into his performance as King Lear.

From that point on, the pursuit of "nature" became integral to Garrick's conception of acting, and on days when he was due to play a part he would closet himself away, running through dialogue and slowly acquiring the manner-

Garrick imitates nature

isms and gait he would use, while developing those pieces of incon-
sequential business that helped to build a sense of a consciousness
beyond the lines. "The only Way to arrive at *great Excellency* in
Characters," he wrote in his *Essay on Acting*, published anonymously,
"is to be very conversant with *Human Nature*, that is the noblest
and best Study, by this Way you will more accurately discover the
Workings of Spirit." Conscientious study bore fruit. "When Garrick entered the scene," wrote Murphy, "the character he assumed,
was legible in his countenance, by the force of deep meditation he
transformed himself into the very man. . . . When he spoke, the
tone of his voice was in unison with the workings of his mind."
"He was so natural," concurred the dancer Georges Noverre, "his
expression was so lifelike, his gestures, features, glances were so
eloquent and convincing, that he made the action clear even to
those who did not understand a word of English . . . he lacerated
the spectator's feelings, tore his heart, and made him weep tears
of blood." To an anonymous writer in *The Gentleman's Magazine*,
Garrick performed "Parts so *naturally*, as that in Truth they are
not *perform'd at all*."

With his earnest approach to craft and capacity for hard work,
David Garrick rose so rapidly that it unsettled the conservative
hierarchy of the theatre, a profession in which "seniority was considered with as much jealousy in the green-room as in the army or
navy." By the time he stepped on stage alongside Bellower Quin
in Nicholas Rowe's *The Fair Penitent* at the close of 1746, it was
clear that times had changed and that a new era was about to begin.
Quin, in his full-bottomed periwig, high-heeled shoes, and an elab-
orately embroidered beryl-green frock pulled over his great swag
belly, seemed ponderous and heavy, jerking his hand like a saw and
rolling "out his heroics with an air of dignified indifference." Garrick, by contrast, was "young and light and alive in every muscle and

David Garrick by Thomas Gainsborough, 1770. © *National Portrait Gallery, London*

in every feature." "It seemed," wrote Richard Cumberland, "as if a whole century had been stept over in the transition of a single scene; old things were done away, and a new order at once brought forward, bright and luminous, and clearly destined to dispel the barbarisms and bigotry of a tasteless age."

2

Of James Boswell, complex Scot

If there was one man for whom the Shakespeare Jubilee was guaranteed to appeal, it was James Boswell. The idea of it was tailor-made for the sociable Scottish lawyer who considered himself finely attuned to the sensibilities of art and literature, and loved nothing more than to be at the heart of the fashionable swell. He first made Garrick's acquaintance nine years earlier, when Boswell was twenty and the actor was forty-three. Meeting "the man who from a boy," he said, "I used to adore and look upon as a heathen god" had made an indelible impression on him, and the two men had maintained a friendly relationship ever since, mediated often through Samuel Johnson, Boswell's mentor and Garrick's former tutor.

However, when Garrick announced the Jubilee from the Drury Lane stage, Boswell had no intention of attending at all. He was on a mission of his own, newly arrived in Ireland in pursuit of a potential bride named Mary Ann Boyd, a young woman he nicknamed "*La Belle Irelandaise*," "formed like a Grecian nymph," with a father worth ten thousand pounds. It was not the first time that Boswell had fallen dotingly in love, and as he raved about Mary Ann to his friends, many of them predicted he would fall out of love just as quickly. True to form, having anticipated the meeting for months, he found Mary Ann to be a disappointment

Courts a wife

and rather too childish and obeisant in person—"so much *yes* and *no*." He had traveled to Ireland in the company of his cousin Margaret Montgomerie, who attended as chaperone, confidante, and ally. She was the perfect companion for a wife hunt, humoring him, consoling him when he drank too much or let himself down, and happily accompanying him down the cart tracks of speculative conversation along which he frequently ambled. Comparing Margaret with Mary Ann in a letter to his friend George Dempster, it dawned on Boswell that it was Margaret he truly loved. "Her most desirable person," he wrote, was "like a heathen goddess painted alfresco on the ceiling of a palace at Rome" when compared with the "reserved quietness" of Mary Ann. "I am exceedingly in love with her," he told another friend, William Temple. She was perfect for him, "but the objections are She is two years older than me. She has only a Thousand Pounds."

Boswell was now twenty-nine years old and eager to secure his growing reputation and take his place as a respectable and upstanding laird, just like his father. He was enjoying a period of celebrity, what he called his "newspaper fame," thanks to his *Account of Corsica*, a book that recounted his visit to that embattled island four years earlier, as well as his friendship with Pasquale Paoli, leader of the Corsican fight for independence against the Genovese. Corsica was wild and unknown to British readers, and the journey, undertaken at the recommendation of the philosopher Jean-Jacques Rousseau, had become a defining moment that drew the line between his youth and adulthood: "I had got upon a rock in Corsica," Boswell wrote, "and jumped into the middle of life." Success had not been effortless, and neither had he left it to chance. His book's reception had been built on foundations he had begun *Courts fame* to lay in January 1766, by sending anonymous letters about himself to the *London Chronicle*. The letters falsely purported to come from various Italian cities and were intended to give the impression that his trip to Corsica had been the talk of mainland Europe. These he followed with a series of letters to politicians and further reports sent to the papers detailing the purported travels of "Signor Romanzo," a nonexistent diplomat whose visits to foreign capitals and embassies were invented by Boswell in an effort to manufacture interest in the plight of his Corsican friends. In reality, Boswell's trip had lasted only six weeks, two of which were spent with General Paoli, with another three spent recuperating from a fever. But by the time the truth had been massaged and mythologized, Boswell had become so synonymous with his adopted island that he had taken on the nickname "Corsica Boswell."

Celebrity was sweet. "I liked to see the effect of being an author," he wrote in his journal as the *Account* entered its third edition on the eve of the Jubilee. "It is amazing how much and how universally I have made myself admired." With fame came famous acquaintances and the satisfaction of knowing the known. "I am really the *Great Man* now," he told Temple, listing the writers, philosophers, and military men with whom he now socialized:

> I have had David Hume in the forenoon and Mr Johnson in the afternoon of the same day visiting me, Sir John Pringle, Dr Franklin and some more company dined with me today and Mr Johnson and General Oglethorpe one day Mr Garrick alone another and David Hume and some more Literati dine with me next week. I give admirable dinners and good Claret. . . . This is enjoying the fruit of my labours, and appearing like the friend of Paoli.

It was a giddy period. Even his father had begun to treat him like a man.

Fame was important to Boswell as it shored up the moorings of a frequently wavering identity. As a boy, climbing the ancient trees that stood fieffal watch around his family's estate at Auchinleck in west Scotland, he surveyed a landscape that presented him with dual visions of who he and his family were. Bounded on one side by the river Lugar and on the other by a swift brook that ran through red sandstone, the estate was the site of both the square and respectable Palladian manor house his father had built and the ruins of an old moated castle to which his ancestors—favorites of

A mature James Boswell, painted by Sir Joshua Reynolds in 1785.
© *National Portrait Gallery, London*

James I and kinsmen to the powerful Douglas clan—had cleaved in former years. The contrast between the orderly present and the wild past affected Boswell deeply, giving form to the internal forces that would pull at him in different directions throughout his life. It was green and rained often.

A fertile imagination offered vital respite from a cheerless family life. Boswell's devout mother taught him "the gloomiest doctrines" of her Calvinist catechism, his brother John was subject to periodic contentions with lunacy, while his father was distant and disapproving. Alexander Boswell was one of the high judges of Scotland and the archetype of a stolid Scotsman, a respectable Tory landowner with an impatient and pragmatic view of the world. His title, Lord Auchinleck, had come as the result of his status within the legal profession as opposed to aristocratic sanguinity—a fact that, like his mother's distant relationship to Scottish royalty, Boswell chose to fudge. Displays of affection were not indulged between the laird and his son, and their conversation came marbled with reproof. Boswell chose, to the extent one can, to be a sickly boy, as only when sick did he receive the attention he craved.

Studies in Edinburgh At thirteen, Boswell left home to study a broad curriculum of languages and liberal arts at the University of Edinburgh, a medieval city of wet slate and steep wynds as taciturn as the horseshoe crags that ringed it, still a moping boy, weighed down with grim, salvational preoccupations hewn from the cheerless Calvinist granite of his mother's devotions. At sixteen, he fell into a deep depression, one of the many "hypochondrias" that would abduct him for sustained periods of his life. Carried back to convalesce at Auchinleck, he became attached to a sheep farmer and self-taught philosopher named John Williamson, who lived in the nearby village of Moffat. Williamson was an oddity in that barely literate farming community. Fascinated by geology and philosophy and the religions of the Far East, he read deeply in the history of the

Hindu Brahmins, many of whose customs he adopted as his own. Williamson's vegetarianism brought him into conflict with his profession as a sheep farmer, and his refusal to make a profit from his lambs or allow them to be slaughtered so frustrated his landlord that he was evicted from his farm and sent away to live on a small annuity. With no flock to tend, he adopted the life of a peripatetic prophet, reading and developing his beliefs in alchemy, polygamy (although he never married), the transmigration of souls, and the importance of worshipping on hillsides and moors. Boswell accompanied Williamson on these reverential hikes and, whether in spite of his association with him or because of it, he emerged from his depression almost a different person: "I do not know how," he wrote, "I think by yielding to received opinions." Gone was the reticent boy plagued by night terrors, to be replaced by a sociable young man who wanted to know everyone and do everything. As a template for his new persona, he looked to the example shown by *The Tatler* and *The Spectator*, the famous periodicals written by Joseph Addison and Sir Richard Steele published between 1709 and 1712, to which he had been introduced by a tutor. These magazines concerned themselves with the variety of metropolitan life, of opera and fine arts, fashion, coffeehouses, and satirical caricatures of aristocrats, businessmen, and oft encountered London types. Through the editorial persona of Mr. Spectator, Boswell found an urbane masculine archetype, known for his faultless critical judgment, wit, taste, and gentility. Mr. Spectator was cultured and clearheaded, ruled by a disciplined but unprissy morality, and capable always of self-reflection and improvement.

It was this Boswell who would return to study once again in Edinburgh. Almost immediately, he began to frequent the theatre, passing through the low gate and along the narrow gulley made by high tenement walls and dark windows to the city's playhouse, established in 1747 as an unlicensed enterprise protected from legal censure by influential backers, but still subject to intermittent bouts of puritanical approbation and antitheatrical rioting. Prior to his nervous illness, Boswell had regarded the players "with a mixture of narrow-minded horror, and lively-minded pleasure," wondering at the "painted equipages and powdered Ladies" as they passsed down Canongate. Now watching them perform, they far exceeded his expectations. Three actors in particular made a strong impression— the graceful James Love, who spoke so well Boswell would go to him for elocution lessons; the captivating Mrs. Cowper; and the rakish actor-manager West Digges, best known for his portrayal of the highwayman Macheath in Gay's *Beggar's Opera*, whose polished manners, irresistible charisma, and chaotic personal life Boswell found enormously attractive. "The impression he made upon a warm youthfull imagination is strong and permanent," Boswell once told Garrick of Digges. "It was he who threw open to me the portals of Theatrical Enchantment, and therefore He and Pleasure are insepa-rably associated in my mind."

Theatre's importance to Boswell

"Theatrical Enchantments" would not only remain dear to Boswell throughout his life, they introduced him to many of his life's most abiding themes—most notably, the cultivation of a large social circle, journalism (by way of his earliest publications, theatrical reviews), as well as his greatest literary achievement, his journals, which were begun at the urging of James Love. Just as important, the theatre gave form and vista to an urgent emerging sexuality. Characters like Macheath provided the template for a sexually commanding masculinity that the shy boy found desperately appealing, while the opportunity to sit and watch afforded a license to gaze upon women with a linger-ing, libidinous eye, assessing them against his urges and providing space to understand better the roles he hoped to play in the sexual game. One of the first objects of his passion was the actress Mrs. Cowper, of whom he wrote, "She has the finest Person, the most agreeable Face, and the politest Carriage of any Actress we remember to have seen on this stage."

Lord Auchinleck did not approve of the way his son spent his time and, in 1759, recalled him from Edinburgh to send him instead to the University of Glasgow. By far a more sober and studious setting, Glasgow provided Boswell with the opportunity to attend lectures on moral philosophy delivered by Adam Smith, then on the verge of publishing his *Theory of Moral Sentiments*. In his lecture hall, Smith expounded on his belief that through their craving for "fellow feeling" human beings acquire a sense of right and wrong by shaping their actions to win the approval of others and attuning their emotions according to an internalized sense of how an impartial observer might judge them. This idea of values attained through collective experience, and of becoming by being seen, resonated strongly with Boswell, affirming his dedication to theatrical communality and the urbanity he encountered in *The Spectator*.

Although Boswell found Smith to be a generous and inspiring lecturer, the puritanical environs of Glasgow provided little opportunity to practice his philosophy, and loneliness weighed heavily on his mind. Depressed, his thoughts swung toward their other polarity, piety, and a small cache of Catholic tracts presented to him in Edinburgh by a Jesuit named Père Duchat. In March 1760, Boswell sent his father a letter declaring his intention to travel to London and become a Catholic priest, a decision that may have been inspired in part by his pining for the Catholic Mrs. Cowper. This announcement alarmed his father more than anything else his troublesome son had ever done. Conversion to Catholicism was a capital offense, and while the penalty was rarely imposed, Catholics were discriminated against in *Discovers London via bout of religiosity* every walk of life, barred from practicing law or holding public office, joining the army or navy, or legally inheriting their family's wealth. Boswell made good on his threat of going to London, so Lord Auchinleck contacted Lord Eglinton, a neighbor from Ayrshire who was himself resident in the capital, and pleaded with him to intercede. It was a stroke of genius on the elder man's part, as Eglinton was a libertine bachelor who immediately managed to shake the teenager from his pious introspection by exposing him to the glamor of London life. Under Eglinton's tutelage, Boswell attended the races, was introduced to writers and dramatists (among them Garrick), and socialized in the company of the Duke of York, brother to the future George III (to whom Boswell developed an immediate dislike).

After three heady months, Boswell returned to Scotland, where he published an anonymous poem in praise of theatre, "Ode to Tragedy," most notable for its dedication to James Boswell, to whom the author (James Boswell) offers profuse thanks "for your particular kindness to me; and chiefly for the profound respect with which you have always treated me." Three years later, having finally completed his studies, he returned to London again, this time with his father's blessing. Once again, he met Garrick, and was overcome when the actor told him "you will be a very great man." Boswell took Garrick by the hand. "Thou greatest of men," he replied, "I cannot express how happy you make me." In his journal, he admitted, "I was quite in raptures, to find him paying me so much respect."

Garrick made "particles of vivacity" dance within Boswell "by a sort of contagion," but never so much as when Boswell saw the actor perform. May 12, 1763, was particularly memorable.

A night at the theatre

This was the night Boswell attended Drury Lane to see Garrick in *King Lear*, a performance that was due to begin at six, but "so very high is his reputation," he recorded, "that the pit was full in ten minutes after four." On any given evening the theatre was filled with representatives of all but the meanest classes, from the aristocrats who peopled the boxes, to the maids and footmen who waited for them in the highest galleries and the prostitutes and orange sellers "who lurk about the house avenues and parts adjacent." The pit held around five hundred people, so crammed together that they often sat on one another's laps while others walked over them, hopping across from bench to bench. This was the part of the house frequented by those who considered themselves theatrically literate—critics, opinion formers, and men who took an interest in the traffic of the stage—as well as "plain, sober Tradesmen, their Wives and Children," army officers, and men about town. It suited Boswell perfectly. With two hours to wait, the audience had to entertain themselves. Many brought their dinners wrapped in handkerchiefs, played with their dogs, or amused themselves by dropping walnut shells and orange peel over the balconies onto the heads of those below. Once while waiting, in what he described as "a wild freak of youthful extravagance," Boswell began lowing like a cow. The audience members cried out, "*Encore* the cow! *Encore* the cow!" and | *Farm animals impersonated* encouraged by his success, he tried imitating a range of other animals, although none were as well received. "My dear sir," said his friend, "I would *confine* myself to the cow!"

At six o'clock, the bell rang and Garrick stepped out to deliver the evening's prologue under the light of six wide-circumferenced girandoles suspended above his head, their sputtering tallow lighting both stage and auditorium. The audience quieted, although never really settled. People came and went throughout the performances, their evening plans assisted by guidebooks such as John Brownsmith's *The Dramatic Time-Piece: or Perpetual Monitor*, which provided exact timings for each act of each play in the current repertoire so that patrons might plan their arrival and departure precisely (and demand a refund for whatever portion of the bill they didn't see). At the close of the third act, a second wave of spectators was admitted to fill the empty seats, paying half price for their tickets.

This was such a feature of the theatrical landscape that it shaped the writing of plays, many of which contained a summary of the plot at the beginning of Act 4.

The constant interruptions were especially annoying to Garrick, who every season tried to impose more order on the auditorium. When playing Lear, he demanded the attention of his audience to the extent that any conversation above a whisper was checked by "hush men" he had strategically placed around the theatre. Despite the distractions, Boswell primed himself to receive the emotion that Garrick injected into every performance—the gasps and pauses, the emphatic weeping and windmilling arms, the deployment of the "fright wig," a hairpiece controlled by wires that could be raised at moments of extreme distress. Boswell "was fully moved, I shed an abundance of tears." There then followed an afterpiece named *Polly Honeycomb*, after which the orchestra led the audience in a rendi-

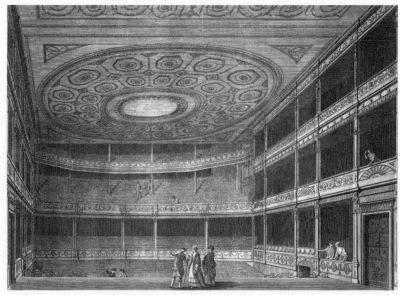

Drury Lane Theatre, as it appeared from the stage.
Used by permission of the Folger Shakespeare Library

tion of "God Save the King" before everyone pressed for the exits and the unpredictable London night, their ways illuminated by link boys padding ahead with lighted torches.

For all the chaos and inconvenience a night at the theatre entailed, it was the kind of experience that Boswell held to be transcendent, his belief in its civilizing influence vindicating the teachings of Adam Smith. There was his "soul refined" by "the exalted pleasure resulting from the view of a crowd assembled to be pleased, and full of happiness." To experience theatre was to experience the formation of community, as to a "generous contemplative mind," he wrote, "nothing can afford a more sublime satisfaction than to see happiness diffused thro' a number of our fellow creatures mutually participating of the same entertainment." Given the strength of his commitment to these principles, it was a shame he would miss the Jubilee.

3

A visit to Stratford A month passed between the announcement of the Jubilee and the start of any planning. It was early June by the time Garrick visited Stratford-upon-Avon with a retinue that consisted of his wife, Eva, his younger brother George, and the architect Richard Latimore. The party was greeted with the ringing of church bells and a civic dinner at the White Lion Inn, Stratford's largest coaching inn, which stood on the Great North Road close by the house in which Shakespeare had been born. The dinner cost the Corporation almost fifteen pounds, money largely wasted as Garrick detested events of any kind in which he "considered himself as under the necessity of being a very delightful companion," and "supporting his character as a wit." After dinner, the party toured the environs, led by William Hunt, the industrious and hardworking town clerk. They began at the birthplace, before moving on to King's New School, where Shakespeare had studied, and the remains of New Place, the home he had purchased for his retirement. As they walked, Garrick consulted with Latimore, pointing out sites that might be useful and the number and size of buildings that could be used for dinners, dances, and other repasts. Such had been the response that people had already started trying to reserve rooms, and now Garrick was wondering if the two days he had allotted would be enough as "every body will be there." He told Hunt, "There is much talk, and great Expectations, and we must take care to answer them as well as we possibly can."

The town was not designed for crowds. Situated in gentle hills beside the banks of the river Avon, it was a compact municipality of twelve streets and four hundred half-timbered houses sheltering two thousand souls. Its size and character had changed little in the two hundred years since Shakespeare had walked reluctantly from his home in Henley Street to take his place on his school's narrow benches, just as the open fields that lay beyond remained largely unaltered since the once mighty forest of Arden had been cleared away by Anglo-Saxon handsaws. Its sovereign smells were lanolin and fresh air; its loudest sound the knelling of Holy Trinity's bells.

*Account of
that parish*

Stratford rarely made the news and, prior to Garrick, its most recent appearance in the London papers was the report of a man who, walking home to Birmingham, had saved a baby owl lying in the road only to be attacked by its mother "with such violence as to

The quiet town of Stratford-upon-Avon, with a view of Holy Trinity Church across the Warwickshire fields. © *The Trustees of the British Museum*

deprive him of the sight of one eye." Neither had it done much to exploit its connection to Shakespeare. The house in which he had been raised, for example, had been altered many times, with new rooms and extra kitchens, and the greater part of it being converted into an inn called the Maidenhead. Catering to visitors was not a priority, a fact that had dismayed the writer Horace Walpole, who passed through in 1751 and declared it "the wretchedest old town I ever saw, which I intended for Shakespeare's sake to find snug, and pretty, and antique, not old."

The most extreme example of indifference, however, had been displayed by the Reverend Francis Gastrell, the vicar of Frodsham in Cheshire, who had retired to Stratford and purchased New Place with its ten fireplaces, five gables, two orchards, two barns, and two gardens, one of which contained the famous mulberry tree, planted around 1609 after King James I had thousands of them imported from France. Although slow growing, in the course of the intervening one and a half centuries the mulberry had become a thick and intervolving town landmark, attracting occasional tourists like David Garrick who would come up from London to stand beneath it while contemplating Shakespeare's genius, helping themselves in summer to commemorative sprigs and branches and staining their

The Reverend Gastrell's fury lips in autumn with its wine-dark fruit. These intrusions so aggrieved Gastrell that, in 1756, he hired the carpenter John Ange to fell the tree and dismember it for firewood, so angering the townsfolk that they in turn formed an avenging mob who descended on New Place and broke all its windows. This did nothing to alter the reverend's strong conviction that he could do whatever he wanted with his own property, irrespective of who had owned it before. Three years later, when faced with a bill for the monthly assessments toward the maintenance of the parish poor, he refused to pay on account of the fact that he spent a large part of the year residing in Lichfield. When the Corporation insisted, Gastrell vowed that his house would never be assessed again and had the entire building demolished, leaving a fresh stump and an exposed foundation as all that remained of Shakespeare's estate.

While the citizens of Stratford went on living, largely unconcerned about the many ways in which they were failing to honor the literary ghost imprinted on their walls, the country around them was changing. One would not have had to travel far to find a starkly different version of British life, where sleepy parishes of wool combers and ribbon weavers, high hedgerow and rutted country lanes, gave way to towns black with soot, the din of cart wheels over crocodilian cobblestones, and the angry chattering of looms. Just twenty-two miles north of Stratford sat Birmingham, which in the course of a few short decades had grown from a small town into the most densely populated city in the country after London. Birmingham's population had doubled in the 1760s alone, transforming itself into a hive of commercial invention that burned fifteen thousand tons of coal a week. The principals of Birmingham's rise were the forge and the foundry: iron had been worked in the hills around the city since the sixteenth century, feeding the "toy-makers" to whom the city owed its great affluence. These manufacturers did not produce playthings for children, but rather an array of metal goods considered essential to modern living, from shoe tacks to belt buckles and the buttons on a waistcoat, as well as an infinite catalogue of other small and useful items, such as "Trinkets, Seals, Tweezer and Tooth Pick cases, Smelling Bottles, Snuff Boxes, and Filigree Work such as Toilets, Tea Chests, Inkstands &c. &tc. Cork screws, Buckles, Draw and other Boxes: Snuffers, Watch Chains, Stay Hooks, Sugar knippers &c." Toy work employed over twenty thousand people in an industry worth over £600,000 a year, exporting its goods via a network of waterways that connected Birmingham

The wonders of Birmingham

to the world. "The West-Indies, and the American world," observed the local historian William Hutton, "are intimately acquainted with the Birmingham merchant."

As those merchants grew rich, they badgered at modernity, pushing the pace of invention while searching for efficiencies that would maximize their profits and increase their leisure. With income rising and tastes becoming more cultivated, Birmingham retailers stocked Persian rugs, finely tooled guns, enamels, and furniture finished with exquisite japanning. Speculators arrived, looking to fund their schemes through practical demonstrations of steam engines and condensers, magnetism, lenses, and hydraulics, jolting themselves with electric shocks while discursing on the properties of the Leyden jar, or experimenting with forms of horseless transport like Mr. Moore's carriage, a self-propelling, four-wheeled vehicle that moved by means of a crankshaft.

Stratford's economy, meanwhile, had been stalled for years due to the collapse of its trade in harrateen, a kind of linen used for curtains and the canopies that enclosed four-poster beds and kept the sleeping safe from the mice that fell from the rafters stupefied by wood smoke. Led by its mayor, Samuel Jarvis, the Corporation of Stratford had failed to raise sufficient volunteers to sit on the town council, which consistently numbered fewer than the twelve aldermen and twelve capital burgesses required by its charter, in spite of the thirty-pound fine levied against those who refused to serve. Even those who did agree to sit attended so sporadically that the council was often forced to disperse without conducting its business. "Surrounded with impassable roads, no intercourse with man to humanize the mind, no commerce to smooth their rugged manners," wrote the historian of Birmingham of his provincial neighbors, "they continue the boors of nature."

In the face of such apathy, the economic fate of Stratford came

increasingly to rely on a handful of men—most notably, the town
cler, William Hunt. Hunt's efforts to bring investment to | *The Town*
Stratford had begun when the Corporation sought to | *Hall*
rebuild the town's market house, which had been in a state
of near ruination since lumps had been shot out of it during the
Civil War. Having received a builder's quote for £678, and commit-
ting £200 of its own funds toward construction of a new building,
the Corporation gave Hunt the job of raising the rest from local
worthies. A list of potential subscribers was compiled that included
the town's biggest landowner, the Duke of Dorset, and the Earl of
Warwick, who gave £21. Hunt himself gave £5, 5 shillings.

When completed in 1767, the new Town Hall emulated the
Georgian elegance of many English market towns with its golden
frontage of smooth Cotswold stone. Standing in marked contrast
to the eaved and timbered dwellings that surrounded it, it boasted
a spacious ballroom on its top floor, "sixty feet long thirty foot wide
and twenty feet high . . . plastered with a good handsome plastering
of light yellow colour," separate card rooms for gentlemen and ladies,
and—a sign of the greatest modern convenience—two purpose-
built water closets complete with lead basins and brass fittings. On
the ground floor were kitchens, a pantry, and the town prison, while
the front portion of the building was left as an open colonnade
to house the corn market. Although a source of great civic pride,
one small detail prevented perfection: a recess that had been built
into the exterior of the second story on the building's north side.
This concave space, the ideal home for some kind of statue or bust,
remained unfilled, and standing noticeably empty, looked forlorn.

Just as the Town Hall was being finished, a man named George
Alexander Stevens came to town. After an unsuccessful stint as an
actor in Garrick's company, Stevens had attained fame as a singer of
comic songs and "spouter" of mock orations that he crafted into

one-man shows like the wildly popular *Lecture upon Heads*, a satirical performance in which he performed characters such as lawyers,
doctors, and gamblers, and historical figures including Cleopatra,
Alexander the Great, and a Cherokee chief, with the aid of several
wigs and busts of pasteboard and wood. The show had taken him all
over the country and even to America, enabling him to amass a fortune close to ten thousand pounds, "the greatest part of which
melted from his hands" according to *The Gentleman's Magazine*. Stevens was a friend of John Payton, landlord of the White Lion, and,
along with William Hunt, one of the Stratford's more ambitious
citizens. Payton—"as hearty, as sensible, and as polite a being as any
man who loves and relishes society would wish to be acquainted
with," according to one guest who had stayed at his inn—had been
one of the few who had tried to capitalize on Shakespeare's reputation by showing visitors around the remains of New Place and taking them to "Shakespeare's Canopy," a crab tree growing from a
hedge that the playwright had reputedly slept under after a night of
drinking (the tree collapsed in 1824, another victim of relic hunt-
ers). It was during a convivial dinner with Payton and several members of the Stratford Corporation that Stevens first suggested that
A statue the Town Hall's empty nook should contain a statue of Stratford's peerless son. The matter was discussed, and it was
decided that Stevens would approach Garrick, his former employer,
with the idea of holding a benefit night at Drury Lane to raise
funds. Although Garrick declined, he did share his regret with Stevens that nothing had been organized in 1766 to mark the 150th
anniversary of Shakespeare's death.

Ambitions at this stage ran no further than obtaining a statue
for the empty nook, and with a line of communication successfully
opened, William Hunt charged Francis Wheler with following up.
As steward for the Court of Records, Wheler's business often took

him to London's Middle Temple, where he kept chambers at the spacious Jacobean house at 1 Brick Court. A fellow resident was Oliver Goldsmith, the popular author of *The Vicar of Wakefield* currently at work on his groundbreaking poem, the harbinger of Romanticism that was "The Deserted Village." Wheler may well have passed Garrick on the stairs, since the actor and Goldsmith were good friends, and Goldsmith often hosted parties in his rooms. One acquaintance he certainly made was Garrick's friend the poet George Keate, who agreed to intercede on the Corporation's behalf. As degrees of separation diminished, Wheler felt confident that he was nearing his quarry and reported back to Hunt with a plan. "In order to flatter Mr Garrick into some such Handsom present," he wrote, "I have been thinking it would not be at all amiss if the Corporation were to propose to make Mr. Garrick an Honourary Burgess of Stratford and to present him therewith in a Box made of Shakespears Mulberry tree." The Corporation approved, delivering fifty-five pounds and a parcel of mulberry wood to Thomas Davies of Newhall Walk, Birmingham (and not to be confused with Garrick's first biographer), commissioning him to carve both a box and an ornamental standish—a desk set for pen, ink, and writing materials—as a gift for Keate to thank him for his part in their plan.

George Alexander Stevens, meanwhile, paid Garrick a second visit, this time finding that the actor had grown more amenable to the idea of presenting a gift *Petitioning Garrick* to the town of Shakespeare's birth. Writing to Payton, Stevens declared,

> I am Certain Mr Garrick; (at least as well as I can guess,) will present ye Town and Town Hal with either a Statue or Bust of Shakespear—but by all means address Him by Letter properly.

Set forth his great merits, and that there is not a man in England (except himself) to Whom you can apply with equal propriety for a Bust, or Statue. Say Shakespear the father of the English Stage, Garrick the Restorer of Shakespear—and some other such phrases for all great Men Love to be praised.

Flattery was a proven method for dealing with Garrick, who, in the words of one rival, "never failed to enjoy adulation." The hint was passed on to Wheler in London, who in December 1767 wrote to Garrick to formally request a "Statue Bust or Picture" of Shakespeare to be displayed in the Town Hall, along with "some Picture of yourself That the memory of both may be perpetuated together in that place wch gave him birth and where he still lives in the mind of every Inhabitant." Moreover, continued Wheler,

The Corporation of Stratford ever desiring of expressing their Gratitude to all who do Honour and Justice to the memory of Shakespear, and highly sensible that no person in any age hath excelled you therein would think themselves much honored if you would become one of their Body; Tho this Borough doth not now send Members to Parliament perhaps the inhabitants may not be the less virtuous, and to sending the Freedom of such a place the more acceptable to you the Corporation propose to send it in a Box made of that very Mulberry tree planted by Shakespear's own hand.

Doubly besieged, Garrick relented, and the next time Stevens saw him, "He told me he thought himself obliged to the Corporation etc. of your Town for their application, and declared He would present you as fine [a statue] as London could make." Offering to write a dedicatory ode for the statue's eventual unveiling, Stevens signed off with a promise to send his ice skates to Payton's son, John junior, and retired from the negotiations.

When it came to Shakespeare statues, Garrick had form. The garden of his house at Richmond contained what Hor- *Garrick's* ace Walpole called a "grateful temple to Shakespeare," *temple to* a domed octagonal structure close to the riverbank that *Shakespeare* housed a fine statue by the French sculptor Louis François Roubiliac: "A most noble statue of this most original man," wrote the playwright Hannah More, "in an attitude strikingly pensive— his limbs strongly muscular, his countenance strongly expressive of some vast conception, and his whole form seeming the bigger from some immense idea with which you suppose his great imagination pregnant." The temple was unique, for while it was not uncommon in grand British gardens to find picturesque rotundas, pavilions, and exedrae like the Temple of British Worthies at Stowe in Buckinghamshire (built in 1734), Garrick's was the only one devoted solely to a single writer. It was indeed, as Walpole claimed, "grateful," an expression of thanks for the earthly rewards Shakespeare had bestowed upon the house of Garrick. It also served to flatter Garrick himself. The actor, it was said, had posed for the statue, suggesting that he was more than just a willing vessel. If not exactly a reincarnation of Shakespeare, it implied, the two artists were somehow collocated, existing in one body: "SHAKESPEARE revives! In GARRICK breathes again!" as the writer Richard Rolt would have it. The temple was equipped with a dozen chairs—including one made from mulberry wood—in which visitors were invited to sit and admire. Tea was served.

Garrick's statue took as its template the Shakespeare monument installed in the southeast corner of Westminster Abbey in 1741, for which Garrick himself had helped to raise subscriptions. Sculpted by the Dutch artist Peter Scheemakers from sleek, lactescent marble, the Westminster Shakespeare was similarly pensive and elegant. The poet was depicted with a sheaf of paper pinched between forefinger and thumb, leaning casually on a pile of books as though inviting inspiration to come and read to him, surrounded by the symbolism of poetical solemnity—a dagger and a laurel wreath, and busts of the monarchs featured in his history plays. Both statues had been prohibitively expensive, so when it came to commissioning a statue for Stratford, Garrick turned prudently to John Cheere, maker of mass-produced statuary at his god-filled yard at Hyde Park Corner. Cheere sold to the price-conscious gentleman eager to stock his parks and halls with "frisking satyrs" cast from lead. The result was a close approximation of Scheemakers's statue at a far more reasonable price, and with one notable improvement: when Scheemakers's original had been unveiled, the parchment Shakespeare held in his left hand was blank, leaving a tantalizing space for any pencil-wielding Pasquino to scrawl rude and satirical verses. This was curtailed when the dean of Westminster Abbey had the empty page inscribed with lines from *The Tempest* (which in the event were misquoted). To ensure that the Stratford statue wouldn't endure the same fate, it would display lines from *A Midsummer Night's Dream*.

Next, Garrick attended to the paintings that Wheler had suggested might be hung in the Town Hall ballroom. A portrait of Shakespeare was produced by Benjamin Wilson, the tutor of John Zoffany and the current incumbent of the office of sergeant-painter to the king, a role that required him to produce royal portraits and adornments for celebrations. A second painting by Garrick's friend Thomas Gainsborough depicted the actor gazing mistily into the invisible realms with his arm around a bust of Shakespeare in the grounds of Prior Park, the home of William Warburton, the bishop of Gloucester and an editor of Shakespeare. The painting was masterly, but Garrick, concerned that it might smack of vanity to present the town with a picture of himself and Shakespeare so lovingly

David Garrick with a bust of Shakespeare in the grounds of Prior Park,
Somerset. This is a copy of Thomas Gainsborough's original, hung in the
Town Hall at Stratford-upon-Avon until destroyed by fire in 1946.

© Shakespeare Birthplace Trust

entwined, suggested that the Corporation pay for it directly. With little choice, the town fathers complied, paying also for a magnificent gilt frame obtained by Wilson for a total cost of £137 and 4 shillings. Dealing with celebrities was expensive: when tallied alongside with Thomas Davies's commission for the mulberry box, the cost of wooing David Garrick had almost doubled the Corporation's investment in the Town Hall.

◀§

Somewhere in the course of these negotiations, the idea of staging a festival around the presentation of the statue had been born. As with the artistic commissions, Garrick made sure this wouldn't leave him out of pocket. Growing up under the perpetual threat of poverty had made him careful with money, and one of his first orders of business on arriving in Stratford was to determine the

Financing the Jubilee

finances for the Jubilee. Forty years earlier, if such an event could have been conceived, the Jubilee would have been the product of patronage, paid for by an aristocratic sponsor and offered in the spirit of *noblesse oblige*. These days, it was an entirely private venture. Just as the economy was modernizing, the way in which high culture was consumed was in transition too, and the opportunity to venerate Shakespeare had to balance the books like any other commodity.

The aristocracy still played an important role, smoothing over with their presence any anxieties that might exist about the commercialization of culture, and invoking an older relationship between actor and patron that placed Garrick in the role of courtier rather than businessman. Garrick played the role impeccably by being studiously deferential and accommodating, but cash was now king. Garrick proposed that he and the Corporation cover all the expenses between them, including footing the bill for food and lodging for the performers, sharing any losses equally, but allowing any profits that might be made to be invested in Stratford and "entirely laid out in the Honor of Shakespeare."

It was a generous offer, but the men of the Corporation were uneasy. Having sunk money into the paintings and mulberry box, and already committed themselves to making improvements to the house of Mr. Hatton next to the site of New Place in order to accommodate the Duke of Dorset for the duration of the Jubilee, they were reluctant to spend further.

If that were so, said Garrick, he would be better off turning the entire production over to London speculators, in which case any profit would leave Stratford entirely. He wondered aloud if there might be a small coalition of local "adventurers" who would be willing to shoulder the risk, a broad hint that was taken up by both William Hunt and John Payton, the landlord of the White Lion. Hunt and Payton were keen to speculate and perhaps emulate in some small part the success of men like their Birmingham neighbor Matthew Boulton, a captain of industry whose newly opened Soho Manufactory on Handsworth Heath had been designed to look like "the stately Palace of some Duke" in order to emphasize the braided strands of affluence, consumption, and taste that together formed the bonds of social progress. Men like Boulton understood the connection between the arts and industry, as evinced by his own attempts to bring a licensed theatre to Birmingham, arguing to the Earl of Dartmouth that it was an essential means of civilizing the people. "All well regulated states have found it expedient to indulge the people with amusements of some kind or another," Boulton had told the earl,

> and certainly those are most eligible that tend to improve the morals, the manners, or the taste of the people, and at the same time to prevent them from relapsing into the barbarous amusements which prevailed in this neighborhood in the last century, when Birmingham was as remarkable for good forgers and filers as for

their bad taste in all their works. Their diversions were bull bait-
ings, cock fightings, boxing matches and abominable drunken-
ness with all its train. But now the scene is changed. The people
are more polite and civilized, and the taste of their manufactures
greatly improved. There is not a town of its size in Europe where
mechanism is brought to such perfection, and we have also made
considerable progress in some of the liberal arts, which hath been a
means of extending our trade to the remotest corners of the world.

Boulton continued, "It is certainly in our interest to bring a [theatri-
cal] company to Birmingham, as it contributes so much to the public good, not only from the money they leave behind them, but from
their explaining their wants to the manufacturers, and giving hints
for various improvements, which nothing promotes so much as an
intercourse with persons from different parts of the world." In the
minds of Payton and Hunt, a jubilee would provide a similar stimulus for Stratford, resulting not only in short-term profit but in a rising tide of gentility that would connect the town to the new
economy—or so they hoped. A "determinate and final answer is
desired on this matter as soon as possible as there is no time to lose,"
insisted Garrick, eager to close the deal before leaving town and
encouraging Hunt to put up one hundred pounds of his own money.
The *Whitehall Evening Post* agreed. "The money which this Jubilee
will cause to be circulated in Stratford and its environs," it wrote,
"will be very serviceable to many of the inhabitants of that town as
they stand more in need of it than those of Bath, Bristol, Margate,
Brighthelmstone, etc., many of whom have already become rich by
the expensive pleasures of the opulent."

Everybody loves George Garrick

Having taken his tour, Garrick returned to London,
leaving behind his brother George to oversee the preparations. Six years David's junior, George Garrick was a
devoted sibling, albeit somewhat lacking in initiative and

unable to capitalize on the many professional openings his brother had arranged for him. For the past twenty years, George had been the managerial assistant at Drury Lane, a job that involved little direct management but enabled him to serve as a counterweight to the demanding attention to detail that often alienated the actors from his brother. Managing such a talented group of performers was a constant strain, and Garrick frequently lost his temper with his "large family, in which there are many froward [sic] Children," tiring of their green-room arguments, feuds over preeminence, and chronic underpre-paredness, leaving it to his brother George to soothe their wounded feelings and get them ready to perform. Some, like Spranger Barry, who had for a short while been considered Garrick's rival in the role of Romeo, required every ounce of George's détente, since he and his wife made increasingly outrageous demands of Garrick, or arrived at the theatre drunk or not at all. Others, like Giuseppe Grimaldi, master of the corps de ballet and a pantomime clown with enormous energy and a generous dash of insanity, had to be approached with the same caution one might approach a dangerous beast. Garrick, who labeled Grimaldi a "Tartar" and "impudent fellow," considered him "ye worst behav'd Man in ye Whole Company and Shd have had a horse whip," for his serial seduction of young dancers, the sadistic punishments he would inflict on the children of the company, and the beatings he would dole out to those who crossed him.

Fortunately, even Garrick's avowed enemies found it hard to hate George—he was affable and easygoing and "had so many admirable traits of real goodness," according to the librettist Charles Dibdin. In addition to serving as house mollifier, George was fre-quently employed as saboteur and spy, talking down plays that Gar-rick did not want to stage but didn't want to see his rivals to perform either, and keeping watch on his brother's servants, especially one named Molly at Southampton Street, a woman Garrick considered "particularly bebitched," who took men back to the house and was "a great peeper into papers." All this came with a salary of £200 a year, topped off by an allowance from his brother for another £100, as well as an unwritten agreement that Garrick would provide for George's numerous children. Like many in the company, however, George knew what it was to enjoy a bohemian lifestyle in which time was of little consequence and money was thought to evaporate if left unused too long. He was constantly in debt.

Preparations begin | In Stratford-upon-Avon, George headquartered himself in a large stone building known as the College, "capacious, handsome, and strong," which in turn abutted Holy Trinity Church. The College was owned by Mrs. Kendall, a sickly widow recuperating in Bath. While now empty, it had once been the habitation of priests, and with its absentee landlord, large rooms, long gallery-like corridors, and monastic garden surrounded by a high stone wall that discouraged prying eyes, it was the perfect place from which to plan Jubilee surprises. To work on these marvels, George was joined by John French, a leading Drury Lane scenery maker, and his assistant, Porter. French was a talented artist and a heavy drinker. "Being addicted to inebriety," wrote one account, "it was with difficulty that Mr. George Garrick could induce him to proceed, as French frequently made it necessary that drink should be sent to the painting rooms to secure his attendance there." Deep in his cups, French hated to be left alone, and because George was known for being such a good fellow, he insisted that he stay with him throughout his long binges. In London, George was usually so assiduous in following out his brother's commands that he "was always in anxiety, lest in his absence his brother should have wanted him; and the first question he asked on his return was, 'Did DAVID want me?'" In sleepy Warwickshire, with no brother to superintend him, it was easy just to let the days pass in drinking and chat.

This was a problem as Garrick had left his brother with a long list of to-dos, including liaising with the locals, making arrangements for two public dinners, and commandeering vessels for the use of day-trippers on the river Avon (which amounted in the end to just "2 barges and Fishing Boat"). In addition, George was to find stalls for all the horses the visitors would bring, measure the span of the river (a measurement Garrick was inexplicably eager to learn, and which George was particularly tardy about delivering), and design a plan of decoration for the town's sole bridge with its fourteen arches. He was also supposed to ensure that all the houses in the town would be adorned with streamers and flowers, and to arrange for the presence of the local militia to enforce public order and provide the fête with some martial dignity. Jubilee ribbons were to be commissioned from Mr. Jackson in Coventry, and a commemorative medal was to be engraved by Westwood in Birmingham with versions cast in copper, silver, and gold, to suit each pocketbook. George was to supervise French in the construction of a "triumphal car" that would bear the muses of Comedy and Tragedy at the front of a grand procession of Shakespeare characters Garrick had planned, as well as to arrange for the men of the Corporation to march in costume and audition some local children for parts. "We shall want 8, 10, or a dozen of the handsomest children in ye Town, by way of Fairies and Cupids for our pageant," Garrick had written to William Hunt, "will you be so obliging to cast an Eye upon ye Schools for this purpose?—We must likewise collect as many seemly fellows as we can get to assist in ye Pageant."

The pageant was going to be one of the most important parts of the Jubilee. Audiences loved processions and parades, especially after a long night of drama, and when done well they offered a shimmering vision of distant ages and exotic locales, accompanied by waving banners and stirring music that afforded the senses the pleasures of luxuriation without need for either close listening or critical discernment. One hundred and fifty boxes of dresses and scenery were sent up from Drury Lane to furnish the pageant, accompanied by an assortment of leather-aproned scene men and understrappers who would barrack in the College and spend the day knocking and sawing.

The Rotunda   By far George's most important commission was to bring into reality Garrick's vision for a space large enough to fit more than one hundred performers and up to two thousand guests. The architect Richard Latimore had decreed that none of Stratford's existing buildings would be sufficient, so it was decided that a temporary rotunda would be built under his direction similar to the one that stood in Ranelagh Gardens, a popular pleasure spot owned by James Lacy, Garrick's business partner and co-owner of the patent of Drury Lane. Opened in 1742, on the site of a former mansion, Ranelagh was a private landscape of shady walks, formal plantings, and water features designed for al fresco entertainments. Located at the edge of the Thames and most charmingly approached by water, for two shillings and sixpence anyone could enjoy music, dancing, and firework displays, or spend time alone on its private paths and bowers before partaking of "fine imperial tea and other refreshments." This ornate wooden pavilion, described by Horace Walpole as "a vast amphitheatre, finely gilt, painted and illuminated in which everybody that loves eating, drinking and staring is admitted," was 150 feet in diameter and contained fifty-two dining boxes lit by a thousand lamps.

Garrick had initially intended his rotunda to be built behind the White Lion Inn, but the site did not provide good access, and so a spot on Bankcroft Mead, a meadow at the edge of the Avon, was chosen. This would permit of the prettiest aspect and, just like Ranelagh, allow visitors to enjoy the romance of approaching an illuminated palace from the water. To achieve the desired effect, it was necessary to remove more than one hundred willow trees that stood on the land. William Hunt sought permission to fell the trees, which was jointly granted by the Duke of Dorset, who owned them, and a lawyer named Dionysus Bradley, who held the lease. Once they were removed, an unobstructed view from the site to the bridge and so across to town was revealed.

Having seen the newly opened meadow, Hunt was moved to build a Chinese summerhouse on the opposite bank, which he would open to visitors. Hunt's friend and fellow "adventurer," John Payton, similarly busied himself. As the landlord of the White Lion, Payton took on the role of official caterer and hotelier for the duration. Garrick had asked him to rename his inn the "Shakespeare's Head," even offering him a good price on a new sign, but Payton was reluctant to give up the established reputation he had built. Nonetheless, he invested heavily, renaming his rooms after Shakespeare characters and hastily adding to his property by constructing an assembly room, card room, coffee room, and a suite of private apartments he would reserve for the Garricks. Even the menu was revised so that visitors might enjoy meals such as "Jubilee chicken." To cater to the expected crowds, he had ordered 3600 pewter plates and cutlery to go with them, 1000 gallons of wine for his cellar, and (what had been the height of London culinary fashion five years earlier) a 327-pound sea turtle that until recently had supported its full weight in the green waters of the Caribbean.

The enthusiasm for the Jubilee shown by Hunt and Payton was not universally shared around the town. As George Garrick's residency continued and the streets began to fill with strangers, many Stratford locals could be found "either pursuing their occupations in the old dog-trot way"

Indifference and anxieties of locals

(in the words of *The Gentleman's Magazine*) "or staring with wonderful vacancy of phis at the preparations, the purpose of which they had very few ideas about." "The low People of Stratford upon Avon are without Doubt as ignorant as any in the whole Island," reported a correspondent for the *St. James Chronicle*,

> I could not possibly imagine that there were such Beings in the most repost, and least frequented Parts of the Kingdom. I talked with many, particularly the old People, and not one of them but was frightened at the Preparations for the Jubilee, and did not know what they were about: Many of them really thought that Mr. G_____ would raise Devils, and fly in a Chariot about the Town. They ordered those whom they had Power over, not to stir out the Day of the Jubilee. . . . It is impossible to describe their Absurdity; and indeed Providence seems, by producing Shakespeare and the rest of his Townsmen, to shew the two Extremes of Human Nature.

The townsfolk's anxiety was exacerbated by the fact that even with all this activity, no one had any real idea what the Jubilee would actually entail. *Town and Country Magazine* had announced that it would last five days and consist of concerts, masked balls and "riddotoes [sic] alternately." An unsigned letter in *The Gentleman's Magazine* made it sound entirely different, "an intellectual feast" akin to an academic conference whose first day would be devoted to a "eulogium . . . on the wonderful dramatic Genius," the second to "an examination of the Poet's verification," including lectures on harmony and rhyme and "much delightful instruction" on the "errors of some modern performers in respect to accent, emphasis, and rest." The whole was to conclude with an opportunity to view a copy of "the Stratford Swan," a periodical devoted to literary criticism, which, according to this correspondent, Garrick intended to edit after retiring from the stage.

In August, two weeks before the Jubilee was supposed to begin, Joseph Cradock, a writer, amateur performer, the high sheriff of Leicester, and friend of David Garrick, took a ride over to Stratford to check on its progress but found that hardly any had been made. A tour of the sites found nothing but "desolate appearance." Of particular concern was the Rotunda. "If that great and striking object, turns out as it ought to do," Garrick had said, "it will make other matters very Easy." However, not only had construction not begun, but a price for the wood to make it had still not been agreed with the Birmingham lumberyard. Cases of lamps sent up to illuminate the interior had arrived "shivered to pieces" and been dumped on the riverbank. Calling at the College to speak with some of the Drury Lane men there, Cradock was told, "We never were so uncomfortably circumstanced in our lives."

> We are sent down here to make some preparations for the entertainment, but we are absolutely without materials, and we can gain no assistance whatever from the inhabitants, who are all fearful of lending us any article whatever. We would do any thing in the world to serve our good Master, but he is entirely kept in the dark, as to the situation of everything here, and we only wish to return to London again, as soon as possible, to save expenses.

At a dinner with the Corporation, the message of doom was repeated. The Jubilee promised to be the largest single congregation of people outside London in living memory, and the locals, understandably nervous about the size of the crowd, were anxious that they would open their houses only to have their hospitality abused by vicious Londoners and "have all their plate stolen, and their furniture destroyed." Most wanted only to lock up their houses and abandon the town for the duration, pleading with Cradock to take their concerns back to Garrick and ask that he cancel the Jubilee.

A dire prognostication

"Sure, you cannot think that any Jubilee will take place here," a local told him. "I doubt whether any one was ever seriously intended; but if it was meditated, you may depend upon it, that it is entirely given up."

Cradock assured the man that the Jubilee was definitely going ahead.

"There will be no Jubilee," replied the man. "There will be a riot."

4

The threat of disorder was real. The Jubilee was set to take place in a country in the midst of a constitutional crisis, bringing thousands of people together at a time when public violence was commonplace. As the American in London Benjamin Franklin wrote in 1769,

> I have seen, within a year, riots in the country about corn; riots about elections; riots about work-houses; riots of colliers; riots of weavers; riots of coal-heavers; riots of sawyers; riots of sailors; riots of Wilkesites; riots of government chairmen; riots of smugglers, in which custom-house officers and excisemen have been murdered, the King's armed vessels and troops fired at, &c.

The unrest was so frequent, he wrote, "one would think riots part of the mode of government."

It had not always been this way. The 1760s had begun with an emphatic series of victories over France in the Seven Years War, which had dismantled the French empire overseas and seized for Britain half the world's trade. But instead of assuring prosperity, victory was followed by a sharp economic decline as repatriating soldiers found little work and industries lacked the stimulus of war. A recessionary slump caused a wave of inflation that was further deepened by problems in food production; more than ten years of poor harvests had resulted in shortages of meat and bread that pushed many to the brink of starvation. Concerned at "the exhausted state

Burdens of taxation

of the public revenues," George Grenville, first lord of the treasury, compounded the misery by raising taxation. "In England," wrote one foreign observer,

> the people are taxed in the morning for the soap that washes their hands; at nine for the coffee, the tea and the sugar they use for their breakfast, at noon, for the starch that powders their hair; at dinner for the salt that savours their meat; in the evening for the porter that chears their spirits; all day long for the light that enters their windows; and at night for the candles that light them to bed.

By 1768, the price of bread had doubled, making it hard even for working families to feed themselves. Crime worsened in spite of a penal system that listed more than two hundred offenses punishable by death, among them damaging fruit trees and impersonating a Chelsea pensioner. "The papers are filled with robberies and breaking of houses," wrote *The Gentleman's Magazine*, "and with recitals of the cruelties committed by the robbers, greater than ever known before."

Political shortcomings of George III

The crisis had come about through the systematic dismantling of a political establishment that had once been considered the most open and stable in Europe. Since the accession of George I in 1714, Britain had been ruled by a claque of Whig politicians who had considered it their divine commission to defend Britain against France, Catholics, Jacobites, and Pretenders Old and Young. Yet when the twenty-two-year-old George III came to the throne in 1760, this reliable faction was pulled apart. The new king was a lonely and isolated man who did not learn to read until he was eleven, and at the time of his coronation still wrote like a child. He despised the ministers who had counseled his predecessors and was determined to replace them with his adored boyhood tutor, Lord Bute. In 1761 he forced the resignation of the popular William Pitt, tormentor of the French, who was then serving as both foreign minister and war minister, installing in his place his beloved Bute and instructing him to end the war and make peace with France. Bute did as he was told, but proved unequal to the task of governance, and as the old, reliable, political machine began to unravel, infighting and incompetence led to seven governments rising and falling in quick succession. It was, in the words of the statesman and philosopher Edmund Burke, "a tessellated pavement without cement . . . utterly unsafe to touch, and unsure to stand on," with a political establishment "dreaded and contemned" by the people, and stripped of all legitimacy. "The laws are despoiled of all their respected and salutary terrors," Burke continued,

> and all the solemn plausibilities of the world, have lost their reverence and effect; that our foreign politicks are as much deranged as our domestic oeconomy . . . that hardly any thing above or below, abroad or at home, is sound and entire; but that disconnection and confusion, in offices, in parties, in families, in Parliament, in the nation, prevail beyond the disorders of any former time.

From the discord rose a man who would become the most divisive figure in Britain, loved and loathed in equal measure. He also happened to be a good friend of James Boswell. Named John Wilkes, he was the son of a London distiller who had overcome the significant social barriers of modest birth *Of Wilkes and liberty* and unfortunate features thanks to great charm and wily intelligence. Wilkes had made his first foray into politics in the 1750s, having bribed his way to become the MP for Aylesbury, squandering his wife's fortune and destroying their unhappy marriage in the process. Having secured his seat, he seemed content to live as an idle carpetbagger, paying more attention to his appetites than his duties while espousing the popular patriotism that supported Pitt's aggression in the war against France.

Once Pitt was ousted, Wilkes's life was turned around. The king sued for peace with France, thus angering many bellicose populists, among them Wilkes, who discovered in himself a profound talent for troublemaking and political agitation. As a parliamentarian and orator, he had never done well—bad teeth, cross-eyes, and a distracting lisp ensured that his few performances in the House of Commons had been awkward and unpopular affairs—but as a writer of polemic, he was exceptional. In 1762, together with the poet Charles Churchill, he founded a weekly newspaper they called *The North Briton*, ostensibly in support of Lord Bute (who was Scottish, and therefore "North British") but actually a savage and thinly veiled critique of his policies, bullient with antigovernment bile. Like many, Boswell followed the *North Briton* avidly—despite his own conservative politics, which were based on a sentimental reverence for ancient ties rather than a formal ideology. During his extended sojourn in London between November 1762 and August 1763, Boswell would walk to the printer's shop in Ludgate Street to secure his copy as it came off the press at four o'clock, enjoying the paper's "poignant acrimony" that he found "very relishing."

Following Bute's resignation in 1763, *The North Briton* fell contentedly silent, pleased with a job well done. Until, that is, George III offered his customary speech at the closing of Parliament, during which he praised the Treaty of Paris—the diplomatic agreement that had official brought hostilities with France to a close and returned many conquered territories to the French—as "honorable to the crown, and so beneficial to my people." This statement enraged Wilkes, who like many supporters of William Pitt considered the treaty to be a betrayal of British sacrifices and a negation of its victories. And so *The North Briton* went back to the press. Unable to attack a

R. E. Pine pinx.ᵗ   *W. Dickinson fecit.*

The Right Honᵇᵉˡ JOHN WILKES Esq. Lord Mayor
of the CITY of LONDON.

London, Publish'd Novʳ 9ᵗʰ 1774, at Mˢˢ Sledges Henrietta Street Covent Garden.

Politician, polemicist, campaigner, hedonist—John Wilkes.
© *National Portrait Gallery, London*

reigning monarch, Wilkes used his magazine to argue that the king was himself a victim, the unwitting puppet of spineless ministers and despicable men who had used him to ventriloquize their own treacherous policy of surrender. "I am in doubt," he wrote, "whether the imposition is greater on the sovereign, or on the nation. Every friend of this country must lament that a prince of so many great and amiable qualities, whom England truly reveres, can be brought to give the sanction of his sacred name to the most odious measures, and to the most unjustifiable public declarations, from a throne ever renowned for truth, honour, and unsullied virtue."

The piece, which appeared in issue 45 of *North Briton* on April 23 (Shakespeare's birthday), 1763, indirectly accused the king of treason by way of the rhetorical device known as litotes in which speech affirms its opposite by means of understatement. (A famous Shakespearean example is Antony's repetition of the phrase, delivered over the corpse of Julius Ceasar, "But Brutus is an honorable man.") It was an audacious slice of effrontery that earned a furious retaliation from the government and a general warrant for the arrest of the "Authors, Printers and Publishers of a seditious and treasonous paper intitled, the North Briton Number 45." Wilkes's house was ransacked, hundreds of documents were seized, and forty-nine people were arrested, including children.

After a nervous standoff at sword point, Wilkes allowed himself to be escorted to the Tower of London, but he was soon released. Drawn to the excitement of current events, Boswell joined the crowd that had gathered outside the Tower to meet him, defying his mentor, Samuel Johnson—the recipient of an annual pension of three hundred pounds from George III "solely as the reward of his literary merit," Johnson believed that Wilkes should be ducked in the river by a troop of footmen. In its disproportionate fury, the government had miscalculated the legality of its warrant and its blanket call to round up unnamed individuals irrespective of any evidence of their guilt, which—when combined with Wilkes's own claims to immunity from prosecution as a sitting MP—caused their case to become quickly snagged in confusion. Wilkes seized the initiative by seeking damages for wrongful arrest, presenting himself in the process as the champion of a political system considered the freest and most enlightened on earth, thanks to a mixed constitution that had traditionally balanced monarchical power, aristocratic oligarchy, parliamentary democracy, and a system of laws to create what Edmund Burke called an "isthmus between arbitrary power and anarchy."

As a self-styled victim of tyranny, Wilkes became a political idol. In his home constituency of Aylesbury, he was escorted into town by an honor guard who hailed him in a long series of boozy toasts. Impressed by his bravery and willingness to endure hardship without complaint, more and more people came to his cause—"the middling and inferior set," he called them, "who stand most in need of protection," a yeomanry of fiercely independent and patriotic supporters who adopted "Wilkes and Liberty!" as their rallying cry. In London, he was applauded in the streets, receiving the support of the freemen of the City of London and County of Surrey. Not everyone was convinced. "This hero is as bad a fellow as ever hero was," wrote Horace Walpole to his friend Sir Horace Mann, "abominable in private life, dull in Parliament, but, they say, very entertaining in a room, and certainly no bad writer."

Wilkes's initial ascendancy was short-lived. When Parliament reopened, he was openly insulted by the MP *Wounds groin* Samuel Martin, resulting in a duel in which Wilkes took a shot in the groin that almost killed him. Believing with just cause that this was a bungled attempt at assassination, he fled to Paris and was expelled from Parliament, declared an outlaw, and found guilty of libel in absentia. It was during this exile that Boswell came to know Wilkes well. At the end of his long stay in London in 1763, Boswell had been ordered by his father to study law at the University of Utrecht, a miserable sentence made endurable only by the promise that he would be allowed to travel in Europe once his studies were concluded. It was then that he crossed paths with Wilkes in the customs office in Rome, and decided to follow him and his mistress, Gertrude Corradini, to Naples, where they spent three weeks together, talking, calling on William Hamilton, the British envoy to the court of Naples, visiting the tomb of Virgil and the sites of Herculaneum and Pompeii. At Mount Vesuvius, Wilkes had to be pushed and pulled by five porters to make sure he reached the top, but once at the summit, he and Boswell lay on their bellies and gazed into the crater surrounded by clouds of sulfurous smoke.

Boswell found Wilkes to be a "rough, blunt fellow, very clever" and considered his company to be "boisterous" but enjoyable— "the phoenix of convivial felicity," as Johnson mockingly described him. As their friendship grew, Boswell, a habitual writer of letters, diaries, and memoranda, recorded surprisingly little of it, a signal perhaps of his concern that a friend like Wilkes might bring the scrutiny of the authorities upon himself. While Boswell's politics would not allow him to think of Wilkes as anything other than "an enemy to the true old British Constitution, and to the order and happiness of society"—a phrase he addressed to Wilkes directly—a personal regard for his companion grew daily, fueled by respect for his unrelenting candor and unflagging spirits, and for his ability to pay heed only to the demands of the present. "Never think on futurity," Wilkes told Boswell, "as not data enough."

Even more intriguing, Wilkes appeared to be immune to the pressures of social conformity, especially around sex. When Boswell read Wilkes an excerpt of a letter from Belle de Zuylen, a Dutch woman he had met in Utrecht and over whose affections he had been obsessing, Wilkes's only comment was "Go home by Holland and roger her." Wilkes, too, had been sent to Holland to study as a young man, but where the young Scot had spent his time struggling to master his senses and control every urge, Wilkes had gloried in his dissipation: "three or four whores: drunk every night." For the hypochondriac Boswell, the matter-of-factness with which Wilkes owned his desires was thrilling. "Thank heaven for having given me the love of women," he told Boswell, reveling in the feeling of freedom sex gave him, especially given that "to many she gives not the noble passion of lust." Taking the elder man's mentorship to heart, Boswell tried to sleep with as many women as possible in Italy, writing in his journal, "Be Spaniard: girl every day." As he later told Rousseau, "I sallied forth of an evening like an imperious lion." One night he even arranged an orgy, recording the payments in his account book under the heading "badinage."

After three weeks, he and Wilkes parted company. Boswell returned to Rome to study antiquities, with Wilkes telling him that he hoped that the "champions of liberty will in time pluck out of your lairdish breast the black seeds of Stuartism, etc., with which you are now so strongly impregnated." Boswell himself largely hoped to be rid of the nuisances he had acquired in Naples—namely, crabs and gonorrhea.

❦

Boswell returned to Scotland in 1766. Wilkes's exile lasted until the spring of 1768, just as Parliament was dissolved to prepare for fresh elections. In his absence, the government

Runs for Parliament

had continued to change hands, with one weak minister following another and the king experiencing the first bout of the madness that would dog him for the rest of his life. Reasoning that the dissolution of Parliament meant that his expulsion was no longer valid, and seeking to gain fresh immunity from prosecution by getting himself reelected, Wilkes announced an audacious plan to vex his enemies by standing as a candidate. Boswell, who had not seen his friend since Naples, went to see him on the hustings, where "the confusion and the noise of the mob roaring 'Wilkes and Liberty' were prodigious." He made no attempt to speak to Wilkes: he was a lawyer now, a famous author, and an advocate for Corsican independence, for whom it would do no good to be seen fraternizing with a seditious fellow. Boswell was happy to be mistaken for Wilkes two days later, though, while wearing a suit of green and gold not unlike his friend's.

Gold Badge commemorating issue number 45 of the *North Briton*,
inscribed with the word "LIBERTY." © *The Trustees of the British Museum*

"Sir, I beg pardon, is not your name Wilkes?" asked a man coming up
to him. "Yes, Sir," replied Boswell, who proceeded to cheerfully stroll
the length of Long Acre with the man, stringing him along with talk
of liberty and general warrants and telling him that the king secretly
held him in high regard, before finally admitting that he wasn't Wilkes after all. When he recounted this tale to Samuel Johnson, Johnson inquired why he hadn't asked the man to lend him money.

Against all expectations, Wilkes won the Middlesex election.
His supporters celebrated for two days, demanding that every house
in London from Temple Bar to Hyde Park Corner illuminate its
windows or risk having them broken. The lord mayor's residence
was attacked, causing more than two hundred pounds of damage as supporters passed through the city taking aim at the houses
of prominent courtiers, among them Lord Bute and the Duke of
Newcastle. The Austrian ambassador was pulled from his coach and
manhandled by the crowd, who chalked "No. 45" on the soles of

his shoes to commemorate the issue of the *North Briton* that had sparked their revolution. The Duke of Northumberland narrowly averted a disaster by hastily putting lights in his windows and ordering the Ship alehouse to serve free beer to the mob. After the second night of disorder, Boswell surveyed the damage for himself. Feeling in the "very sink of vice" after spending the night with a "red-haired hussy" in a "horrid room" that lacked fire, curtains, and had "dirty sheets," he crept out at dawn, the broken windowpanes and riotous devastation mirroring his own self-loathing.

Having embarrassed his enemies, Wilkes announced that he would surrender himself and answer for the charges leveled against him prior to his exile. After a series of anticlimactic hearings, he was ordered to be detained in the squalid and overcrowded King's Bench prison, a medieval slum where 700 inmates scuffled over 250 beds. On the way, a crowd barred the passage of his coach, unhitched the horses, and carried him to the Three Tuns tavern in Spitalfields for a night of celebration that put Wilkes in the unusual position of having to escape a party to attend a prison. The next day, crowds began to amass in St. George's Fields, the Lambeth marshland that abutted the jail, shouting encouragement and sending in gifts. Like previous Wilksite assemblies, it had the feel of an impromptu fair, with ballad singers, ribbon sellers, and speeches in favor of liberty, albeit tinged with an air of expectation and menace. Wilkes's supporters camped out for the next two days, growing in number and testing the nerve of the Surrey magistrate, who requested the assistance of a hundred soldiers of the Third Regiment of Foot. As rumors circulated that the prison was about to be stormed, the crowd continued to swell, growing from one thousand in the morning of the second day, to as many as twenty thousand in the afternoon. The mood remained largely peaceful until the magistrate tore down a piece of Wilksite verse that had been pinned to the prison doors. Shouts went up: "Wilkes and Liberty," "Damn the King," and (according to one account) "This is the most glorious opportunity for Revolution ever offered!" Samuel Gilliam, a justice of the

Reading of the Riot Act

peace, came forward to read the Riot Act, a piece of legal verbiage intended to be read aloud whenever twelve or more persons were thought to be assembled for riotous purposes, ordering them to disperse in the name of the king or be guilty of a felony punishable by death. Gilliam was jeered and hit in the head with a stone, prompting three soldiers to give chase to a man they believed was the assailant. Losing sight of him, they shot and killed William Allen, an innocent boy exiting his father's cowshed.

At the doors of the jail, the roars and hissing rose to a deafening pitch. Gilliam read the Riot Act a second time, and the foot guards, now reinforced by a troop of horse, began shooting into the crowd, recharging their muskets up to three times and bayonetting those who came too close. Eleven people were killed. The crowd fled, flooding into the city for another night of vengeful destruction.

The St. George's Fields Massacre, as it came to be known, served only to make martyrs of Wilkes's supporters and bring more people to his cause. Wilkes himself was convicted of libel and handed a sentence of twenty-two months. His imprisonment meant that his parliamentary seat became vacant, but his support was such that he emerged from the subsequent by-election victorious nonetheless, prompting a nullification of the vote and a ridiculous sequence of events in which repeated elections were held and voided after Wilkes won every one. By the beginning of 1769, the government's attempts to mute the popular voice had become so egregious that even those who found Wilkes personally objectionable could not fail to agree with Edmund Burke's assessment that he had become the "object of persecution," for "his unconquerable firmness, for his resolute, indefatigable, strenuous resistance against oppression."

In the London Tavern, Bishopsgate, a group of men styling themselves the "Society of the Supporters of the Bill of Rights" drafted a document that demanded wide-ranging redress against all kinds of

Society of the Supporters of the Bill of Rights

government abuse, calling upon the king to uphold the rule of law, assert the constitutional right of trial by jury, investigate the abuse of military power, shorten the duration of Parliament, and resolve the grievances of the American colonies. Similar meetings took place in taverns and public houses across the country, their members drafting petitions that framed the farce of the Middlesex elections as a constitutional crisis that mocked the basic principles of free election. Fifteen county petitions and eleven borough petitions were generated, containing more than sixty thousand signatures from every corner of the country, including Buckinghamshire, Derbyshire, Devon, Durham, Gloucestershire, Herefordshire, Kent, Middlesex, Northumberland, Somerset, Surrey, Wiltshire, Worcestershire, and Yorkshire.

In Warwickshire, where the Wilksites were described as "the restless offspring of the cruel murderers of Charles I," the many parallels that might be drawn between the Jubilee and a Wilksite rally caused concern. The thousands of people preparing to descend on Stratford wearing ribbons, bearing banners, and singing ballads in praise of a national icon were virtually indistinguishable from a political mob. One newspaper even reported a fable in which Garrick's mulberry box and Keate's mulberry standish attended a meeting at the London Tavern to conspire on behalf of Wilkes, intending to use the celebration as a smoke screen for revolution. Others held that Wilkes was merely an excuse, and what people really wanted was an outlet through which to let off steam. "The people of England were always falling out of one fit of madness into another," wrote one commentator, "and that the passion for Mr. Wilke's politics had totally given place to the Shakespeare mania."

∽§

Having initially resisted it, Boswell caught the Shakespeare mania himself. This was not the only thing he had caught, having returned from his Irish wife-hunting trip in the late spring of 1769 with another case of venereal disease and the realization that his cousin Margaret Montgomerie was the woman he should marry after all. He proposed

Boswell proposes, seeks a cure

to her and went immediately to London to consult with Dr. Gilbert Kennedy, a physician he considered "very old, large and formal and tedious," but who he hoped could "purify my blood from every remain of vicious poison," and get him ready for marriage. Once in London, the lure of the Jubilee took hold. "When I left Scotland I was resolved not to go," he wrote. "But as I approached the capital I felt my inclination increase, and when arrived in London I found myself within the whirlpool of curiosity, which could not fail to carry me down." Still undecided, he asked his friend George Dempster for advice, who replied merely that "it belonged to the chapter of whims, as to which no advice should ever be given."

Next, Boswell called on his mentor, Samuel Johnson, hoping that they might make the journey to Stratford together, but Johnson was away visiting a friend in Brighton. Mrs. Williams, the blind old lady who shared Johnson's house, encouraged Boswell to go by him-

Johnson's scorn for the Jubilee

self, knowing that Johnson had already dismissed the Jubilee with scorn and denounced the *Dedication Ode* that Garrick proposed to deliver over the gifted statue as "terrible." Johnson and Garrick's relationship was particularly tense around the topic of Shakespeare, pitting as it did actor against scholar. Johnson had every claim to know Shakespeare just as well as Garrick, having published his own edition of the collected works in 1765, prefaced with perhaps the strongest critical essay on Shakespeare written to date. This essay had sought to introduce some objective critical distance to evaluations of the poet's merit without (in Johnson's words) "envious malignity or superstitious veneration," a countermand to what Boswell called "a blind indiscriminate admiration [that] had exposed the British nation to the ridicule of foreigners." Eyeless esteem of any kind irked Johnson, and he would bait the genuflecting Garrick by proclaiming that "Shakespear

Samuel Johnson in the year 1769. © *National Portrait Gallery, London*

never has six lines together without a fault," and that William Congreve was the superior poet. Even more pointedly, Johnson claimed he could teach a boy of eight to read "To be or not to be" just as well as Garrick could "in a week."

It was a shame that Johnson would not "partake in the festival of genius," and "upon this occasion," wrote Boswell, "I particularly lamented that he had not that warmth of friendship for his brilliant pupil." Johnson "insensibly fretted a little," he said,

> that *Davy Garrick*, who was his pupil and who came up to London at the same time with him to try the chance of life, should be so very general a favorite and should have fourscore thousand pounds, an immense sum, where *he* has so little. He accordingly will allow no great merit in acting. Garrick cannot but be hurt at this, and so unhappily there is not the harmony that one would wish.

Despite this disappointment, the very thought of the Jubilee, Boswell told Dempster, "makes all my veins glow." Promising his friend that he wouldn't write any anonymous articles about himself and send them to the press while he was there, he went on to consult with Dr. Kennedy, who allowed him to defer his cure—two bottles daily of his patent Lisbon Diet Drink, a miracle beverage composed *Boswell prepares* of sarsaparilla, licorice, and guaiac wood—until his return from Stratford. Next, he made a quick tour of the shops to ensure he had all he needed. He found a musket, a pistol, and a stiletto, and paying a visit to Mr. Dalemaine, a Covent Garden tailor, asked him to run him up a makeshift cap. Finally, he went to a shop in Cheapside, where he purchased a walking stick that looked like "a very handsome vine with the root uppermost, and upon it a bird, very well carved." The price was six shillings. "Why, Sir," he told the shopkeeper, "this vine is worth any money. It is a Jubilee staff. That bird is the bird of Avon."

5

As the summer of 1769 progressed, the number of
goods and people arriving in Stratford started to cause
alarm. The townspeople were "in general, much dissat-
The people of
Stratford
isfied," wrote Benjamin Victor, a theatrical historian and the trea-
surer of Drury Lane, "and greatly afraid of Mischief—they had not
the least Comprehension of *what*, or about *whom* such Preparations
were making:—They looked upon Mr. *Garrick* as a *Magician*, who
could, and would raise the Devil! And, instead of being delighted
with the approaching *Festival*, many of them kept at home, and
were afraid to stir abroad."

George Garrick passed it all on to his brother, who in turn wrote
to William Hunt, the town clerk. "I heard yesterday to my Surprise," said Garrick, shocked at the absence of gratitude, "that the
Country People did not seem to relish our Jubilee. . . . I suppose this
may be a joke, but after all my trouble, pains, labor and Expence for
their Service and the honor of ye County, I shall think it very hard,
if I am not to be received kindly by them—however I shall not be
the first Martyr for my Zeal."

At least one group who would welcome Garrick warmly
were those who stood to make a profit. Upholsterers from
Birmingham and London commissioned a convoy of wag-
Fears of
profiteering
ons laden with fifteen hundred beds to be bought to town, there

to be knocked up the stairs of any house that would have them and rented out at a guinea a night. Back kitchens, landings, outhouses, and closets large enough to hold a bed became bedrooms, so that "no hovel almost remained unappropriated to visitors for some weeks previous to their occupation." Cooks came from all over the country, as did hairdressers. Sedan chairs came up from Bath and London, including one owned by a Mr. Hart, who claimed descent from Shakespeare's sister, Joan Hart. This, too, unsettled Garrick, who feared not only condemnation in the press but the violence that many felt was inevitable. Writing to Hunt of this "ill consequence," he shared his fear that

> the exorbitant price that some of ye People ask, will Effect the whole Jubilee, and rise up a mortal Sin against us—such imposition may serve ye Ends of a few selfish people, but the Town will suffer for it hereafter, and we for the present—I was in hopes that you and ye other Gentlemen of the Corporation might have prevented this. Again if your Innkeepers intend to raise their victuals and liquour, it will be abominable, and perhaps occasion riot and disorder.

The press attacks the Jubilee | As Garrick was no doubt aware, accusations of veniality and greed were already being used to attack the Jubilee, with the earnest efforts of Hunt and others being gleefully leapt upon in London. "The Fame of Shakespeare is at present made subservient to the low Cunning of a Set of Men," wrote one correspondent,

> who have suffered his Memory to sleep unhonor'd for more than half a Century. Now indeed they propose to revive their ancient Trade of *shearing close*, as well as to make the first Experiment on the Company whom they can tempt thither by a promise of Pageantry, which they could neither contrive, nor can execute, them-

selves proving at the same Time incontestably, that their late *wooden Presents* are only to be rewarded as *Begging Boxes* manufactured for their own Benefit.

A writer calling himself "Insomnis" claimed to have stayed at John Payton's White Lion during a meeting of the mayor and the Corporation of Stratford. At four in the morning, he said, he was woken by the company singing:

> Come brothers of Stratford, these flocks let us shear.
> Which bright as if wash'd in our Avon appear.
> The coolest are they who from fleeces are free;
> And who are such trimmers, such trimmers as we?
>   Sing Tantararara, shear all, etc., etc.
>
> We harbour no lodgers but such that can pay,
> We ask for a room but two guineas a day;
> On the length of each pocket we fasten our eyes
> And learn from Al Fresco's to rob in disguise.
>   Sing, etc.
>
> By mode and caprice are these Londoners led,
> For dinner they'll pay what we charge them a head:
> Our wives and our daughters will most of them tell,
> For where ven'son's plenty, the flesh will rebel.
>   Sing, etc.
>
> The giant from Dublin we never can dread,
> Our hall is too high for so lofty a head:
> Little David and George take the cash at the door,
> Their gold from the rich, and their pence from the poor.
>   Sing, etc.

As soon as they're gone, all our gains we'll reveal;
As light as the flocks we have shear'd they shall feel;
While we with their money are jolly and gay,
And leave to next year the return of the day.
            Sing, etc.

Such satires stung Garrick, and as the *Public Advertiser* warned that the ghost of Shakespeare would walk the streets and bring terrible retribution upon the Corporation as "a dreadful example to those who tempt the Vengeance of an injured Poet by prostituting his Fame to their private interest." Garrick wrote to Hunt, telling him that that they only had themselves to blame. Their eagerness to woo him and promote the Jubilee had upset the press, he said, especially when they rewarded George Keate for his part in the negotiations with a mulberry standish along with effusive thanks for "his very elegant and spirited Defence of that first of English poets in his *Ferney,* an epistle in verse to Monsieur de Voltaire." Keate, known for being highly affable, would have been an unlikely target of abuse aside from the fact that he had befriended Voltaire, not only a Frenchman, and thus an enemy of Britain, but even worse, an avowed enemy of Shakespeare. Voltaire, Europe's leading man of letters, conceded there were "pearls" to be found in the Shakespearean "dunghill," but had for years been broadly critical of his work, accusing him of provinciality in his themes and technical barbarism compared with the theoretically disciplined and mannered exemplars of the French school headed by Corneille and Racine. Shakespeare, concluded Voltaire, was nothing more than a literary relic, a step to be passed over on the way to better things. ("I'll tell you why we admire Shakespeare," Boswell had said to Voltaire while visiting him in Ferney, readying to deliver an irrefutable blow. "Because you have no taste," parried Voltaire before his guest could draw breath.)

To the proud men of the English press, Voltaire was no better than

a common brigand, a "French Plunderer," who would "rob and mur-
der afterwards." To the press, Keate had committed the ultimate act
of treason when, in order to honor their friendship, he had composed
Ferney, a poem that celebrated Voltaire's genius and described in detail
the eponymous bucolic hamlet in which he lived, where "beauteous
Nature fills th' admiring Eye / With all the Charms of wild Variety."
In the face of such vitriol, it was no surprise that the gentle rebuke
Keate nested in *Ferney*, in the form of his claim that Shakespeare was
"Above Controul, above each classic Rule, / His Tutress Nature and
the World his School," was drowned out in the noise. The gift presented to him by the Stratfordians was a grave miscalculation. "Your
present to Keate of ye Ink Standwork," scolded Garrick, "has brought
ye scribblers upon us, who think their title superior to his. I felt it wd
be so—when the gift and ye reason of bestowing it was so displayed in
ye Papers—I hinted to you what I thought, which I find is ye opinion
of Every body." He was relieved only that it was not worse. "Keate's
affair has been unlucky," he told Hunt. "I foresaw it—what wd it have
been had you given him ye Freedom too?"

　　Garrick's friends urged him to ignore the "*asthmatic* and *intermittent* nibblers," those "little critics that shall carp." "Was the Roman
Conqueror lessened, by the abusive Slave appointed to follow his
Triumph?" asked the librettist Isaac Bickerstaff. "Proceed, and let
Envy rail on." Newspapers, though, were hard to avoid. London
had four dailies and eight or nine triweekly evening papers, supplemented by nearly forty provincial titles and a host of short-lived
periodicals (like *The North Briton*) that dealt with specific issues as
they arose. All of these encouraged anonymous submissions, which,
given the oppressive political climate, was one of the only ways
to ensure freedom of expression, as illustrated by a series of letters that was currently appearing in the *Public Advertiser* under the
name "Junius," which openly attacked the government and policies
of George III through grievances broadly parallel to Wilkes's. The

papers ensured discretion by having their post boxes face the street
to receive unsigned intelligences, not unlike the ominous lion's
mouths that adorned the Doge's palace in Venice. In spite of such
measures, *Lloyd's Evening Post* claimed to know who was responsible for "the contemptible and indecent attacks upon Mr. Garrick,
Mr. Keate, and some other Gentlemen, in relation to the Jubilee at
Stratford-upon Avon," writing that

> A Correspondent assures us, that they are the productions of a
> Writer, who some time since offered a very dull Tragedy to our Eng-
> lish Roscius [a nickname for Garrick, after the celebrated Roman
> actor Quintus Roscius Gallus], and upon the latter giving it as his
> opinion, that it was totally unfit for the stage, the disappointed
> Scribbler declared himself his enemy, and has since empaled himself
> in several impotent attempts to blacken characters which are too
> well established in the public opinion to suffer from his malice.

A thorn for Garrick

A prime suspect was George Steevens (not to be mistaken
with Payton's friend, the actor George Alexander Stevens),
who, while not a dramatist, was a superb Shakespeare
scholar, editor, and antiquarian. Steevens was a doryphore—one who
delights in the small mistakes of others—and baiting people gave
him doryphoria. He was an obsessive needler, a scourge to all those
he considered guilty of pomposity or scholarly imprecision, joying in
rancor for rancor's sake by allegedly writing libelous notes about his
innocent neighbors and throwing them over their garden walls for the
thrill of their mortification. Steevens was the author of an ironic ode
named "Shakespeare's Feast" that described Garrick and the mayor
and aldermen of Stratford gorging themselves and falling asleep while
Keate recites *Ferney*, including the elegant couplet "At length, as sunk
in Sleep's soft Arms he stretches / The snorting Magistrate b[eshi]t his
breeches." Keate thought of Steevens as a friend.

Garrick felt that would be enough to cover general admission and that extra charges should be levied for meals and balls. ny should not there be taken 10:6 Ordinary for it including a wn for ye Expences of ye Jubilee," Garrick asked Hunt, "or if Ball and Masque are omitted, and paid separately, it will answer same thing—consider it well with my brother if he is with you, d a few days more, or less, for ye delivery of ye Tickets—I have ally half kill'd myself wth this business, and if I escape Madness, fevers I shall be very happy."

Rumors of the program made many scratch their heads, among hem a correspondent to the *Public Advertiser*, who wrote, "I am unable to learn how Oratorios, Races, or Fireworks, are to be conducted in such a Manner as to add Reputation to the Poet, tho' there needs no Ghost to inform us how they may be managed so as to feed the Vanity of an Individual, or the Avarice of a Fraternity of Tradesmen." Garrick continued to work tirelessly nonetheless, although not without emphasizing his martyrdom. "If I come off with only a fever dash'd wth Rhumatism," he wrote to Hunt, "I shall think myself very much befriended above." Garrick's focus turned now to the moment that would form the centerpiece of the entire celebrations, the *Dedication Ode* that would formally accompany his presentation of the statue to the town. This was to take the form of a musical hymn in praise of Shakespeare performed with the backing of the entire Drury Lane orchestra. The composer Thomas Arne "works like a dragon about it," Garrick told Hunt. "He is all flame and fire," in return for his fee of forty-five pounds. After a full rehearsal with the company, Garrick was satisfied that the piece "has a great effect." Rumors of his achievement spread quickly, with the result that he was invited to read the ode before the king and queen at St. James's Palace, where, he said, it "met with much approbation. I was three hours and a quarter with them."

Steevens denied the allegations at the tim
the editors of the *St. James Chronicle* that he ha
or forty" of the offending pieces, and *"that it w*
Garrick. He can't have imagined that Garrick
out, such was Garrick's hold on the press. Garrick
James Chronicle and had shares in the *Gazetteer,*
and (ironically) the *Public Advertiser,* counting its e
as well as being on intimate terms with the proprie
Critical Review and the *Monthly Review.* So few per
print anything negative toward him save *The Gentlem*
and *London Review* that it was assumed by many that l
manufactured the controversy purely for the purposes
ing the Jubilee. That would certainly explain why Garri
taken the time to advertise the Jubilee in any convention.
fact that Hunt reminded him of, receiving yet another
note in return: "I am so busy, and have been for some tim
never thought of the advertisem', why did you not send to me
about it." On the other hand, it was often said of Garrick th
precipitancy of his temper often hurried him into engagem
which he either could or would not, and, indeed, sometimes, o
not, to fulfill."

On August 10, 1769, just four weeks before the Jubilee, notices finally appeared naming the places where
tickets might be ordered. Five days later, surrounded
by musicians entreating him on issues of "Catches, Glees, &c Lord
help me," Garrick finally provided Hunt with an inventory of the
events he was planning: an oratorio in Holy Trinity Church, a suite
of new songs entitled "Shakespeare's Garland," grand illuminations
and firework displays, a horse race and sports upon the meadow, formal breakfasts and dinners, and balls on the first and second nights.
Such a packed program necessitated a reconsideration of the ticket
price. Initially, it was thought that a guinea would be sufficient, but

Shakespeare's Jubilee.

Wednesday, SEPTEMBER 6th.

FIRST DAY.

Began at 6 o'Clock in the Morning, with a grand Discharge of Cannon, ringing of Bells, &c. At Seven, o'Clock a Grand Seranade consisting of Guittars, German Flutes, &c. accompanied with several good Voices. At Nine o'CLOCK, was a PUBLIC BREAKFAST at the TOWN-HALL: During which, the Drums of the *Warwickshire Militia,* beat several fine Marches, accompanied by the Fifes.

From thence they proceeded to the CHURCH to hear

The ORATORIO of JUDITH,

Which began exactly at ELEVEN.

From Church there was a full CHORUS of VOCAL and INSTRUMENTAL MUSIC to the AMPHITHEATRE; where, at Three o'Clock, was

An ORDINARY for Gentlemen and Ladies.

About Five o'Clock, a Collection of NEW SONGS, BALLADS, ROUNDELAYS, CATCHES, GLEES, &c. was performed in the AMPHITHEATRE; after which was a BALL, which began at Nine, with NEW MINUETS, (composed for the Occasion) and played by the whole Band.

SECOND DAY

Was a PUBLIC BREAKFAST, at Nine o'Clock, accompanied as before, from thence they proceeded to the Amphitheatre, where

A N O D E

(Upon Dedicating a BUILDING and Erecting a STATUE to the Memory of *SHAKESPEARE*) was performed.

This Day was to have been a PAGEANT of the principal Characters in the inimitable Plays wrote by the Immortal *Shakespeare,* but the Weather being bad was obliged to be omitted.

At Four An Ordinary for Ladies and Gentlemen.

At Eight, The following FIREWORKS:

FIRST FIRING.

No.
1 Twelve Half-pound Sky Rockets.
2 Four Tourbillons.
3 Two Vertical Wheels, illuminated.
4 Two Cascades, with Reports; one Fir Tree, in Chinese Fire.
5 Two regulating Pieces of three Mutations each; viz. Sun and Stars; Porcupine's Quills; and, large double Stars of eight Points.
6 Two Pidgeon Wheels, with seven Pidgeons each.
7 Two Horizontal Tables, with six Vertical Wheels and Globes illuminated,

SECOND FIRING.

8 Twelve Pound Sky Rockets.
9 Four Tourbillons.
10 Two regulating Pieces of three Mutations; 1st, Brilliant Wheels with yellow and blue Lights. 2d, A brilliant Sun. 3d, A brilliant Star with eight Points.
11 Two Diamond Pieces of Stars and Fountains, to finish with Mines.

No.
12 Two Pyramids of twenty-one Chinese Fires and Boxes, each.
13 Two new Pieces of changeable Fires, intersecting each other.

THIRD FIRING.

14 Twelve Pound Sky Rockets, with Flames, Tails, Stars, &c.
15 Four Tourbillons.
16 Two large horizontal Wheels, changing into a vertical Sun illuminated,
17 Two Figure Pieces, containing sixteen Furibonies of brilliant Fires, and vertical Wheels in the Centre, with yellow Fires.
18 Two regulating Pieces of three Mutations each, viz. A large Wheel, illuminated, two brilliant Suns; fix Branches of new Fires, representing Ears of Corn.
19 Two Pieces called the Fort, consisting of brilliant Fountains, Roman Candles, and Chinese Jurbs, with Reports.

And at Eleven the MASQUERADE, the most brilliant ever seen.

THIRD DAY.

At Twelve o'Clock, a Race for a *Jubilee Cup,* of 50l. Value, for which the following Horses started:

Mr. *Pratt*'s Brown Colt, *Whirligig,* J. *Pratt,* Blue - - - - 4	1	1
Hon. Mr. *King*'s Bay Colt, Name unknown, T. *Camel,* White - 1	4	4
Lord *Grosvenor*'s Colt, *Scholes* - - - - - - - - - 2	3	3
Mr. *Fettiplace*'s Bay Colt, *Pompillion,* E. *Freeman,* Green - - 3	2	5
Mr. *Watson*'s Grey Colt, *Lofty,* John *Rider,* Red. - - - 5	5	2

At Nine o'Clock the following Fireworks, which, thro' the badness of the Weather, could not be let off the Night before, viz.

1 Four Balloons.
2 Four Air Balloons.
3 Four Tourbillons.
4 Two Figure Pieces, consisting of five vertical Wheels and Spiral Wheels, illuminated.
5 One Figure Piece, consisting of five vertical Wheels, &c. four Spiral Wheels, illuminated.

6 Twelve large Chinese Jurbs.
7 Four Dozen of Water-Rockets.
8 Twelve Mortars with Air Balloons, illuminated.
9 One large Sun on the Top of a transparent and illuminated Building, with six Pots d'Aigrets, &c. and a Flight of six Dozen Half-Pound Sky Rockets.

And, at Eleven, by the Request of the LADIES, was a BALL, at the HALL, now call'd SHAKESPARE's-HALL.

A handbill from Garrick's own collection, seemingly printed after the fact, announcing the order of events at the Jubilee.

᠀§

The company departs | Six days before the Jubilee was scheduled to begin, Garrick finally published the order of its entertainments, along with a list of places tickets might be purchased in London and Stratford. Three days later, at four in the morning, sixteen coaches, six post chaises, a team of men on horseback, and the statue of Shakespeare wrapped in sackcloth and strapped to a cart left the London home of the actors William and Hannah Pritchard, senior members of Garrick's company. Together, they constituted the orchestra and players of Drury Lane that would be performing at the Jubilee. There were sixty-eight principal actors in Garrick's company that season, as well as sixteen dancers and twelve singers, more than half of whom were being sent to Stratford, mostly to sing in the chorus of the *Dedication Ode* or to appear in the pageant of Shakespearean characters scheduled for the second day.

The company that year was not the best Garrick had ever built. It was aging and had recently lost one of its strongest performers in Catherine "Kitty" Clive, who had decided to retire at the age of fifty-seven to live a peaceful life close by the Garricks in Twickenham. Garrick found younger actors capable of meeting his exacting standards difficult to come by, thus enabling his rivals to accuse him of deliberately keeping good actors out of his company lest another of "marking genius" might steal away the audience's affections. Generally speaking, the public's view of the company was mixed, if a pamphlet entitled "A Critical Balance of the Performers at the Drury-Lane Theatre" is any guide. Providing each of the actors with end-of-season grades for their performances, only the celebrated Mary Yates received a round twenty out of twenty for "Figure," "Grace," "Spirit," and "Ease."

Garrick himself had reached a pivotal moment in his life. When he looked in the mirror, he still saw one of the most famous faces in England—he had had his portrait painted more times than the king—but it was aging. Bareheaded, his scalp shaved close save for a stumpy pigtail at the back for tying on wigs, he looked haggard and ill, and far too advanced in years for many of the roles he continued to play. Neither did the increasingly generous layer of makeup he applied conceal the fact. As one reviewer unflatteringly put it, "Your mouth has no sweetness; your voice is growing hoarse and hollow; your dimples are furrows; a coarse and disgustful dew-lap hangs from your chin; your lips have lost their softness and pliability; the upper especially is raised all at once, like a turgid piece of leather."

Despite his long career and public profile, Garrick had found it difficult to acquire a thick skin, listening intently to everything that was said about him in a virtual "*whispering gallery*," according to William Cooke, a writer and theatre critic. Garrick was "more affected by any pleasantry against himself, than by the highest eulogiums in his favor," wrote another, while according to Boswell, the actor kept copies of every unflattering letter, pamphlet, and newspaper article ever published against him, inking his own indignant commentaries in the margins and transferring them to a ledger in which he recorded the names of all of those who praised or abused him. Such was the effect of always needing to be approved of, and of always seeking approval. As Samuel Johnson said of his former pupil, "Another man has his dram and is satisfied but Garrick must have a sip every quarter of an hour."

Long careers breed resentments, especially when successful, but many of the complaints against Garrick were not without foundation. Rival managers alleged that he paid "place men" and "puffers" to applaud his new plays and ensure their success while paying others to hiss his rivals at Covent Garden. Playwrights protested the numerous obstacles he placed in the way of writers and his evident prejudice against new plays (indeed, one of the reasons he loved Shakespeare so much, it was muttered, was because he never had to pay him). Getting an appointment to see him was an impossibility. "Admittance, is frequently more difficult, than to come at a Prime Minister," complained the actor Theophilus Cibber, while Oliver Goldsmith claimed that an audience with David Garrick was a "privilege reserved only for the happy few who have the arts of courting the manager as well as . . . adulation to please his vanity." Actors disliked the way Garrick would lampoon them, undermining those whose stars were on the rise by torturing them "on the rack of ridicule" or stabbing them with "a misrepresented anecdote, or an exaggerated foible." The treatment was doubly cruel if the actor in question happened to be tall. One of the reasons the "*diminutive chief*" was believed to delight so much in the company of George Colman, the manager of Covent Garden, was that Colman was even shorter than he was. Garrick, complained Colman, "is fond of sidling up to me in all publick places, as second-rate beauties commonly contrive to take a dowdy abroad with them for a foil."

An Irish nemesis

This unusually combative profession had been especially challenging recently. Garrick had suffered acutely at the hands of an affected young Irishman and self-appointed critic of independent means named Thaddeus Fitzpatrick. Fitzpatrick had announced himself as a nuisance as early as 1752, when during a performance of *Harlequin Ranger*, he had thrown two apples at Harlequin: the first had smashed the window of the sedan chair in which Harlequin sat, while the second had hit him square in the face. Although initially supportive of Garrick, Fitzpatrick had fallen out with him in the early 1760s at a meeting of the Bedford Coffee House Shakespeare Club, after calling him "the most *insignificant* person that belonged to their society." Given that "anxiety for his fame was the manager's reigning foible," according to Arthur Murphy, and that "on the slightest attack, he was *tremblingly alive all o'er*," Garrick immediately demanded an apology, further riling Fitzpatrick who was moved to pen a series of poisonous reviews under the name "X.Y.Z." These pieces accused Garrick of strange locutions and arrhythmic pauses in his speech, as well as chronically underpaying his actors, running his theatre like Nero, and using "the revival of expiring and the introduction of expired plays" as a means of keeping emerging authors off the stage. To respond, Garrick denounced Fitzpatrick in a satirical poem entitled "The Fribbleriad," which labeled him a "mincing" "namby-pamby" "lady-fellow." Fitzpatrick retaliated, and one night in January 1763, as Garrick attempted some of the more moving passages in *King Lear*, the Irishman climbed on top of his bench in the pit and began to whinny like a horse.

The disturbances might have been easily handled, had not Garrick unwittingly gifted Fitzpatrick a platform around which he could rally support. This was the same season Garrick had decided to end the custom of taking half-price admissions after the third act, thus allowing a second wave of patrons into the theatre to socialize and enjoy the afterpiece. Naturally, the half-price crowd caused a disturbance, and Garrick saw its discontinuation as just another of the necessary reforms he was bringing to the acting space, just as he had previously removed the spectators who used to sit behind the actors onstage, banned the gentlemen who paid to loiter behind the scenery and watch from the wings, and removed the light above the actors' heads, all as a means to draw a clearer distinction between the auditorium and the world of the play. To the mutinous Fitzpatrick, emboldened by the rhetoric of John Wilkes and his rallying cry of "Liberty," Garrick's decision to end half price was nothing less than a tyrannous attack on freedom. His claim was not extraordinary, because, while the theatre was technically a private business in which Garrick could do as he pleased, it was popularly viewed as a public place, subject to the will of the people. "Whatever notions modern performers may have imbibed, by inflated applause and profuse recompense, actors are neither more or less than the servants of the public," wrote

Fitzpatrick. "As Englishmen, it is our duty, and what we owe our-selves and posterity, to be tenacious of our rights and privileges, and to keep a watchful eye to any, the least innovation of our liberties and prerogatives."

Fitzpatrick's whinnying transmuted into a chant that spread across the pit and called on Garrick to show himself and submit to the will of the people by reversing his decision on half price. When Garrick asked for time to consult with his co-owner James Lacy, he was greeted with more noise. The actors came out several times, but as soon as they did they were pelted with apples and dirt and met with cries of "Off! Off! Off!" The king and queen were in the audience that night, as was Gia-como Casanova, the famous Venetian lover. Casanova heard a shout of "Clear the house," at which point the audience pushed for the exits in a panic while Fitzpatrick's group wreaked havoc on the building. The glass lusters were smashed and lighted candles fell to the floor. Benches were torn up and thrown onto the stage. "In less than an hour," wrote Casanova, "everything inside the building was wrecked, only the four walls were left standing. The sovereign people destroyed everything it could lay hands on, just to show its sovereign power; then, satisfied with its work, went off to swill beer and gin."

The following night the chant went up again, only this time the actor John Moody was called onstage to answer for the offense of stamping out a candle that had been deliberately set against the wainscot by a rioter intent on burning the building to the ground. When he appeared, the crowd chanted, "Knees, knees! Down on your knees!" forcing him into supplication for the offense of not per-mitting arson. Bravely, Moody refused. Terrified at the prospect of renewed violence, Garrick abandoned his plans to end half price.

His health | The feud with Fitzpatrick had taken its toll and, going to confer with his friend the Duke of Devonshire in his mansion, Chatsworth House, he made the decision to leave Drury Lane and take his wife, Eva, on a tour of the Continent. The trip, which lasted two years, coincided which a serious decline in Garrick's health. In Munich in the summer of 1764, he was confined to his bed for a month with a blood infection and "the most dangerous bilious Fever," that so convinced him he was about to die that he drafted his own epitaph, concluding it with the line "Fitzp——k was my foe." He recovered, only to succumb immediately to a fit of the "Gravel and Stone." "I am most truly ye Knight of ye Woefull Countenance," he wrote to the Reverend William Arden, "and have lost legs arms belly cheeks &c and have scare any thing left but bones and a pair of dark lack-lustre Eyes that are retir'd an inch or two more in their Sockets and wonderfully set of ye yellow Parchment that covers ye cheek bones." Ministered to by eight doctors (three German, three French, and two English), Garrick lost a significant amount of weight and all desire to perform. "I have at present lost all taste for ye Stage," he wrote to George Colman, in whose hands he had entrusted Drury Lane. "It was once my greatest Passion, and I labor'd for many years like a true Lover—but I am grown cold—should my desires return, I am the Town's humble Servant again—tho she is a great Coquette, and I want Youth, vigorous Youth, to bear up against her occasional Capriciousness."

Garrick returned to London in the spring of 1765 to find that, while he ailed abroad, death had stalked his friends and family at home. His sister Linney, the artist William Hogarth, and the poet Charles Churchill had all passed away, as had his great confidant the Duke of Devonshire. Theatrical trouble followed almost immediately, this time orchestrated by a publication entitled *The Theatrical Monitor*, which questioned Garrick's financial management and urged him to open the Drury Lane books in order to demonstrate "to the world the uprightness of your intentions and the justness of your laws in this *important* but *tempting*, therefore *dangerous trust*." Along with questioning his financial probity, *The Theatrical Monitor* drew attention to Garrick's age and ailing health. "If we weigh his merits in the scale of reason," it wrote,

> It has long been observed by the judicious, that he no longer plays in tragedy with the same fire and spirit that he did fifteen or sixteen years ago. G—— in Lear or Hamlet now, is no longer the same G—— that once excited the admiration of the town. When I saw him about seven or eight years ago play the character of Richard, I could hardly believe that he was the same man, whose performance almost raised astonishment when he appeared for the first time in that part at Goodman's Fields. The decline of his abilities in Tragedy is indeed visible to the most superficial observer, and naturally accounts for his playing it so seldom, for a man generally grows tired of what he is unfit for!

Abilities questioned | It was the beginning of a whole new campaign. "GARRICK, attend!—be prudent,—quit the stage," chirped a poisonous little verse. "Nor let advice provoke thy little rage . . . / Retire at once, and to thy fame be just, / Lest we our former judgments should distrust."

An average season at Drury Lane ran for 190 nights, each night featuring at least two plays, or a play and a one-act afterpiece. In the season before he left for the Continent, Garrick had performed on 111 of those evenings, not including the many prologues and epilogues he had spoken to introduce new plays and close out the night. In the four years after his return, he performed an average of 17 nights a season, and always in old, familiar roles. By 1769, battered by illness and public barbs, the waning of his powers at fifty-two years old felt like a diminution of himself. Understanding that his greatest triumphs were past, the thought of irrelevance terrified him. "We know that each Apartment in the Temple of Fame is held upon Lease only," wrote an anonymous contributor to the *Public Advertiser*,

> The Celebrity we derived from having appeared with Success in the Characters of Hamlets or Lears, will probably be denied to us when we have ceased to represent them in Public. . . . If to be talked of should be as necessary to us as to be fed, we must seek out new Lights in which to exhibit ourselves, or Opportunities of doing something which may still preserve our Fame alive.

The Jubilee represented those "new Lights" and "Opportunities." This was Garrick's chance to rally a fractured country under a unifying idea and assert his rightful place at the center of the nation's cultural life—if not as its favorite actor, then as the man who lay the foundation on which the artistic legacy of Britain would be built.

A ticket for the Jubilee, featuring an image of the Shakespeare statue intended for an exterior alcove on the Town Hall. Each ticket was signed by George Garrick as a guard against forgery. © *Shakespeare Birthplace Trust*

Only Garrick had the status to cement Shakespeare's place as a literary god and, in so doing, proclaim himself as his high priest. But so much depended on the Jubilee. As Garrick made his way down to Stratford on Friday, September 1, bearing a basket of fruit from his Hampton garden, he was filled with anxiety. The Jubilee could secure his legacy or cement his decline. It had to succeed.

6

At five in the morning of September, 6, 1769, Domenico Angelo emerged from behind a chinoiserie screen set on the meadow beside the river Avon. Vulpine, slim-waisted, x *The Jubilee begins!*

and spring-kneed, he surveyed the field like a general plotting a siege, issuing orders in a mysterious accent to a regiment of grizzled stagehands who wheeled a battery of thirty cannon behind them, sixteen of which were thirty-two pounders, guns most usefully deployed hulling ships.

One of Europe's greatest swordsmen and the proprietor of an exclusive *academie des armes* in London's Soho, Angelo had come to Stratford to help his friend David Garrick realize his Jubilee vision. Although not an employee of Drury Lane, as a younger man Angelo had helped to produce the grand civic-aquatic festivals staged on the canals of Venice under the direction of the artist Canaletto. Garrick consulted him on matters of spectacle often. With his fine poise and straight back, Angelo was also considered one of the most graceful men in Europe, handsome enough that Garrick had cast him as Antony in a grand procession of characters and had considered sailing him down the Avon in an Egyptian barge with a Drury Lane Cleopatra by his side.

Garrick had charged Angelo with responsibility for the firework displays that were to conclude each evening. Accompanying

Angelo were his thirteen-year-old son, Henry, enjoying the final week of vacation before returning to Eton, and his assistant for the Jubilee, Benjamin Clitherow, a man whose blackened fingertips and brimstone-infused overcoat signaled his calling as a specialist in pyrotechnics. From his house in Moorfield's Rose and Crown Court, Clitherow advertised himself as "the Britannic artist," making and selling fireworks with names like "Gold Flower Pots," "the Pyramids of Fire Pumps," and "the Metamorphose Wheel, or Wheel of Folly." His address somewhat belied these grand titles, as the nearby fields that had long been the site of London's dunghills now nurtured other forms of liminal commerce, from the buoyant trade in homosexual prostitution conducted at their northern end to the Bedlam lunatic asylum at the south. Manufacturing fireworks was a dangerous profession in the close-set warren of small and malodorous courtyards where Clitherow worked alongside a go-cart factory and secondhand bookstalls, as his wife discovered the day she blew herself up, along with three houses and ten people, while taking stock ahead of Guy Fawkes Night. To avoid a similar accident, Angelo had been careful to store the two large casks of gunpowder he needed well away from the Jubilee, placing them in the cellar of the Bear Inn, Bridgetown, a small hamlet a mile outside Stratford. Not that the weather was especially conducive to explosions. The clouds were hung low, heavy with rain.

This morning, Angelo needed to worry only about firing the cannon that would officially announce the opening of the Jubilee, and at six o'clock sharp he gave the signal for three volleys to be fired across the river. The report in turn prompted a team of bell ringers who, for a fee of three guineas each, had been retained to peal the bells of Holy Trinity at regular intervals throughout the day. The combined booms and ringing woke the town, although Garrick, in his rooms at the White Lion, had hardly slept. According to the program, Angelo's cannonade was supposed to be followed by musicians taking to the streets and singing serenades written and set for the Jubilee by the composer Charles Dibdin. Garrick had brought Dibdin and his writing partner, Isaac Bickerstaff, to Drury Lane to perform their new comic opera *The Padlock*. Dibdin had written the songs for the opera and also performed the part of the drunken African servant Mungo, the first comic blackface role to appear on a British stage.

The Padlock proved to be one of the most popular plays of the period, with a libretto that sold 38,000 copies, netting Garrick and Bickerstaff around £1500 each. Dibdin, however, made less than £45. Instead, Garrick had offered to clear the debts the composer had accrued paying to have his brother released from debtor's prison and start a new life in India. As far as Garrick was concerned, it was not only a fair deal but a great favor, and one he wouldn't let Dibdin forget. "The circumstance followed me," wrote Dibdin, "to the end of my whole connection with that man. It was a spell upon me, and many years elapsed before its influence left me; for, from that moment, I led a life of mental slavery, and *Dibdin's resentments* suffered a perpetual conflict between my duty and my inclination." Throughout the summer of 1769, Garrick set Dibdin to work on the music for the Jubilee, rejecting multiple drafts and demanding frequent revisions and rewritings according to his regular practice. Should Dibdin voice complaints, his "pecuniary obligations" were "hit in my teeth." Disgusted by Garrick, he saw the Jubilee merely as an exercise in vanity. "The ostensible motive was to pay a honorary tribute to the talents of SHAKESPEAR," wrote Dibdin in his autobiography,

> Had the public, however, known what I did; had they known that, with all his enthusiasm for SHAKESPEAR, he had the fame, the

honor, the interest of no human being in view but GARRICK; had they known that various arts he put in practice to entice patronage, to raise volunteers without bounty-money; had they known in what manner he tickled the vanity of the great, his private friends, his professional connections; had they known the abuse he wrote against himself in the newspapers, that men of abler talents might take up the matter upon principle, and defend him against what evidently appeared to be a pre-judgement of his conduct; in short, had they known that the whole business was concerted to levy contributions on his friends, retainers, dependents, and the public in general, for no other motive upon the earth but to fill his own pockets, it is more than probable that the *Jubilee* would have given a severe shock not only to his reputation but to his strong-box; a circumstance certainly more material to feelings like his. As it was, the tomb of SHAKESPEAR was stript of laurels to adorn the brow of GARRICK.

Determined to humiliate the man who kept him in perpetual indebtedness, Dibdin let it be known that he intended to boycott the event and withdraw his songs from the Jubilee. Garrick was sick with concern and immediately commissioned pieces from two new composers, neither of which he liked. Yet Dibdin experienced a last-minute change of heart, thinking that his own reputation would suffer at what would "appear a meditated insult to the public." With only a day to spare, he set the words and accompaniments for guitars and flutes and went down to Stratford the evening before the Jubilee, making the musicians sit up all night rehearsing until the first flush of daylight. Upon hearing the cannon, the musicians—dressed as peasants with dirt smeared across their faces, and playing guitars, hautbois, clarinets, and "German flutes"—began to walk about the streets, "and to the astonishment of GARRICK serenaded him with the very thing he had set his heart upon, but which he had given up as lost." They sang, addressing themselves to the females of the Jubilee:

Let Beauty with the sun arise,
    To Shakespeare tribute pay,
With heavenly smiles, and speaking eyes,
    Give grace and lustre to the day.
Each smile she gives protects his name;
    What face shall dare to frown?
Not Envy's self can blast the fame,
    Which Beauty deigns to crown.

"The Morning Address to the Ladies"

A relieved Garrick thanked Dibdin profusely, telling him that he would never forget this generous change of heart. "I knew what credit to give to his protestations," wrote Dibdin, who received £21 for the music, "which, he said, as I was a good boy, he gave me to buy apples." The journey and accommodations alone had cost him £26.

From beneath Garrick's window, the musicians moved on to those of Lord and Lady Spencer, one of the richest couples in England and friends to the Garricks, who had explored the slopes of Mount Vesuvius with them in the wake of the troubles at Drury Lane. The Spencers were also parents to twelve-year-old Georgiana who, as Duchess of Devonshire, would become the most famous society lady of her day. As more guests came to their windows to look out, the musicians began a second tune that would become one of the best known of the Jubilee:

Ye *Warwickshire* lads, and ye lasses,
See what at our Jubilee passes,
Come revel away, rejoice and be glad,

"A Warwickshire Lad"

For the lad of all lads, was a *Warwickshire* lad,
  Warwickshire lad,
   All be glad,
For the lad of all lads, was a *Warwickshire* lad,

Be proud of the charms of your country,
Where Nature has lavish'd her bounty,
Where much she has given, and some to be spar'd
For the bard of all bards, was a *Warwickshire* bard,
  Warwickshire bard,
   Never pair'd,
For the bard of all bards, was a *Warwickshire* bard.

Each shire has its different pleasures,
Each shire has its different treasures;
But to rare *Warwickshire*, all must submit,
For the wit of all wits, was a *Warwickshire* wit,
  Warwickshire wit,
   How he writ!
For the wit of all wits, was a *Warwickshire* wit.

Old Ben, Thomas Otway, John Dryden,
And half a score more we take pride in,
Of famous *Will Congreve*, we boast too the skill,
But the *Will* of all *Wills*, was a *Warwickshire Will*,
  Warwickshire Will,
   Matchless still,
For the *Will* of all *Wills*, was a *Warwickshire Will*.

Our SHAKESPEARE compar'd is to no man,
Nor *Frenchman*, nor *Grecian*, nor *Roman*,
Their swans are all geese, to the *Avon*'s sweet swan,

And the man of all men, was a *Warwickshire* man,

    Warwickshire man,

      Avon's swan,

And the man of all men, was a *Warwickshire* man.

As ven'son is very inviting,

To steal it our bard took delight in,

To make his friends merry he never was lag,

And the wag of all wags, was a *Warwickshire* wag,

    Warwickshire wag,

      Ever brag,

For the wag of all wags, was a *Warwickshire* wag.

There never was seen such a creature,

Of all she was worth, he robb'd Nature;

He took all her smiles, and he took all her grief,

And the thief of all thieves, was a *Warwickshire* thief,

    Warwickshire thief,

      He's the chief,

For the thief of all thieves, was a *Warwickshire* thief.

"A Warwickshire Lad"—a jigging roundelay accompanied by an excited tambourine suggestive of jester's bells—established Shakespeare's primacy among his literary peers and laid out the terms under which the guests were being invited to interact with their surroundings. Garrick's place-making left no doubt that this was Shakespeare's country, the nursery of genius, a pastoral space that imbued its gifted son with a rustic power so strong it bested all other civilizations. But Shakespeare was not only a product of nature. As the song's final stanza suggested, he had improved on her power of creation and thus challenged her monopoly for bringing tears and laughter to the world. This argument turned on its head the criticisms of Voltaire and others, who accused Shakespeare of a lack of sophistication for his failure to adhere to the formal rules of classical literary composition. For the Warwickshire Lad, ignorance of classicism was proof of his organic genius, a wholesomeness and purity free from artifice. Shakespeare, it was claimed, followed no rules for the simple fact that he was, in the words of Alexander Pope, "an instrument of Nature; and 'tis not so just to say that he speaks from her, as that she speaks, thro' him." His work could be unruly because nature can be unruly and, like nature, possessed of such sublime poetic beauty that all other work by comparison seemed fussy and contrived.

The music gradually enticed sleepy revelers out onto the streets, where they found handbills left by the musicians announcing the day's order of events, beginning at eight o'clock as Garrick and his wife, Eva, made their way down Henley Street and onto Chapel Street toward the new Town Hall, now dubbed "Shakespeare's Hall" for the duration of the Jubilee. Waiting for them was a delegation of Stratford dignitaries led by John Meacham, the current mayor, who, it had been faithfully reported by the London papers, had commissioned a new wig for the occasion while also insisting that a detachment of guards be present in case the resentful townsfolk attempted to snatch it from him. Fortunately, a regiment of the Warwickshire militia—staunch anti-Wilksites every one—was there to protect him, men whom Garrick had obtained through a special dispensation from the Ministry of War. They beat a reveille as the town crier, also wearing an ostentatious new wig, called the meeting to order. Eva

William Hunt's address

Garrick took a place next to her friend Lady Spencer. William Hunt, the town clerk, then stepped forward to address Garrick. "Sir," he said, "you, who have done the memory of Shakespeare so much honour, are esteemed the fittest

Commemorative silver medal forged by Westwood of Birmingham.
© *The Trustees of the British Museum*

A Jubilee ribbon. These rainbow-colored rosettes were designed
to allude to Samuel Johnson's praise of Shakespeare's art.
© *Shakespeare Birthplace Trust*

person to be appointed the first steward of his jubilee; which we beg your acceptance of: permit me, Sir, in obedience to the commands of this corporation, to deliver to you this medal, and this wand, the sacred pledges of our veneration for our immortal townsman, whereby you are invested with your office." The wand Hunt presented Garrick with was a short baton made of mulberry that would serve as his staff of office. The medal was a large medallion also of mulberry, ringed with gold and carved with a bust of Shakespeare. Garrick made a polite speech by way of reply, after which those gathered applauded, the cannon fired, and the church bells rang again. Inside the Town Hall, a public breakfast had been prepared, available to all ticket holders on payment of an additional shilling.

A troop of drums and fifes struck up as the guests filed in. Tea, coffee, and chocolate were served, with many of the participants already sporting commemorative ribbons and medals of their own purchased from Mr. Jackson, who had

Jubilee mementos

come over from Coventry and set up shop in Chapel Street. The medals showed Shakespeare in profile with an epigraph that echoed *Hamlet:* "WE SHALL NOT LOOK UPON HIS LIKE AGAIN." The reverse read, "JUBILEE AT STRATFORD IN HONOUR AND TO THE MEMORY OF SHAKESPEARE SEPTR. 1769. D. G. STEWARD." The ribbon, explained Jackson, "is in imitation of the Rainbow, which, uniting the Colours of all Parties, is likewise an emblem of the great Variety of his Genius. 'Each change of many colour'd life he drew.'" This last line was a quote from the prologue Samuel Johnson had written for Garrick at the start of the 1747 season: "When Learning's Triumph o'er her barb'rous Foes / First rear'd the Stage, immortal SHAKE-SPEARE rose; / Each Change of many-colour'd Life he drew"— the prologue that had marked the beginning of Garrick's managerial career at Drury Lane. It was ironic, Boswell would remark, how the

Jubilee's sole trace of the great Johnson should be "the whimsical advertisement of a haberdasher."

The crowd was dispiritingly small, although still heavy with dignitaries—a sign of how deep Garrick's *The breakfast* connection to the aristocracy ran. Arrayed in their ribbons and medals were the Duke of Dorset; the high sheriff of Warwickshire; and Francis Seymour-Conway, Viscount Beauchamp, who served as lord chamberlain to George III. Lord Grosvenor, the landlord of the enormous Grosvenor estate in west London's Mayfair and a founding member of the Jockey Club was there, minus his wife, with whom he was currently at war. Grosvenor organized his life around horse racing, keeping the most impressive stud in the nation at his home in Eaton Hall, Cheshire, allowing it to consume so much of his time that when he was ennobled by the king, he chose to watch a trial at Newmarket instead of attending the ceremony at St. James's Palace. He had come to Stratford directly from the York races and had agreed to attend the Jubilee only after Garrick had assured him that it would not clash with the Shrewsbury races the following week. Lord Archer was present—for many years MP for Coventry, before taking a seat in the House of Lords. Garrick's friend Sir Watkin Williams Wynne, a Welsh antiquary and drama enthusiast whose home was equipped with a fully functioning private theatre, had come to take his mind off the recent death of his wife, Lady Henrietta. His sister-in-law had hoped to accompany him, but she had been thrown from her chaise and broken her leg just days before.

The disappointing numbers were the result of demand rather than indifference. Traffic coming into *Roads, clogged* Stratford was backed up for miles, with one traveler writing that "all the inns and roads from London are filled as if an army was upon its march." Ease of travel had been a concern for months, with the commissioner of turnpikes urging William Hunt to attend to the completion of a new road that had been languishing for years. The call was taken up by the local aristocracy, who drafted extra men to rehabilitate a long neglected stretch known as the Portway, first laid by the Romans and now renamed "Shakespeare's Road." This helped somewhat, but the volume of traffic was far beyond anything anyone might have predicted. Those arriving from London on the Banbury road had to wait hours to cross the sole bridge that spanned the Avon, before merging with the traffic coming in from the Warwick road and trying to force itself up the narrow passage of Henley Street, which was wide enough only for two carriages to graze past each other. Any chance of that was rendered impossible by the addition of chairmen who weaved their sedan chairs through the blockade, having carried them all the way up from London with the promises of heavy profits. This noisy, inching progress stalled entirely when a London stagecoach overturned while maneuvering into the yard of the White Lion. To compound troubles, six horses had gotten loose and were making circuits of Stratford, outrunning the waiters sent to corral them. Neither was there respite for those who had decided to sail to the Jubilee, as boats already filled the width of the river from the bridge to the Bankcroft meadow, leaving no room for mooring. That it had started to rain made everything worse.

Bankcroft itself was now the site of the Rotunda, its imposing form having taken shape in a matter of weeks. Workmen still scurried over its roof, hammering in loose boards as they raced to complete it and affix the eight pennants and large flag that read "Shakespeare" to its crown. Nearby, traveling showmen pitched tents and unloaded carts, unpacking the worlds of wonder they carried on the back of their wagons promising rope dancers and strongmen, sword swallowers and acrobats. To the din of driving nails and the curses of carriage drivers were added the pops of firecrackers let off by boys who had begged them from Benjamin Clitherow.

Rooms at the White Lion had been sold out for weeks, and with so many people trying to cram themselves into town, every available closet and

Price and quality of lodging

landing was being offered as a lodging. Local carpenter Thomas Taylor put up actors in his house on Church Street, while his colleague Thomas Sharp housed a party of his own that included Lord and Lady Pembroke and the future prime minister of Britain, Charles James Fox, then a nineteen-year-old member of Parliament with a reputation for drunken wildness. Admiral George Rodney, who had fought successful naval campaigns in the Seven Years War but was currently leveled by debt and political failure, was at the house of Mr. Whitmore in Swine Street. With so many lodgings taken in advance, the shortage of decent rooms encouraged price gouging, leading Garrick to insist that "no more shall be taken than a Guinea a Bed." While the price cap was enforced, quality was not. "Musidorus," a correspondent for the *Public Ledger*, named for the prince who disguises himself as a shepherd in a play wrongly ascribed to Shakespeare in the 1664 edition of his Folio, wrote of the trouble he had encountered finding a "sleepable" bed. "An innkeeper [meaning John Payton] was kind enough, in his public Advertisement, to promise us good beds, for a guinea a night," he wrote.

> The Innkeeper, however, who was a mighty great man on the occasion, like most great men, forgot his promise. So far from getting decent accommodation, by his means, we could not get a civil answer at his house; a most wretched shed in the town, that had a few rags patched into a bed, was estimated at one guinea a night, and many who would not part with a single crown to relieve a dis-

tressed family, advanced five pounds with the utmost chearfulness, for an apartment at a green shop.

Those so indisposed included several "great families" who were lodged in the wretched medieval almhouses or forced to share a bed with strangers. Some groups found themselves starved and sleeping in a stable with cows. "Neglected by the waiters, and insulted by their master," complained a correspondent for the *Whitehall Evening Post.*

> If we humbly request a class of wine, you will find us treated like beggars indeed; and, when fainting through lassitude, hunger and thirst, you will find us giving, as I have already hinted, a guinea for the indulgence of a single night in sheds, where desperation only would venture, and where, if we escape from the ruin that hangs seemingly ready to tumble on our heads, we have a very tolerable chance of being devoured by the original possessors of our delectable dominions.

A shrewd party of ten Covent Garden mercers solved this problem by hiring a large, broad-wheeled wagon which they stocked with food, wine, chairs, and tables, and slung with hammocks so they could use it "for parlour, for kitchen, for hall."

The mangy accommodations had Musidorus and others considering an early return to London, especially as "the then appearance of the company made me heartily sick of my journey." His sentiment was echoed by another correspondent for the *Whitehall Evening Post*, who called himself "Vindex." His first impression of Stratford was to compare it to the worst of the London slums, "the Ruins of St. Giles, with a set of people equally needy." The town, he said, was "amazingly full,"

> but the company consisted not of persons whose rank in life was likely to do honour to the Festival; on the contrary they consisted

chiefly of itinerant Hairdressers and Figure-dancers from the Theatres. At every corner, Monsieur le Friseur was either thrusting into
my hand a card, soliciting the honor of my commands, or Monsieur
Coupée, in his magnificent laced waistcoat and elegantly powdered
head, was scandalizing my rusty black coat, and putting my old
fashioned grizzle out of countenance. In short, Sir, the worthy
Gentlemen of these two respectable orders monopolized almost
the whole accommodations.

Joining the hairdressers and *maîtres de ballet* were those who came to
the Jubilee purely because it was the thing to do. As the playwright
Francis Gentleman wrote in a satirical piece published just weeks
after the Jubilee,

> Smart beaux, whom stern cynics call rational apes,
>> Haste hither to shew their fine cloathes and fine shapes,
>>> They know *Shakespeare's* name,
>>> And have heard of his fame,
> Though his merit their shallow conception escapes.

The gulf between guests and locals could not have been more
pronounced. Stratfordians were unsure what a "jubilee" was meant
to be, and worried whether it might "notify and misdecorate a new
Species of Bacchanalian Revelling at Stratford Upon Avon." Preach-
ers condemned the event for its idolatry, calling it (according to
Garrick) "a plot of the Jews and Papishes," and using
the words "Jubilo," "Juvilum," and "Jew Bill" inter-
changeably. The last term struck many as dangerous

"A plot of the Jews and Papishes"

and heretical through its evocation of the Jewish Naturalization Act
of 1753, the "Jew Bill" that had ended some legal discriminations
against Jews by opening up a way for them to own property and
become British citizens. The bill had been so unpopular and the

resulting backlash so fierce that it had been repealed the following year. Others, like a man from Banbury, hired to carry a double bass into town, suggested that the instrument would be used to play liturgical music celebrating "the resurrection of Shakespeare." The most threatening symbol was the giant wooden rotunda that had appeared in their town, but for what purpose, nobody seemed to

Garrick in his regalia as the Steward of the Jubilee. In his left hand is his wand of office, in his right the carved Mulberry medallion presented to him by William Hunt. © *The Trustees of the British Museum*

know. As Garrick's own parody would have it: "Why to drive all us poor folks in, to be sure, like cattle into a pound. Then lock us in, while they may be firing the town and running away with and ravish—ay, that's what they will—ravish man, woman and child! How can one sleep with such thoughts in one's head?"

The sense of doom was amplified when a strange point | *A comet*
of impossible light suddenly appeared in the heavens. It was a comet, whose arrival spread tales of ill portent around the country. Some said it was an inhabited world, traveling the universe at a speed of three thousand miles per minute to harm the Earth. Others claimed that it appeared to warn against "the enormous increase of Papists and Popery" in Britain.

7

Boswell makes his way | Boswell did not make it to Stratford in time for the serenades. It was not the fault of the traffic so much as absentmindedness induced by a combination of anxiety and sexual tension. Having started out in a rush of excitement, he had made it as far as Oxford before realizing that he had mislaid his watch, his money, and the letter from his cousin Margaret accepting his offer of marriage. Virtue was to blame. Since his betrothal, Boswell had promised himself he would become more vigilant against the sexual urges that had dogged him since childhood. There had been many such resolutions throughout his life, reached after long bouts of self-analysis and morning after penitent morning. He was an expert at fresh starts and vows that, starting tomorrow, he would be a better Christian, more resolute and stronger than the desires that perpetually unskinned him. On Monday, he began anew, and by Sunday, had let himself down again, a cycle of failure and recrimination that brought him to the brink of despair. One night, he and Samuel Johnson had watched a moth fly into the flame of a candle. "That creature was its own tormentor," said Johnson, "and I believe its name was Boswell."

As a student in Holland, Boswell had sought to better know himself by writing daily memoranda addressed in the third person, observing his behavior in the disinterested style of Mr. Spectator: "you labored hard yesterday"; "persist firm and noble"; "spend not so much time in sauntering"; "if the day is good, put on your scarlet clothes and behave with decency before fair lady." When he failed to uphold the

Boswell in dialogue with himself

high standards of conduct and piety he set for himself, he would write stern prescriptions for improvement, telling himself to get more exercise or wear a nightcap in order to preserve his teeth and thus avoid an unattractive lisp. He wrote extensively on the best kinds of breeches, the need to perfect his French, and guarding against prattling "too foolishly and too freely." The memoranda culminated in a piece Boswell titled the "Inviolable Plan," a three-page document composed on October 16, 1763, that was "to be read over frequently" as it set out the steps required "to form yourself into a man." The plan required Boswell to be sober and studious in defense of his family's reputation, avoid sarcasm and self-aggrandizement, uphold the Church of England, and pursue the path his father had laid out for him in the legal profession to become a member of Scotland's Faculty of Advocates. Every Saturday morning he went over it, reinforcing his will by reciting to himself, "Your great loss is too much wildness of fancy and ludicrous imagination. . . . The pleasure of laughing is great. But the pleasure of being a respected gentleman is greater."

One year on, following the conclusion of his legal studies and granted license by his father to travel, Boswell arranged to meet Jean-Jacques Rousseau, sending him, by way of introduction, another introspective text. This "Sketch of My Life" was the companion piece to the "Inviolable Plan," but whereas the first was intended to shore up his resolve, its sequel looked to understand the source of his frailties. It was searching and confessional, an exercise aimed at identifying a path to reconciling the warring aspects of his personality. In Rousseau, he was meeting the master of this style, then hard at work on his *Confessions*, a masterpiece of self-scrutiny that would mark a significant evolution in the language and structures of introspection with which Europeans were able to examine their inner lives.

As a cartographer of the interior life, Rousseau had towering appeal. "O great philosopher, will you befriend me?" wrote Boswell in his journal, "Am I not worthy? I tell you that the idea of being bound even by the finest thread to the most enlightened of philosophers, the noblest of souls, will always uphold me, all my life." Pilloried in his native France and banished to Geneva, the great philosopher was unfortunately not in the best of spirits or health, experiencing constant pain from a urethral stricture that required the frequent and unsatisfactory use of a chamber pot and the need to administer a dilator to his penis to relieve the discomfort. Visitors were strictly limited to fifteen minutes at a time, which Boswell, ever persistent and unrelenting in the face of rejection, successfully bartered up to twenty minutes and then twenty-five over the course of the next few days. As the young Scot shared his struggles and burning desire to make something of himself, Rousseau replied in a distinctly Johnsonian fashion. "Yes," he said. "Your great difficulty is that you think it so difficult a matter."

◄◦§

It is true that Boswell had a difficult time reconciling himself to being Boswell. He thought too much and worried about how he seemed and acted to others and what he said and did. Sex especially disturbed his equilibrium. On the way to Stratford, while changing coaches at the Angel Inn at Oxford, he had recalled the effort it had taken him to resist the

Misadventure in Oxford

attentions there of the beautiful Miss Reynolds, refusing the invitation to sleep with her and contenting himself instead with drawing his hand "gently along her yellow locks," and encouraging her to become a milliner. Pressing on with his journey intending to post the last forty miles to Stratford, the darkness made him uneasy. As he left the town and jolted through the open country, the pleasant residue of resolve gave way to a fear that the flat terrain might encourage some agile young highwayman to jump on the step of his carriage, hold a pistol to his chest, and demand his money. Slipping his purse, watch, and letter from Margaret into the upholstery, he allowed himself to relax and to think about the effect he would create in Stratford with his "fine, striking appearance."

Sleepily, he changed carriages at Woodstock and again at Chipping Norton. It was hours before he realized what he'd done. Beside himself, he retraced his steps all the way to Woodstock, where the innkeeper handed him his missing effects. By now it was past six in the morning. Angelo had fired his volley and Dibdin's musicians had started their procession through the town but Boswell was still miles away, stranded. "Such crowds had passed that there was no post-chaise to be had," he wrote. "Here then was I, on the very morning of the Jubilee, in danger of not getting to it in time." Increasingly agitated, he hired two horses and a postilion to carry his bags and set out on horseback. The rain fell like nails. With no boots and a borrowed coat, he splashed off toward Stratford, with water filling his buckled shoes, carrying nothing but a small traveling bag, a musket without ball or powder, and a staff with a looping handle representing the bird of Avon. The clouds hung damp and low, breaking infrequently to reveal the comet, blue and livid, its tail as sharp as the blade of a sword.

After six miles of riding, Boswell managed to find a post

chaise, and "partly by threatenings, partly by promises, prevailed on the post-boys to drive fast." At last he reached Stratford, only to be turned away from the White Lion and be sent instead to the house of Mrs. Harris, who lived across the street from the Shakespeare birthplace. There he rented "a tolerable old-fashioned room with a neat, clean bed at a guinea a night, the stated Jubilee price." Without changing, he went immediately to Holy Trinity Church, where Garrick had led his guests to hear *Judith*, an oratorio to be performed in the chancel by the full orchestra of Drury Lane. The performers obscured Shakespeare's grave, set in the floor behind them and marked with a plain stone inscribed with a curse against any who would demote his remains to the charnel house when space was needed for new graves: "Good friend for Jesus sake forbeare / To dig the dust encloased heare / Bleste be ye man y^t spares thes stones, / And curst be he y^t moves my bones." In a niche on the north wall overlooking the grave was a waist-length bust of the poet supported by black marble columns. To some, its rudimentary execution made it look as if it belonged more to a pub sign or coconut shy than a temple of British worthies. Eva Garrick and the singer Mary Barthélémon had attempted to cheer it up by festooning it with garlands of flowers and evergreens, although the effect, wrote *The Gentleman's Magazine*, left Shakespeare looking more like the god Pan than the genius of British literature.

Boswell arrived just before the performance began, his bedraggled hair falling about his ears, his legs and back splashed with mud. Seeking out Garrick, he struck a pose, shook him warmly by the hand, and passed him a note that asked him not to reveal his true identity but simply state that he was "a clergyman in disguise." The conceit was Boswell's attempt to delay his formal entrance until such time as he could be sure it would flatter his own sense of celeb-

Shakespeare's gravesite (second flagstone from the left) inside the chancel at Holy Trinity Church. The commemorative bust, garlanded for the duration of the Jubilee, oversees it from the wall. © *The Trustees of the British Museum*

rity. That he was a "clergyman" was a joke, no doubt, about his worshipful intentions and resolution to be chaste.

With Boswell settled, the oratorio began with a bustling overture of violins that scrambled furiously up and then *Judith* down to meet the coppery thumps of the harpsichord that punctuated every musical thought. Based on the apocryphal story of the beautiful widow Judith of the Judean city of Bethulia besieged by Assyrians, it related her visit to the Assyrian camp and meeting with their general, Holofernes, who entertains her with a banquet and is lulled into sleep by her singing. As the Assyrian king rests his head in her bosom, Judith, "drawing from its sheath his shining faulchion," decapitates him, fleeing the camp and displaying his head from Bethulia's city walls. The music was by Thomas Arne, another collaborator with whom Garrick had a difficult relationship, with the latter accusing the manager of speaking ill of him. Arne had only recently lost his wife, "so young and so blooming," which made his participation particularly difficult. He was a professional, however, and his performers were some of the most elite in Britain, including the Midlands-born Joseph Vernon; Samuel Champness, who had been trained by Handel; and a popular singer and actress, Sophia Baddeley, who came to Stratford alongside her estranged husband, Robert, an actor and singer. François Barthélémon, husband of the singer Mary, provided a solo on his violin; a young performer from Bordeaux with a serious interest in mysticism and alchemy, his first London appearance had been on the same bill as an eight-year-old Wolfgang Amadeus Mozart.

Although it was the first formal event of the Jubilee, *Judith* bore no obvious connection to Shakespeare. The piece had not been specially commissioned and neither was it especially notorious or successful on the London stage, having been performed only a couple of times before—most notably, at a benefit for the New Lock hospital, an institution that specialized in the treatment of venereal diseases. It was seen there by the preacher John Wesley, the founder of the Methodist Church, who wrote that "some parts of it were exceedingly fine; but there are two things in all modern pieces of music which I could never reconcile to common sense. One is, singing the same words ten times over, the other, singing different words by different persons at one and the same time." Garrick's friend Joseph Cradock didn't like it much either. "The choruses were almost as meagre as the appearance of the audience," he wrote, "and I felt much hurt of all that were engaged to perform in it. The company of any rank had not half arrived; and an Oratorio was but a cold introduction to a tumultuous Jubilee." Boswell, still damp and steaming from his journey, nonetheless allowed himself to be overcome with pious thoughts, regretting only "that prayers had not been read, and a short sermon preached. It would have consecrated our jubilee to begin it with devotion, with gratefully adoring the supreme Father of all spirits, from whom cometh every good and perfect gift."

The performance concluded, Garrick led the guests out through the churchyard and along a loop through town and back toward the Rotunda. As they walked, Mr. Vernon sang:

> This is the day, a holiday! A holiday!
> Drive spleen and rancour far away,
> This is the day, a holiday! A holiday!
> Drive care and sorrow far away.

They stopped at the house in which Shakespeare was born. "Here Nature nurs'd her darling boy," sang Vernon:

> From whom all care, and sorrow fly,
> Whose harp the muses strung:
> From heart to heart let joy rebound,
> Now, now, we tread enchanted ground,
> Here SHAKESPEARE walk'd, and sung!

The procession paused to look around the birthplace, there to be greeted by the owner, an old woman who had recently changed her name to Shakespeare in an effort to claim descent. The house inspired invention, just as earlier that summer Garrick had visited in the company of William Hunt and declared, based on nothing but his intuition, that the large room at the front of the house was the room in which Shakespeare had been delivered into the world. Such decisive specificity was much appreciated by the visitors, since "the Joy and the Satisfaction which they felt at being in the very Room in which the great Man was born," reported the *Public Advertiser*, "exceeds all Description." Filing through the birth room, a wooden cave of warped walls plastered with a mixture of mud and hair, they were greeted near the exit by the smiling face of Thomas Becket, a bookseller who had set himself up with a large supply of books and pamphlets including *An Ode upon Dedicating a Building, and Erecting a Statue, to Shakespeare*, the piece that Garrick would debut the following day, as well as a collection of the Jubilee songs written by Garrick, Dibdin, Bickerstaff, and others that they had been hearing as they walked around. Also for sale were printed portraits of Garrick and Shakespeare and a commemorative issue of *The London Magazine* containing twin biographies of both men.

The Rotunda　　The crowd was now beginning to fill out. At three o'clock, there was a public "ordinary" in the Rotunda, a meal at which the guests were given the first opportunity to see inside the building. Despite the panic there had been to finish it, they found it hard to believe that something so beautiful could be fashioned entirely from wooden boards. Garrick's rotunda was only twenty feet smaller in diameter than the one that had inspired it at Ranelagh, with a large, hexagonal roof supported by a circular colonnade of Corinthian columns, in the middle of which hung a chandelier of eight hundred lights. To enter, guests passed through a wide curtained doorway topped by a pediment surrounded by brilliant lamps arranged in the shape of the imperial crown of England. Smaller colored lights served as its gold and jewels. From there, they moved into a large covered space in which tables had been set for the meal, at the end of which was a raked stage large enough to seat the Drury Lane orchestra. The imposing effect was made all the more piquant by the knowledge of its transience. "It would make a lover of art sigh," wrote one attendee, "to think how soon it would be demolished."

As the guests took their places, a stream of waiters appeared from field kitchens constructed on either side of the building to collect money and dispense drinks. The orchestra began to play. Boswell greeted some friends—Benjamin Victor, the actor John

Sketch of Stratford Jubilee Booth or Amphitheatre.

The Rotunda. "It would make a lover of art sigh," wrote one attendee, "to think how soon it would be demolished." © *The Victoria and Albert Museum, London*

Lee, and William Richardson the printer—before taking a seat with a group from Edinburgh comprised of Dr. John Berkeley, whom Boswell may have known as a student, and the actors James Love and his wife, a woman with whom Boswell had had an affair with eight years earlier, using the cipher "Φ" to record their assignations in his diary. Mrs. Love was at least twenty years Boswell's senior, and there is reason to believe that their affair took place with the full knowledge and even consent of her husband, who pressed Boswell for several loans at the time. Boswell, however, chose not to dwell on the past. The party included a woman from Ireland named Mrs. Sheldon, "a most agreeable little woman," he wrote, who after only a few minutes' conversation he could feel "was stealing me from my valuable spouse."

For a person determined to behave himself, the Jubilee was a lair of temptations. "Wenches!" wrote one traveler. "Never was any paradise so plentifully or beautifully inhabited as here at this time." This sentiment would have pleased Garrick, who had himself boasted to William Hunt, "I find we

An amorous spirit

shall have all ye Beauties at ye Jubilee." The whole was conducive to an amorous spirit, which the *Public Advertiser* picked up on when it reported that "last Night, the fat Landlady at the Red Lyon fell out of a Hayloft into the Manger while she was practising the Chamber Scene in Romeo and Juliet with one of the Candle-Snuffers." Others were there to find a good match. Joseph Cradock had sent his wife's sister, Miss Stratford, a "very good young Lady, with a fortune of £12,000," to lodge at the house of Mr. Evetts the baker, hoping that three days of festivity might produce a husband. The courting mood was summarized in verse by Francis Gentleman:

> Miss Tripsy expecting that Stratford will prove
> A delicate region of pleasure and love;
>> Puts on her best face,
>> Adon'd with each grace,
> As ready to bill, and to coo as a dove.

> To the market, old dowagers also repair,
> With borrowed complexions, teeth, eye-brows, and hair;
>> Each woos with her purse,
>> For better for worse,
> The female that's wealthy must surely be fair.

James Boswell wanted only to be good and, intuiting the threat posed by Mrs. Sheldon, he excused himself and moved closer to the orchestra, where Sophia Baddeley sang. Among the most popular

Of Sophia Baddeley | performers of the day, Baddeley had been born Sophia Snow, the only daughter of Valentine Snow, sergeant-trumpeter to George II. Her father had trained her for royal service, but at the age of eighteen she met the handsome actor Robert Baddeley, who lodged above a nearby shop. Robert had been a cook before entering the service of a young nobleman as he embarked on the Grand Tour. Travel had polished his manners and given him an aristocratic deportment that was perfect for the stage. Twelve years Sophia's senior, he persuaded her to elope and subsequently arranged for her to be taken on at Drury Lane, where she made her debut as Ophelia in *Hamlet* in 1764. They shared four pounds a week.

Sophia Baddeley was not an especially good actor, but she had a winning personality and an outstanding voice. She was also very beautiful, a combination of qualities that made her broadly appealing to the audience at large: "one admired her person, another her voice, and a third her acting." According to the Irish playwright Hugh Kelly's poem *Thespis: Or, a Critical Examination into the Merits of the Principal Performers Belonging to Drury-Lane Theatre*—a useful survey, delivering in rhyming couplets an assessment of every player in Garrick's company—Sophia Baddeley's appeal grew the more one watched her:

> Yet of such gifts, tho' happily possest,
> She rather *grows,* than *rushes* on the breast,
> And rather minds the passions to her course,
> Than strives to storm them by immediate force;
> Hence, in the soft and tender walks along,
> Her latent fund of talents must be shewn.

To be so prominently featured at the Jubilee in both *Judith* and again in the Rotunda was a sign of Baddeley's professional rise. She had been much in demand of late, acting at Drury Lane, but also singing at the Haymarket Theatre and in various pleasure gardens including Ranelagh, Vauxhall, and Finch's Grotto, performing popular songs of pastoral love with titles like "My Jockey Is the Blithest Lad." At Ranelagh alone she had supplemented her Drury Lane pay with an additional salary of twelve guineas a week, an inflated number explained by the fact that its proprietor, Thomas Robinson, was in love with her. He was one of many, including George Garrick, who would find himself fighting a duel to defend her honor. Her husband, Robert, more of a pander than a partner, was quick to exploit her appeal, arranging for her to have an affair with a banker named Mendez in return for a loan of three hundred pounds. Once Sophia had been admitted to Mendez's company, however, Robert accused her of having "committed an act that deterred her from going back to her

Sophia Baddeley: "One admired her person, another her voice, a third her acting." © *National Portrait Gallery, London*

own house," and they stopped talking. More suitors followed, among them the king's brother, the Duke of York, and Sir Cecil Bisshop, a gentleman in his late sixties who brought her a silver tea service worth one hundred pounds on condition that she invite him to tea.

At the time of the Jubilee, Baddeley had just emerged from a particularly unpleasant scandal, when, in an effort improve her acting, she had taken lessons from the actor Charles Holland. Holland was a handsome Drury Lane journeyman who had been trained by Garrick himself in the hope that he would be able to take the great man's place as his retirement loomed. The result was that Holland came to be viewed as a mere Garrick impersonator: "GARRICK the body, HOLLAND but the shade." He was the same age as Robert Baddeley and, like him, a serial seducer, even getting himself sued for criminal conversation by one William Earle, steward of the Royal Hospital at Chelsea, holder of the Commissaryship of the Musters, and a shareholder in the Covent Garden theatre; this lawsuit ensued after the landlady in whose house Holland arranged his assignations admitted that she had bored a hole in a closet so she could spy on him with Earle's wife, testifying that she had seen him unbuckle his sword, kneel on the carpet, lift Mrs. Earle's skirts above her head, and kiss her naked knees. Once again, George Garrick was involved, this time called as a witness to affirm that certain incriminating letters had been written in Holland's hand. Holland and Sophia conducted their affair in secret due to the fact that he was betrothed to an actress named Jane Pope. All this had ended, however, when he and Sophia were found in a compromising position on a boat moored not far from Garrick's house.

When Baddeley's song was finished, Lord Grosvenor rose to make toasts to both Garrick and Shakespeare, leading the revelers in three cheers and passing around a cup made from mulberry from which the company took sips. As they drank, Joseph Vernon sang a song in the mulberry cup's honor:

Behold this fair goblet, 'twas carv'd from the tree,

Which, O my sweet SHAKESPEARE, was planted by thee;

As a relick I kiss it, and bow at the shrine,

What comes from thy hand may be ever divine,

    All shall yield to the Mulberry-tree,

        Bend to thee,

        Blest Mulberry,

        Matchless was he

        Who planted thee,

    And thou like him immortal be!

Lord Grosvenor's marriage

Grosvenor was another of Sophia Baddeley's former lovers, with his own scandal unfolding as the Jubilee went on. Immediately prior to setting out for Stratford, he had received a mysterious letter; signed by "Jack Sprat," it claimed that his wife, Henrietta, was having an affair with another of the king's brothers, Henry Frederick, the Duke of Cumberland. The eldest daughter of the MP for Bedfordshire, Henrietta possessed "a good person, moderate beauty, no understanding, and excessive vanity," according to Horace Walpole, who was perhaps turned off by her acute love of fashion and hair *tête de mouton*. She had first met her future husband in Kensington Gardens after an unexpected downpour had cleared the paths and sent everyone running for shelter. Having found the safety of an arbor, she and her friend were joined by a tall, confident man who impressed Henrietta enough that when he offered her a ride home in his carriage, she accepted. It turned out to be the most comfortable and elegant equipage she had ever seen.

Grosvenor had the good fortune to be the grandson of Sir Thomas Grosvenor, whose marriage in 1677 to the twelve-year-old daughter of a cow farmer had made him the sole proprietor of seventy acres of London marshland between Tyburn Lane and the river Thames, land that by the 1720s had been developed into the elite enclave known as Mayfair. With its wide streets and stone-clad buildings organized around a large square named for the Grosvenors themselves, Mayfair quickly became home to aristocrats looking to escape the miasmic purlieus of Soho and Covent Garden. By the time Grosvenor and Henrietta married in the summer of 1764—she nineteen, he thirty-three—he was one of the richest men in England. Wealth was not accompanied by happiness, as Grosvenor was more interested in horse racing than in his wife. When not traveling the country visiting racetracks and stables, he visited prostitutes at a London hotel owned by a man named French George. The idea that his wife might be similarly unfaithful, however, threw him into a rage, and having heard the rumors, he confronted her as she was "lying in," having delivered his son just a week earlier. Henrietta sat in bed with her milliner beside her going through letters, but as soon as Richard demanded to see them, she tore the letters to pieces. They were from Duke Frederick, then cruising to Gibraltar on the aptly named *Venus,* from which he sent poorly spelled notes that made fun of Lord Grosvenor, calling him "Mr. Croper," after the leather strap that passes under a horse's tail to keep the saddle from slipping forward. Grosvenor failed to get his evidence then, but he would continue to keep a close watch on his wife for the rest of the year, all the while planning an elaborate trap.

With all the infidelity and erotic charge that surrounded him, Boswell was struggling. He had moved away from Mrs. Sheldon, only to gaze "steadfastly at that beautiful, insinuating creature, Mrs. Baddeley of Drury Lane." In the case of Baddeley, he knew enough of himself to understand how fleeting attraction can be:

What I feared was love was in reality nothing more than transient liking. It had no interference with my noble attachment. It was such a momentary diversion from it as the sound of a flageolet in my ear, a gay colour glancing from a prism before my eye, or any other pleasing sensation. However, the fear I had put myself in made me melancholy. I had been like a timorous man in a post-chaise, who, when a wagon is passing near it, imagines that it is to crush it; and I did not soon recover the shock.

Tired from his journey, he turned to God. "I recollected my former inconstancy, my vicious profligacy, my feverish gallantry, and I was terrified that I might lose my divine passion for Margaret, in which case I am sure I would suffer much more than she. I prayed devoutly to heaven to preserve me from such a misfortune."

Boswell's struggles

Boswell had internalized the tension between sex and piety at an early age. When, as boy, he sat high up in the trees that ringed his father's estate at Auchinleck, the sensation of shinning up tree trunks gave him a powerful feeling:

Already in climbing trees, pleasure. Could not conceive what it was. Thought of heaven. Returned often, climbed, felt, allowed myself to fall from high branches in ecstasy—all natural. Spoke of it to the gardener. He, rigid, did not explain it. In love at age of eight. . . . I knew about the rites of Venus. But unfortunately I learned from a playmate the fatal practice. I was always in fear of damnation. I thought what I was doing was but a small sin, whereas fornication was horrible.

Having graduated from arboreal frottage to actual masturbation, he was so disturbed by what he dubbed "the Cyprian fury" that he considered the example of Origen, the first-century religious ascetic who had lopped off his penis as a guard against the lures of carnal passion. The complicated welter of guilt and passion similarly characterized his love for the actress Mrs. Cowper, and his subsequent decision to run away and convert to Catholicism. As his sexual experience grew, the polarities of sex and piety bent to meet each other, each encounter convincing him that he had found evidence of divinity in sensuality, with sex providing access to the sublime by putting a fearful, timid boy from Auchinleck in touch with his essential masculinity. "In my mind, there cannot be higher felicity on earth enjoyed by man than the participation of genuine reciprocal amorous affect with an amiable woman," he wrote. "There he has a full indulgence of all the delicate feelings and pleasures both of body and mind, while at the same time in this enchanting union he exults with a consciousness that he is the superior person. The dignity of his sex is kept up. These paradisial scenes of gallantry have exalted my ideas and refined my taste."

Sex soothed him and he became unable to think of it as anything other than proof of God's perfection, as something that made him feel more "humane, polite, generous." There were repercussions, of course. His first visit to a London prostitute, the "Paphian Queen" Sally Forrester, resulted in a dose of venereal disease which took ten stubborn weeks to cure. Having returned to Edinburgh in the summer of 1760, he began courting in earnest, spending time with up to a dozen eligible young ladies whom he would audition for marriage at heavily chaperoned teas. At night, he spent time with girls of a different kind. Determined to keep out of the stews as much as possible, his sexual partners at this time numbered only four—two actresses, Mrs. Brook and Mrs. Love; Jean, the illegitimate daughter of Lord Kames; and a "curious young pretty" named Peggy Doig. Whenever he could, he would see two of them in a day, proudly recording his exploits in ciphers: "rogered Φ forenoon, and P afternoon." In December 1762, Peggy Doig delivered his child, a boy named Charles. Boswell had plans for the boy, but he died at the age of fifteen months, before he had even a chance to see him. Soon enough, Boswell experienced the discharge and telling blotches that signaled his second dose of venereal disease, considerably worse than the first and resulting in a testicle that remained horribly swollen for four months. It was one of the worst experiences of his life, the memory of which plagued him with nightmares for years in the form of a dream in which his surgeon, Andrew Douglas, peered over his genitals saying, "This is a damned difficult case." Determined never to repeat the affliction, he bet three of his friends a guinea that he would remain infection free for the next three years.

On his return to London in 1762, Boswell tried hard to resist prostitutes, despite being surrounded by all kinds "from the splendid Madam at fifty guineas a night, down to the civil nymph with white-thread stockings who tramps along the Strand and will resign her engaging person to your honour for a pint of wine and a shilling." A night at the theatre was frequently combined with a hired coupling. Having failed one night to get into Covent Garden due to the crowd, he ducked into St. James's Park to have sex with Nanny Baker before paying half price to catch the afterpiece at Drury Lane. Often the quality of one performance informed the other. After seeing Charles Holland in a disappointing production of *Macbeth*, he took "a little girl into a court" but failed to get an erection.

Soon enough he met the actress Louisa Lewis, with whom he had first become acquainted when she acted in Edinburgh. Louisa was twenty-four, taller than Boswell, with a good sense of humor and seductive eyes. She liked the same things he did, or at least enough to pass the time when they weren't making love. Within a few short days of their first assignation, Boswell "began to feel an unaccountable alarm of unexpected evil: a little heat in the members of my body sacred to Cupid." While watching a play that was "acted heavily," he felt his testicle swell again, accompanied by a scalding heat. At first, he hoped it was just a "gleet" occasioned by too much venery, but an accompanying discharge confirmed the infection as gonorrhea. Boswell was furious. "Thus ended my intrigue with the fair Louisa," he wrote, "which I flattered myself much with, and from which I expected at least a winter's copulation." Having bet his friends that he could stay infection free for three years, he lost the wager in under three months.

Illness was an opportunity to reform his ways, and never one to do things halfheartedly, he renounced licentiousness and decided to read all 4500 pages of David Hume's *History of England*. The book was not sufficient to abate the fever and self-pity that descended on him frequently, at one point inducing him to write to Louisa to ask for five guineas in compensation. The number five resonated throughout his sickness—it was the number of times he and Louisa slept together, the number of weeks his malady took to cure, and the number of guineas it cost to cure it.

Following this ordeal, Boswell took greater care to always carry his "armour," condoms he purchased from the Green Canister in Half Moon Street, a shop specializing in "implements of safety for gentlemen of intrigue," run by an ex-prostitute named Constantia Phillips. Always capable of ignoring his own best advice, he didn't always wear one. Having picked up "a fresh, agreeable young girl called Alice Gibbs" at the end of his street, he took her down an alley, where "she begged that I might not put it on, as the sport was much pleasanter without it." Meeting Samuel Johnson prompted him to be chaste again. "Since my being honored with the friend-ship of Mr. Johnson," he wrote, two months after meeting him for the first time while drinking tea in the back room of Mr. Davies's establishment in Russell Street in May 1763, "I have more seriously considered the duties of morality and religion and the dignity of human nature. I have considered that promiscuous concubinage is certainly wrong." In a separate memorandum, he wrote, "Swear to have no more rogering before you leave England except Mrs. ——."

Studying in Holland was a chance to cement his chastity, which of course faltered as soon as he left the Low Countries and entered the orbit of John Wilkes. As his tour came to a close, he confessed to Rousseau, telling him "I should like to have thirty women," a Boswellian harem that he could marry off to the local serfs as soon as they bore his children. "If you want to be a wolf," answered Rousseau, "you must howl." The philosopher went on to recommend a life of chastity and spiritual reflection, including more time spent with his father bonding over healthy pursuits like grouse shooting.

Having read of the death of his mother in an English newspaper in January 1766, Boswell prepared to leave Rousseau to return to Auchinleck. He agreed to escort Rousseau's mistress, Marie-Thérèse Levasseur, to London, where she was to go to Hume's house and await Rousseau's arrival. On the second day of travel, they shared a bed, but Boswell, distraught with grief, found himself unable to perform and started weeping. Thérèse, who was only three years younger than his mother, consoled him. The next night they tried again. This time Boswell was more pleased with his performance and boasted to Thérèse of the sexual prowess of the Scots.

Tutored by Mme. Levasseur

"I allow that you are a hardy and vigorous lover," she answered, "but you have no art," and offered to provide him tutelage. For someone who used sex to bolster his sense of masculinity, thanehood, and self-worth, the idea of playing the submissive role of a student intimidated Boswell greatly. He stayed up deliberately late reading, delaying going to bed until she began to insist, at which point he paced up and down asking questions about Rousseau. Unable to delay any longer, he drank a bottle of wine and began the lesson. Her advice was simple—be ardent but gentle, don't hurry, use your hands—but so much of it was new to him and so novel that he doubted her qualifications as a teacher, even to the extent that he thought she wasn't doing it right when she climbed on top of him and began to move "like a bad rider galloping downhill." In the ten days of journey between Paris and Dover, they had sex thirteen times.

8

The audience dispersed after the entertainments in the Rotunda, free to amuse themselves until reconvening for the evening ball. New arrivals filled the town, met by unceasing rain, including many of London's literary set "testifying their reverence for the great Father of the English Drama." Many of them were guests whom Garrick would be pleased to see, including George Colman, the manager of Covent Garden; John Hoole, a translator and civil servant; and Hugh Kelly. Others he was less sure about. Among them was his future biographer, Arthur Murphy, currently an enemy with whom he feuded often, usually over Garrick's refusals to stage Murphy's plays.

Neither would Garrick look favorably upon the unwholesome frame of William Kenrick, who, despite being so devoted to Shakespeare that he had named his eldest son William Shakespeare Kenrick, was considered an oily blot on the literary landscape. A disagreeable degenerate and failed poet, Kenrick set his hand to various forms of literary jobbing, including an English translation of Rousseau's *Julie*, in which he arbitrarily changed Julie's name, and a moralizing guide to female etiquette entitled *The Whole Duty of a Woman; or, A Guide to the Female Sex, from the Age of Sixteen to Sixty*. These days he courted infamy by sniping at authors of note—among them Samuel Johnson, whose edition of Shakespeare he had attacked noisily in the *Monthly Review* as ignorant and inattentive, characterizing Johnson's relationship to Shakespeare as that of "a fungus attached to an oak."

Garrick's worst nightmare, however, was lodged at the Bear Inn, Bridgetown, the hostelry a mile outside of town that had taken in thirty beds to handle the Stratford overspill and whose cellar stored Domenico Angelo's gunpowder. The Bear hosted two men who had traveled to Stratford purely for the pleasure of watching Garrick fail, as so many predicted he would. They were Charles Macklin, Garrick's former acting tutor, and a fellow theatre manager named Samuel Foote.

After nurturing Garrick's talent and being so quickly overshadowed, Macklin had resorted to ridiculing what his protégé had become. "The whole art of acting," he said of Garrick, "is comprized in—bustle! 'Give me a Horse! —Bind up my wounds! — Have mercy Jesu!' —all bustle! —every thing is turned into bustle!" Worse still, he believed that Garrick had conspired to have him fired from Drury Lane in 1743 after Garrick had joined the company at a salary of £500 a year just as the other actors were refusing to work until the then manager, Charles Fleetwood, increased their pay. Under Garrick's leadership, the actors presented a united front, refusing to sign new contracts unless improved terms were agreed for all. An understanding was reached, but only on condition that Macklin, a source of "intractable, unreasonable Obstinacy" (according to Fleetwood), was dismissed. With some reason, Macklin believed that his expulsion had been orchestrated by Garrick and sought to avenge himself by organizing hissing and catcalls from the pit, a ploy that failed when Fleetwood hired "banditti" to menace the protestors. Defeated, Macklin declared himself Garrick's "bitterest enemy" and, reduced to teaching oratory and elocution to tyrannized schoolboys, clung to his resentment for more than two decades. Hungry for any humiliation or embarrassment that he could use to attack his adversary, he kept his pencil ever sharpened.

While Macklin might be yesterday's man, his companion, Samuel Foote, was very much a man of the moment. At the height of his powers as one of the most popular and feared impresarios of the age, Foote was instantly recognizable for his broad belly, wooden leg, and a verbal tic that went "hey-hey-what." He was a ruthless and uncompromising satirist, unafraid to be cruel or break friendships rather than miss the chance to make a good joke. Garrick knew this better than anyone, and while the two had been uneasy friends for years, they regularly exchanged barbs from the stage, although it was no secret that Garrick lived in fear of Foote's ridicule and would timidly try to appease his antagonist before the stakes rose too high. Samuel Johnson considered Foote not only to possess "extraordinary powers of entertainment" but to have an almost feral wit. "Foote is the most incompressible fellow that I ever knew," he told Boswell. "When you have driven him into a corner, and think you are sure of him, he runs through between your legs, or jumps over your head, and makes his escape." Foote was a risk taker who had spent his career skirting the law, expertly evading the 1737 Licensing Act by charging people for a dish of chocolate or advertising his performances as if they were pictures at an exhibition, or dispensing with actors altogether and employing life-size puppets.

The recent loss of his leg had only made Foote more powerful. The accident had occurred during a hunting party with his friends Lord and Lady Mexborough at Methley Hall, their house in Yorkshire. The party was composed of boisterous aristocrats, most of them a decade younger than Foote, including Boswell's loathed Duke of York, who had bet the actor that he could not ride a particularly querulous horse. Foote, out of his element but profoundly competitive, took the bet and was thrown, suffering a severe concussion and fractured leg that had to be amputated above the knee.

To compensate, the Duke arranged for Foote to receive a patent to run the Haymarket theatre during the summer months. With his talent for showmanship suddenly legitimized, Foote became quickly rich, although this did nothing to diminish the delight he took in baiting Garrick. As he had already told the papers, he cared little for Shakespeare and had come to Stratford purely for the purpose of amassing research for a production he intended to call *Drugger's Jubilee* (after Able Drugger, a character in Ben Jonson's *The Alchemist* and one of Garrick's best-known roles), a mocking dismantling of Garrick's pretensions that he intended to have on stage even before Garrick had returned from Stratford. This was the reason, he told anyone who would listen, that Garrick had conspired to make sure he lodged at the Bear Inn atop Angelo's gunpowder—David Garrick was plotting to have Samuel Foote blown up.

Tales of extortion and abuse | The rain fell hard as Foote and Macklin joined the crowds about town to experience the full extent of the profiteering taking place in the name of Shakespeare. "It has cost me above fourteen pounds since I left London, for the pleasure of being grossly affronted, and the satisfaction of being half starved," wrote a correspondent for the *Whitehall Evening Post*. "I love Shakespeare's memory very well, but I cannot bear to be famished out of deference for his character: nor do I see why, because the good people of Stratford are his townsmen, they should be allowed to plunder their well-meaning fellow subjects with impunity."

One guesthouse was charging its patrons eighteen pence each time they used the privy. Nonresidents were required to pay a shilling. The price to tie a horse was half a guinea, the same amount it cost to borrow a coat. One guest was charged a shilling for bringing his dog and nine pence for washing his handkerchief. Foote asked one man the time, only to be told that the answer would cost him two shillings. He readily handed over the money "for nothing more than having it to say that I have paid two shillings for such a commodity." The timekeeper obliged him with the hour but not the minute, informing him that minutes cost extra. With the rain setting a premium on keeping dry and clean, the operators of sedan chairs were able to name their price. A chairman named Larry O'Brien, claiming descent from the ancient kings of Munster, was asking half a guinea for a journey of one hundred yards: "I'll give you a crown, you unconscionable rogue," said his passenger, who was also Irish. The account, published in the *Whitehall Evening Post*, continued:

"Long life to your honour, you know it is Jubilee time," replied O'Brien.

"I'll give you six shillings," said the man.

"The sweet Jasus bless you honour, don't be so hard on your own countryman," said O'Brien.

"I won't give a farthing more than the three half crowns."

"What time shall I call for your honour?"

Despite the extortion, Jubilee favors continued to sell well, as did Jubilee handkerchiefs in white and red, and the gold, silver, and copper medals styled after the one worn by Garrick. Sales of ribbons were accounted at "a thousand pounds," and of medals "it is conjectured treble that sum, even upon a moderate computation," which some in this time of economic depression and national unrest found excessive: "Yet we are distressed all this time our trade is utterly gone, and we are taxed up to the very verge of destruction." At least Musidorus could record one touching "instance of conscience," when the cook in his lodgings sent out the intestines of the chicken he had ordered arranged next to the meat, "and told us, that

Commemorative handkerchief. © *Shakespeare Birthplace Trust*

as her Mistress charged *enough* for every thing, it was but reasonable we should have our property entire."

Mulberry souvenirs of assorted provenance

Of all the souvenirs, none were as profitable as relics from the mulberry tree. Following the Reverend Gastrell's felling of the tree in 1756, much of the timber had been sold to the Corporation of Stratford while another section had been purchased for firewood by Thomas Sharp. Sharp retained a portion in his shop in Chapel Street for parceling out into knickknacks "of Stand-dishes, Tea-chests, Inkhorns, Tobacco Stoppers, etc." He had begun to sell mulberry relics as early as 1756, earning at least three hundred pounds by turning out chairs, toothpick and needle cases, ladles, nutmeg graters, and other kinds of Birmingham-inspired toy work. A third parcel of wood had gone to

An example of the ubiquitous trade in mulberry souvenirs—
a tobacco stopper, used to pack a pipe. © *Shakespeare Birthplace Trust*

a carpenter named George Willes, who had sold four raw lumps of
it, along with a letter proclaiming its authenticity signed by William
Hunt and John Payton, to David Garrick in 1762; Garrick used it
to decorate an ornate chair designed by his friend, the artist William Hogarth. Given the amount of trade that had already taken
place since Gastrell's act of vandalism, it seems unlikely that much
of Shakespeare's original tree was left by 1769, yet a remarkable
amount of it was still offered up for sale. As Domenico Angelo's
son, Henry, reflected in later life, "It is asserted that there are ten or
a dozen skulls, at least, of the same holy saint to be seen at different
convents in various parts of Spain; and it is supposed, that as many
mulberry trees, within the last half century, have been converted
into ink-stands, tobacco-stoppers, and various turnery ware, all as
veritably relics of this identical stump."

For the Jubilee's detractors, the mulberry offered a perfect meta-
phor for the overheated absurdity of Shakespeare mania. Over the

summer, the *Public Advertiser* published a series of pieces, very pos-

The tree speaks!

sibly the work of George Steevens, that were written from the perspective of the tree itself and recorded the many and repeated humiliations it had endured. "Had the keepers of my dungeon been contented only with giving me away to others," complained the tree,

> *I should have found in some place of my soul a drop of patience;* but to be prostituted to their own convenience, to be converted into tobacco-stoppers, handles to knives and forks, and nutmeg-graters, is more than I can bear without expostulation. Not a girl in our town but carries about her a tooth-pick, knitting-sheath, or comb-case fabricated out of my ravaged entrails. Some of the principal wool-combers have cards composed out of my very heart; and one of the most luxurious of my townsmen (an apothecary by professions) to prove his fundamental regard to Shakespeare, has had a branch of me hollowed into a pipe for the most degrading services of the human body.

(One pauses to wonder whether Shakespeare, whose teeming mind engendered worlds, might ever have imagined that a strip of his sapling would be one day used to administer enemas.)

Steevens's pieces not only gave voice to the tree, they animated it too. One of his possible pseudonyms, "Speculator," offered "a very summary Account of the many Hoppings, Hobblings, Jumpings, Skippings, Caperings, Frisks, Curverts and Vagaries, which this sensitive plant is obliged to exhibit every Day," having claimed to have witnessed as much in London's Spitalfields, where the much maligned poet George Keate owned a number of properties. Ever since Keate "first drew the Mulberry tree of Stratford hither," he wrote,

> the whole Place has been an absolute Fair. All Trade is in a Manner suspended and the Efforts of industrious Labour are postponed

till the Violence of eager Curiosity has been gratified to the full. The Carpenter's Yard in which this venerable Relic is preserved, is a very large one, and capable of holding a thousand People at once; yet such is the general Impatience that many have absolutely attempted to untile the Shed where it has taken Shelter, by getting upon the Wall that they may enjoy a Peep at it a few Minutes before it comes to their Turn.

The crowds, he reported, had started to grow, "especially since a Discovery has been made that the old Trunk will put itself into Motion at the bare Recital of a few of Mr. Keate's Verses, from any Mouth as well as his own." Once this miracle had been revealed, no one would leave it alone:

> The Tree is sometimes most cruelly harassed as half a Score People surround it, reciting all at once. The Wood itself appears, during the Ceremony, in the most uneasy Situation possible, as it can hardly move in Obedience to a Couplet before it is summoned another Way by a Stanza. The Strength of a well-conducted Metaphor jerks it seven or eight Yards Westward, from which Place it is no less violently borne back by the Current of a Simile. At a Compound Epithet, however, it seems ready to jump out of it's Bark, and the slightest Allusion to Shakespeare himself has sufficient Power over it to make it follow the Reciter round the whole World.

In a similar vein, "Desqueeze-Oh!" described the tree's reaction as Garrick rehearsed his ode in Stratford's Town Hall, telling the readers how, as he came to the end of the first stanza, "the withered Mulberry began to move. Before the Conclusion of the Ode, the venerable Tree was dancing upon one End thro' the dedicated Hall."

Such barbs sought to place Garrick's celebration on a par with the vulgar fairground sideshows that sprang up around the fringes of the Jubilee, and highlighted the way in which the veneration of relics replaced any sensible discussion of literary merit with slack-jawed wonder. They were also a joke about the power of poetry to "move" its audience, aimed both at Keate's inexpert verse and the scale of presumption implied by Garrick's ode. Another article added the specter of religious heterodoxy to the list of complaints, claiming that part of the timber had been graffitied and left in a lumber room in the old town hall "among mice-gnawn records, mouldy buckets, and tattered ensigns," and an "old figure of the Pope" that had been rescued from a Protestant bonfire by a former mayor who practiced Catholicism. This was a pointed detail, as not only was Stratford known as a center for recusant Catholics in the sixteenth century— including, potentially, Shakespeare's own family—but by associating the mulberry with the remnants of Romish religion, it implied again that Garrick was guilty of the idolatrous worship of false gods. It did not help that since Garrick's announcement of the Jubilee in May, Clement XIV, the newly crowned pope, had declared that a religious jubilee for all Catholics would begin in March of the following year. The coincidence did not pass unremarked, and certainly no one present at the Rotunda as Lord Grosvenor reverentially raised a mulberry cup, treating the "blest relic" as if it were a chalice filled with communion wine, would have failed to appreciate the parallel between this and Catholic rituals, especially Mass. It was also well-known that Eva Garrick was a practicing Catholic who attended Mass her entire life, and for those who sought to ridicule her "mitred" husband as "Saint Mulberry's Priest," serious questions remained.

Illuminations adorning the Town Hall

As the sun began to set, bonfires were lit and Domenico Angelo and the sulfurous Clitherow set to work illuminating the transparencies that had been placed in the windows of the birthplace and of Town Hall. These transparencies were paintings on gauzy canvas whose large frames covered the windows; when lit from behind, they shone through with brilliant colors. Hanging over the window in which Garrick had decided that Shakespeare had been born was a painted device showing the sun struggling through the clouds "in which was figuratively delineated the low Circumstances of *Shakespeare*, from which his Strength of Genius rais'd him, to become *Glory of his Country*!" The illuminations covering the five front windows of the Town Hall were even more ambitious. In the center was a full-length figure of Shakespeare capturing a Pegasus in flight above the inscription "Oh! For a muse of fire." To his left were Falstaff and Pistol from *The Merry Wives of Windsor*, while to his right was Lear in the act of execrating his daughters, and Caliban

Stratford-upon-Avon's High Cross marketplace at the height of the Jubilee.
© Shakespeare Birthplace Trust

drinking from Trinculo's keg from *The Tempest*. A hundred colored lamps shone through these canvases, which Garrick had modeled on ones created by the Royal Academy to illuminate its buildings two months earlier in honor of the king's birthday. Those transparencies, representing painting, sculpture, and architecture, were by the artists Giovanni Cipriani, Benjamin West, and Nathaniel Dance, respectively. Garrick admired the effect and, hoping to save money, asked his friend Sir Joshua Reynolds, the first president of the recently founded academy, whether he could borrow them. Reynolds insisted he "could not part with them," so Garrick turned to the scene makers French and Porter to build some of their own. As they were being built, it dawned on him how usefully these might be used onstage to effect instantaneous scene changes, in which the image seen by the audience would miraculously transform depending on whether the gauze was lit from the back or the front, an effect that would come to be used often at Drury Lane.

George Garrick had successfully persuaded enough Stratford residents to light their windows with candles and, with the musicians balladeering and visitors wandering through the glow in their ribbons and favors, the town took on a special aspect that even Charles Dibdin could not fail to appreciate, despite the rain. "It was magic," he said. "It was fairyland . . . the effect was electrical, irresistible; every soul present felt it, cherished it, delighted in it, and considered that moment as the most endearing to sensibility that could possibly be experienced; when [a person] has said all this and ten times more, he would have given a faint idea of the real impression." "All is Joy and Festivity here," agreed the *St. James Chronicle*, "and what with the Rattling of Coaches, the Blazing and Cracking of Fireworks, the Number of People going and coming from the Mask Warehouse, where they repair to provide themselves with Dresses, my Head is almost turned and I think I may venture to say I shall never see such another Scene in all my Life." Still some locals disagreed. "Notwithstanding the prodigious benefit evidently accruing to the inhabitants of Stratford from the Jubilee," reported Musidorus,

Divergence of opinion betwixt townspeople and others

> it is inconceivable to think how many well-meaning people of the place were in a continual alarm for the safety of the town, which they actually imagined would undergo some signal mark of the Divine displeasure, for being the scene of so very prance a festival. In this opinion they were doubly confirmed . . . when the Town was illuminated for the Assembly, and some transparencies hung out at the window, for the amusement of the populace. . . . These devices struck a deep apprehension on the minds of the ignorantly religious; they looked upon them as peculiarly entitled to the vengeance of Providence, and wished the Londoners heartily at home, though they found our money so highly worth their acceptance.

The ball commenced at ten, with minuets danced until midnight. Refreshments were served and followed by country dances until three in the morning. Boswell, so tired he could hardly stand, made an appearance just long enough to ensure he had been seen. Still rattled from the threat to his chastity, to his great relief he went home alone, where his landlady, "a good, motherly woman," came to him with a bowl of warm, sweetened wine called negus. It was terribly comforting. "I told her that perhaps I might retire from the world and just come and live in my room at Stratford."

9

After such a late night, the next morning's cannon blasts were met with less enthusiasm, as were the trilling of the fife and thumping of the drums. The ladies were again serenaded, but not so many roused themselves from their beds. One grand dame, peering out at the drab sky and immiserating rain, proclaimed, "What an absurd climate!" before retiring again. "It appeared," remembered Henry Angelo, "as if the clouds, in an ill humour with these magnificent doings, had sucked up a superabundance of water, to shower down upon the finery of the mimic host, and that the river gods had opened all the sluices of the Avon, to drown the devotees of her boasted bard."

The second day

Rain threatened the ruination of the Jubilee, although anyone who cared to consult an almanac would have known that September was not ideal for outside pursuits in the weeping climate of England. The past two Septembers had been a washout. "Cloudy, churlish morning" and "smart rain from 6 to 3," read the weather reports, "flying clouds, misty afternoon." It had, however, been a remarkable year for farmers, "the greatest Plenty of Apples," wrote the *St. James Chronicle*, "and other Fruit, ever known in the Memory of Man." Water formed bronze pools in the muddy streets while the fringes of the Bankcroft meadow, on which the Rotunda stood, were seeped in rising river water. "What do you make of that?"

Still raining

Garrick asked Samuel Foote, pointing to a violently running drain. "I think," said Foote, "'tis God's revenge against Vanity!"

The first event planned for the day was a pageant of Shakespearean characters that was to process through the town from George Garrick's base at the College before filing into the Rotunda, where they would line up in anticipation of the *Dedication Ode*. One hundred and seventy actors and local volunteers assembled to dress as directed, milling about in costume as their voices bounced off the high ceilings or they ran outside to shoo the children away from the puddles. Among them was the young Henry Angelo, representing the spirit Ariel, and Francis Wheler, the lawyer who had presented Garrick with the mulberry box, excited to be a part of the procession despite suffering an attack of hemorrhoids that had almost prevented him from reaching Stratford at all.

Pageant of Shakespearean characters

George called everyone outside and hurried about marshaling the group, placing them in the order his brother had ordained. At their head was a large triumphal car carrying actors representing the muses of Comedy and Tragedy—in essence, a cart that had been clad in pasteboard and decorated to befit the occasion, pulled along by six hairy-legged satyrs. Dancers dressed as the remaining seven muses and women playing tambourines and representing the three Graces were to skip alongside. Only nineteen of Shakespeare's thirty-seven plays were included, those plays most commonly performed in Garrick's theatre, with *As You Like It* taking the front and *Antony and Cleopatra* bringing up the rear. Each play was represented by a group of four or five processioners who bore a banner before them while performing in dumb show a scene that presented, in Garrick's words, "some capital part of it in Action." The result was a line of people who together formed the most memorable highlights of Shakespeare's canon as understood by eighteenth-century audiences—Lear in the throes of madness, Macbeth holding a

bloody dagger, Malvolio waving a forged love note, and Fluellen forcing Pistol to eat a leek.

As always, getting organized took time, and the props and costumes, creations of wire and tinsel that looked fabulous under Drury Lane candlelight, began to blister and crease in Stratford's squalling rain. This horrified Garrick's business partner James Lacy, who went immediately over to Garrick's rooms to call the procession to a halt. Lacy had been opposed to the Jubilee from the start, condemning it as an "idle pageant," and was adamant that the weather would ruin the silks and satins of his costumes and all the expensive properties that were needed for the upcoming season.

Garrick clashes with Lacy "See—who the devil, Davy, would venture upon the procession under such lowering aspects?" Lacy said. "Sir, all the ostrich feathers will be spoiled, and the *property* will be damnified five thousand pounds."

Garrick had a strong aversion to Lacy and hated to be challenged by him. The two men quarreled often, with Garrick calling Lacy "the deepest of all politicians" and accusing him of constantly seeking to undermine his authority through "spies, deep researches, and anonymous letters." Furthermore, Garrick complained, "There

Announced in the bills as "A PAGEANT of the principal Characters in the inimitable Plays wrote by the Immortal *Shakespeare*," these promotional images were produced before the parade was cancelled by James Lacy.
Used by permission of the Folger Shakespeare Library

is a rank viciousness in his Disposition that can only be kept under by ye Whip & curb," aggrieved that Lacy was sticking his nose in artistic decisions, a domain Garrick believed to be solely his, by hiring actors and superintending the rehearsals while being "insensible of my Merit and Services"—that is, being insufficiently grateful for the vast profits Garrick brought to the house through his acting and the plays and pantomimes he wrote at no additional fee. Even worse, Lacy mistreated George. "I am quite Sick of his Conduct towards Every body that love Me," said Garrick. "He will never forgive my being the means of his making a figure in the world."

But the rain persisted and Lacy prevailed. Word was sent to the College for the performers to disperse and handbills were printed to announce the change:

A change of plans

To the
Ladies and Gentlemen

at the
Jubilee
Thursday Sep. 7th 1769
As the weather proves so unfavourable for the
PAGEANT
The Steward begs leave to inform them that it is
oblig'd to be deferr'd.
THE ODE
will be peform'd at 12 in the Amphitheatre,
The Doors to be open'd at 11

Garrick was humiliated. When Lacy left, he sat down to be shaved, only for the barber (who had been up late and was not yet sober) to cut him "from the corner of his mouth to his chin." Eva applied styptics to stop the bleeding, but the wound was such that it delayed his getting dressed. The absence of the pageant placed even more pressure on the ode to be successful, the fundamental statement and cultural keynote of the occasion. Having controlled the bleeding, and now dressed in a freshly tailored suit of deep brown cloth embroidered with gold lace and a lining of ivory taffeta finished with thirteen gold buttons, Garrick reached for a slim packet of waxed paper that contained a pair of ivory-white gloves. These had been presented to him at the end of May by an old actor named John Ward, who had himself received them twenty-three years earlier following a performance of *Othello* he had put up to raise money to restore the Shakespeare memorial in Holy Trinity Church. The man who gave the gloves to Ward was a Stratford glazier named William Shakespeare, yet another person claiming descent. "These are the only property that remains of our famous relation," he had said.

Irritated and anxious, Garrick straightened his coat, examined his wound, and stepped out in time for breakfast at the Town Hall at nine. The wind was blowing and the rain came down hard. He ate a meal that ended shortly before eleven and made his way over to the Rotunda. The river, which had been rising steadily for the past two days, sloshed at its banks and seeped deeper into the meadow's long grass.

Close to a thousand people awaited him inside the amphitheatre. The space was beautiful in spite of the torrent outside, hung with crimson curtains and lit with eight hundred lights, which reflected off the gilding on the cornices and pilasters. Some slight adjustments had to be made now that Garrick wouldn't be entering at the head of the pageant, so instead he made his way alone to the front of the rostrum that enclosed the orchestra in a crescent of balusters and sat looking over the audience as they continued to settle in. Behind him sat the entire orchestra and chorus of Drury Lane, more than one hundred performers, banked in a semicircle. Thomas Arne, dressed also in a brown velvet suit, stood to one side, while in pride of place at the orchestra's highest point, stood John Cheere's statue of Shakespeare, commissioned for the Town Hall's empty nook.

Garrick looked nervous as the overture began, some even said "confused or intimidated." He stood, and giving a respectful bow that was received with warm applause, began. "To what blest genius of the isle," he asked his audience, "Shall Gratitude her tribute pay," before presenting them with a verbal image of Shakespeare— "that demi-god"—attended by fey spirits and literary godkins: | *The ode*

> Who Avon's flow'ry margin trod,
> > While sportive *Fancy* round him flew,
> Where *Nature* led him by the hand,
> > Instructed him in all she knew,

And gave him absolute command!
'Tis he! 'Tis he!
"The god of our idolatry!"

This last line, paraphrasing Juliet's "swear by thy gracious self, / Which is the god of my idolatry" from *Romeo and Juliet*, was one that Garrick had been using for years, adopting it as a motto for his own Shakespeare mania. However, given the worship of the mulberry tree and the deep ritualistic reverence he was attempting to convey, opening the ode with such an admission made some listeners uncomfortable. "Pious ears were offended by the boldness of the expression," remarked *Lloyd's Evening Post*, "and others took occasion to compare the whole to the canonization of a Romish Saint." Certainly, it was as if addressing a holy relic that Garrick turned at this point to the statue. "To him the song, the Edifice we raise," he continued,

He merits all our wonder, all our praise!
Yet ere impatient joy break forth,
In sounds that lift the soul from earth;
And to our spell-bound minds impart
Some faint idea of his magic art;
Let awful silence still the air!
From the dark cloud, the hidden light
Bursts tenfold bright!
Prepare! prepare! prepare!
Now swell at once the choral song,
Roll the full tide of harmony along;
Let Rapture sweep the trembling strings,
And Fame expanding all her wings,
With all her trumpet-tongues proclaim,

The lov'd, rever'd, immortal name!
SHAKESPEARE! SHAKESPEARE! SHAKESPEARE!
Let th'inchanting sound,
From Avon's shores rebound:
Thro' the Air,
Let it bear,
The precious freight the envious nations round!

Although set to music, the ode was spoken, not sung. This was an innovation in itself, as audiences were used to hearing this kind of thing as operatic recitative. Garrick, however, thought that "the dullest part of Musick" and had decided to deploy instead his famous gift for oratory and expression. "It is an experiment," he had told the Earl of Hardwicke, "but I think it worth ye Tryal." It worked. Within the space of only a few stanzas, according to Benjamin Victor, it "had so great Effect, that, perhaps, in all the Characters he ever played, he never shewed more Powers, more Judgment, or ever made a stronger Impression on the Minds of his Auditors." Garrick's nerves began to fall away, and he felt himself approaching the height of his powers. "His eyes sparkled with joy," wrote Boswell, who was thrilled to be part of such a defining moment of public spectacle, "and the triumph of his countenance at some parts of the ode, it's tenderness at others, and inimitable sly humour at others, cannot be described." His sentiment was not shared by the *Warwickshire Journal,* who felt that Garrick's "Powers and Tone of Voice" were "much inferior to what they were in his meridian perfection," while quoting a line from the Roman poet Horace, *"Solve senescentem mature sanus equum,"* which advises wise men to rid themselves of aging horses.

After each recited passage, Garrick sat down to make way for

the chorus, who belted out a verse in support of the principal argument. "Swell the choral song," they sang,

> Roll the tide of harmony along,
>> Let Rapture sweep the strings,
>> Fame expand her wings,
> With her trumpet-tongues proclaim,
> The lov'd, rever'd, immortal name!
> SHAKESPEARE! SHAKESPEARE! SHAKESPEARE!

Next Robert Baddeley rose, singing a song that described Shakespeare
being garlanded by the muses (as depicted on the mulberry box that
had initiated the entire Jubilee). Garrick then spoke again, declaring that Shakespeare's achievement was superior to that of Alexander
the Great, as while Alexander conquered earthly realms, Shakespeare
could draw on the limitless resources of his "wonder-teeming" mind
and raise "other worlds, and beings of his own!" By now, the audience
was rapt, applauding every stanza and every song. After another song
from Joseph Vernon, Garrick continued, paraphrasing the opening
chorus of *Henry V.* "O from his muse of fire," he said:

> Could but one spark be caught,
> That might the humble strains aspire
> To tell the wonders he has wrought,
> To tell, —how sitting on his magic throne,
>> Unaided and alone,
>> In dreadful state,
> The subject passions round him wait;
> Who tho' unchain'd, and raging there,
> He checks, inflames, or turns their mad career;
>> With that superior skill,

Which winds the fiery steed at will,
He gives the aweful word—
And they, all foaming, trembling, own him for their Lord.

With each passage, Garrick built on the image he presented of Shakespeare as the commander of the passions, a man who had not only understood the complexities of human nature but tamed them and bound them to his will. "Such is ye Power of Shakespeare," Garrick had written, "that he can turn and wind the Passions as he pleases, and they are so Subjected to him, that tho raging about, and unchain'd they wait upon his Commands, and Obey them, when he gives ye Word." This powerful ability to represent humanity, he argued, not only enriched the humanity of others, it forced them to confront themselves, even to the extent that the guilty would confess their crimes:

With these his slaves he can control,
Or charm the soul;
So realized are all his golden dreams,
Of terror, pity, love, and grief,
Tho' conscious that the vision only seems,
The woe-struck mind finds no relief:

. . . .

Ye guilty, lawless tribe,
Escap'd from punishment, by art or bribe,
At *Shakespeare's* bar appear!
No bribing, shuffling there—
His genius, like a rushing flood,
Cannot be withstood,
Out bursts the penitential tear!
The look appall'd, the crime reveals,

> The marble-hearted monster feels,
> Whose hand is stain'd with blood.

Just as Garrick was asking his audience to examine their con-
Injury to a   sciences, an enormous crack was heard within the Rotunda,
young peer   as an ill-timbered bench split under the weight of the audience and sent a row of people tumbling to the floor. At the
same time, a gust of wind blew a door off its hinges—it fell on a
number of guests, including Francis Wheler and the sixteen-year-
old Lord Carlisle, who was knocked senseless and had to be carried
outside by friends who feared for his life.

The audience reconstituted themselves as Samuel Champness
sang before Garrick returned to compare Shakespeare to *The Tempest*'s Prospero, a "magician" and "Monarch of th'inchanted land."
Waves of repeating applause rang through the Rotunda as Eleanor
Radley now stood to sing of Shakespeare as "the treasure of joy."

Garrick delivers the *Dedication Ode* to a packed audience in the Rotunda, the
statue of Shakespeare taking pride of place at the center of the orchestra.
Used by permission of the Folger Shakespeare Library

A young Drury Lane actress, fittingly known as a "songstress of nature," Radley was a close friend of Sophia Baddeley, who gifted her her old clothes and jewels whenever she received a new set. The song marked a shift in gears as Garrick moved from considering Shakespeare's tragic heroes to a long section reflecting on the genius of Falstaff, a "huge, misshapen heap" and "a comic world in ONE."

Another song from Vernon, called "A World Where All Pleasures Abound," "deserved the thunder of applause which was bestowed upon it" and set up a passage in which Garrick lamented the fact that the poets of Oxford and Cambridge universities had not taken up their pens in praise of Shakespeare's genius, with the clear (and disingenuous) implication that it was a shame that a humble actor had been left to pick up the intellectual slack. This was followed by more of the now familiar mythologizing of the Warwickshire countryside, spiced with some local politics as the ode thanked the Duke of Dorset for permitting the removal of the willow trees to make way for the Rotunda, as well as his decision to forbid the surrounding fields from being enclosed for private farmland. These lines had clearly been inserted at the request of the Corporation of Stratford, "for which after the Performance," Garrick told Hunt, "I expect yr thanks." Robert Baddeley sang again before Garrick started to build toward the crescendo. "Can *British* gratitude delay," he asked,

> To him the glory of this isle,
> To give the festive day
> The song, the statue, and devoted pile?
> To him the first of poets, best of men?
> *"We ne'er shall look upon his like again!"*

This was the cue for the coronation and, as the music swelled, two actors moved toward the statue at the center of the orchestra to crown it with laurel garlands, singing,

Shall the hero laurels gain,
For ravag'd fields, and thousands slain?
And shall his brows no laurels bind,
Who charms to virtue humankind?

To which the entire Drury Lane chorus replied:

We will, —his brows with laurel bind,
Who charms to virtue human kind:
Raise the pile, the statue raise,
Sing immortal *Shakespeare's* praise!
The song will cease, the stone decay,
But his Name,
And undiminish'd fame,
Shall never, never pass away.

Reception As the final notes wavered and the spectators digested all they had seen, Lord Grosvenor rushed to the front, visibly trembling with emotion to tell "Mr. Garrick that he had affected his whole frame, shewing him his veins and nerves still quivering with agitation." Wrote a correspondent for *Lloyd's Evening Post*, "When I saw the Statue of *Shakespeare*, the greatest dramatic Poet, and the living person of *Garrick*, the greatest Actor that England ever produced; when I considered the Occasion, the Scene, and the Company which was drawn together by the Power of *one Man*, I was struck with a kind of Veneration and Enthusiasm."

Boswell was equally in raptures. A lover of solemn ritual and believer in the power of communal artistic experiences to civilize society, he was the ode's ideal auditor. Describing it as "noble," he felt as if he had been exposed to genius, likening it to a performance one might have seen in ancient Athens or Rome. "The whole audience were fixed in the most earnest attention," he wrote,

and I do believe, that if any one had attempted to disturb the performance, he would have been in danger of his life. Garrick, in the
front of the orchestra, filled with the first musicians of the nation,
with Dr. Arne at their head, and inspired with an aweful elevation
of soul, while he looked from time to time at the venerable statue
of Shakespeare, appeared more than himself. While he repeated
the ode, and saw the various passions and feelings which it contains
fully transfused into all around him, he seemed in extacy, and gave
us the idea of a mortal transformed into a demi-god, as we read in
the Pagan mythology.

But what exactly was this thing, half sung, half spoken, filled with
florid pieties and verbal curlicues yet able to move grown men to tears?
Formally, it was a Pindaric ode in varying meters, with eight passages
of recitative, seven songs, and two full choruses. Like Garrick's other
Jubilee texts, it referenced Shakespeare's work only obliquely, through
allusions and half quotations, supplementing those with echoes of
other literary authorities, including John Milton and John Dryden,
whose own ode "Alexander's Feast" was a clear influence. Above all,
it was an actor's poem, a patchwork incantation pieced together from
a commonplace book of half-remembered lines and bits of oratory
that together conspired to sound important. Gauzy and indirect,
it implied the presence of Shakespeare's spirit without tackling the
facts of his textual body and, as such, was a verbal companion to
the abandoned pageant, inasmuch as it aimed to distill the substance
of Shakespeare into a synoptic form. It was the theatrical adaptation par excellence, an apotheosis, the grand summation of a century
of playing and thinking about Shakespeare that stripped him of the
compromising realities of his work and set him on a marble-smooth
throne of genius. Shakespeare had ascended, and it was not necessary
to read a single page of his work to know this to be true.

Garrick was not only delighted by the ode's reception, he was enormously relieved. He had been anxious as to whether his skills as an author were equal to the occasion, consulting with Thomas Warton, the Oxford professor of poetry, throughout its composition. "I must say that his ode greatly exceeded my expectations," wrote Boswell, addressing now the quality of the poetry in the performance he had just witnessed, "I knew his talents for little sportive sallies, but I feared that a dedication ode for Shakespeare was above his powers." Boswell was no doubt thinking of Samuel Johnson's words, who had told him that "Little Davy is a very good actor but as to *poetry*, he never wrote but *one* line in his life." Boswell continued, "What the critics may say of this performance I know not, but I shall never be induced to waver in my opinion of it. I am sensible of it's defects; but, upon the whole, I think it a work of considerable merit, well suited to the occasion, by the variety of it's subjects, and containing both poetical force and elegance."

Critical opinion, in fact, reached a rather swift consensus as to the merits of the ode. "Impartiality," wrote a correspondent for the *Warwickshire Journal*, "obliges me to say, that the Ode in itself will not bear reading to Advantage. . . . His images want magnitude for such an object, nor does he always apply them with propriety." Horace Walpole, Garrick's neighbor, who was then in Paris, was blunter. "I have blushed when the papers came over crammed . . . with Garrick's insufferable nonsense about Shakespeare," he wrote to a friend. "As that man's writings will be preserved by his name, who will believe that he was a tolerable actor?" Back in the audience, meanwhile, the embittered Charles Macklin plotted a more

Macklin's bile

public rebuke, scribbling notes that quibbled with every line. Outraged that Garrick should have the temerity to invite esteem as a poet, Macklin compiled his thoughts into a pedantic letter that accused the ode of imprecise language and botched imagery, deploying scoffing complaints such as saying that while he had heard of raising cabbages, it was preposterous to claim that Shakespeare had "rais'd other worlds."

Garrick penned a long and patient reply, scrawling on the envelope of his copy, "I might have spent my time better than supporting a foolish business against a very foolish man." Macklin's quibbles reappeared, with further elaborations, in a series of four articles published six weeks after the Jubilee under the pen name "Longinus," in reference to the first-century author of an aesthetic treatise that focused on good and bad effects in writing. That the objections are almost identical suggests that Macklin and Longinus were one and the same. "My indignation is at length raised to such a pitch, at the highest insult I have ever known offered to the public taste, that I can contain it no longer," he wrote, before taking the reader through ten dyseptic and closely argued pages that condemned the ode for containing "almost every thing that is false in writing," and being "defective in the small articles of genius, taste, sentiment, language, composition, numbers, (except in the many stolen lines) rhime, grammar, common sense, and common English." It had taken many years, but Macklin had his revenge.

Whatever Garrick's enemies had to say, the general view was that the sense of occasion spared the ode and rendered it "superior to Criticism." This was, after all, a performance, and not merely a man reading his work aloud. *The London Museum* wrote that, while the ode was "not only without sense or poetry, but full of the most displeasing and inapplicable images," Garrick "robs nonsense of its dullness, and impropriety of its defects, merely to convince us of a feature in his character we were not before acquainted with, *that whatever he repeats, requires no collateral assistance.*" Garrick's great skill, it argued, was in "making nonsense agreeable."

After the lengthy applause had died away, a reflective hush fell about the Rotunda. Garrick then thanked Arne and the musicians, apologized for his deficiencies as poet and orator, and told the audience that if they still required a greater authority for the merits of Shakespeare, they should consult their own hearts. "I would not pay them so ill a compliment as to suppose, that he has not made a dear, valuable, and lasting impression upon them!" he said. "Your attendance here upon this occasion is a proof that you felt—powerfully felt his Genius, and that you love and revere him and his memory." Like a preacher asking his congregation to offer testimonials of divine grace, Garrick looked across the many seated faces. "That only remaining honour to him now (and it is the greatest honour you can do him)," he said, "is to speak for him." There was a pause and some embarrassed laughter among the crowd. Garrick continued: "Perhaps my proposition comes a little too abruptly upon you?" he said, and gesturing toward the orchestra, continued, "With your permission, we will desire these gentlemen to give you time, by a piece of music, to recollect and adjust your thoughts."

As the music played, Garrick asked the crowd again: "Now, Ladies and Gentlemen, will you be pleased to say any thing *for* or *against* Shakespeare?" There was a small disturbance, at which point a man stood up and, taking off his great coat to reveal a blue suit embroidered with silver frogs (an audaciously Parisian style), he approached the orchestra and began to complain that Shakespeare was an ill-bred, vulgar author, who excited braying laughter and unseemly tears, "when it was the criterion of a gentleman," he insisted, "to be moved at nothing—to feel nothing—to admire nothing!" This statement was merely a prologue to a fuller harangue, in which the man in the blue frog suit accused Shakespeare of being a debaucher of minds, when, he said, "the chief excellence of man, and the most refined sensation was to be devoured by ennui, and only live in a state of insensible vegetation!" The audience grew restless as he rambled on, slandering Garrick, the Corporation of Stratford, and the entire Jubilee, until eventually it began to dawn on many that the heckler was none other than Tom King, the Drury Lane comedian and one of Garrick's most reliable performers. King was parodying Voltaire, play-

A dissenting Frenchman

ing devil's advocate to such an absurd degree that any lingering opposition to Shakespeare's claim as the greatest writer of all time would be shamed out of existence.

But the anti-masque fell flat, as King was too well-known to be taken seriously and there was no one in the audience who even remotely sympathized with Voltaire. "This Exhibition looked so like a Trap laid on Purpose, that it displeased me," wrote Boswell, who feared the incident lowered the tone. *Lloyd's Evening Post* also found it insipid, "and I could wish that that part of the entertainment had been left alone." King returned to his seat, and Garrick delivered an epilogue addressed to the ladies of the Jubilee, thanking them specifically for the good sense and patriotism their sex had shown by sponsoring Shakespeare's initial return to the stage in the 1730s through the auspices of the Shakespeare Ladies Club, and for helping to fund his monument in Westminster Abbey. And with that, the coronation of Shakespeare as the genius of Britain was complete.

The audience began to leave, no doubt confident that they had witnessed an event that had tilted irrevocably the axis of culture. Charles Dibdin was not so sure. "If GARRICK felt all this extacy, and imparted it to his auditors," he wrote,

> and fraught with nothing more than a noble ardour to lend tribute towards immortalizing his glorious bard, I know that it was called forth by a contemplation of the prodigious remuneration that would result to himself. It was acting; and, while he was infusing into the very souls of his hearers the merits of the incomparable SHAKE-SPEAR, the author of his own transcendent fame, and GARRICK'S ample fortune, his soul was fixed upon DRURY-LANE treasury.

Outside the Rotunda, the rain continued to fall, its fresh chill now mixed with the beefy aroma of roasting turtle.

10

The turtle dinner | Damp guests tried their hardest to amuse themselves until the dinner at four o'clock prepared by Mr. Gill, a cook of Bath, who had come to assist his brother, a drunk of Stratford, along with half a dozen other local cooks. The menu was venison and turtle, the latter an exotic, festive dish, offered on special occasions only. Edmund Burke had treated Garrick to one in 1768, writing to him that it was "an entertainment at least as good for the palate, as the other for the nose. Your true epicureans are of opinion, you know, that it contains in itself all kinds of flesh, fish, and fowl. It is therefore a dish fit for one who can represent all the solidity of flesh, the volatility of fowl, and the oddity of fish." Certainly it presented the diner with options. Three separate dishes could be made from a single animal. Once the head and fins were removed and the guts and belly meat (known as the collops) had been cut from the shell, the collops were stewed with sweet herbs and Madeira and served like veal cutlets, the fins descaled and baked, while the guts were stewed with quince butter and served up in the shell. The taste was reminiscent of neck of beef.

Boswell forwent the chance to feast on turtle, dining alone with the bookseller Richard Baldwin. Baldwin was a literary businessman with shares in a number of newspapers, including the *Public Advertiser*, and spoke enthusiastically of growing its circulation and boosting its value to £2000 a year. Boswell himself was looking to buy shares in *The London Magazine*, a monthly to which he made regular contributions. They ate and discussed business, before Boswell excused himself and returned to the matronly Mrs. Harris's to prepare for the evening's masked ball.

The ball was yet another component of the Jubilee that had nothing to do with Shakespeare, "well enough calculated for vacant minds," wrote George Steevens, Garrick's enemy, in *Lloyd's Evening Post*, "to gratify ostentatious

Boswell prepares for the ball

pride juvenile vanity, and luxurious opulence; and, in short, such as policy directed, in compliance with the vitiated taste of these times." It was also a prime opportunity for Boswell to excel in the business of promoting his person, enlarging his notoriety as a writer among the cream of society and making the world more broadly aware of *An Account of Corsica*. This he would do by attending the ball dressed as a Corsican freedom fighter, although his last-minute decision to attend the Jubilee meant that he had left his authentic Corsican attire in Edinburgh. The costume he brought had been patched together in London and took the form of a scarlet waistcoat and breeches worn beneath a coarse coat of dark cloth, onto which he had sewn the Moor's head crest of Corsica. A tall mitred hat had been commissioned in haste from Mr. Dalemaine, the Covent Garden tailor, and embroidered with the words *"Viva la Libertà"* in gold letters and decorated with a blue feather and cockade, "so that it had an elegant, as well as a war-like appearance." Black splatter-dashes, a kind of legging, were laced up to his knees. Around his waist, he tied a cartridge pouch, into which he shoved a pistol and stiletto, while a musket was slung across his shoulder. He wore no wig, but rather had his hair plaited into a single strand tied with a blue ribbon. In his hand, he carried the bird-headed staff he had come across in Cheapside. Admiring his reflection, he felt certain that dashing figure would reflect just as well on his fiancée as it did on himself. "When I looked at myself in the glass last night in my Corsican dress," he told Margaret,

> I have that kind of weakness that, I could not help thinking your opinion of yourself might be still more raised: "She has secured the constant affection and admiration of so fine a fellow." Do you know, I cannot think there is any harm in such a kind of weakness or vanity, when a man is sensible of it and it has no great effect upon him. It enlivens me and increases my good humour.

So satisfied was Boswell feeling that he broke his promise to his friend Dempster that he would not write anything about himself at the Jubilee for the papers. Not only was he mentally composing the paragraph he would place in *The London Magazine* even as he dressed, he subsequently sat down and wrote some verses to com-memorate his visit, sending them out to a printer who had adver-tised the bold claim that during the Jubilee all printing jobs could be turned around in an hour. Boswell hoped to hand these out as he entered the ball, a live prosodic commentary on the moment, but the printer, distracted by the promise of a fireworks display, had deserted his station. Instead, Boswell sent to the regular printer and found there an adept Scots boy who promised to bring him proofs as soon as they were done.

The fireworks The distracting fireworks were being prepared by Domenico Angelo, hard at work behind his ornamental screen on the far side of the river in the hopes of delivering a display grand enough to mark the end of this special day. It would begin with another transparency lit by hundreds of colored lamps; this one showed Time leading Shakespeare to immortality, flanked on one side by Tragedy and by Comedy on the other—an idea, which while copied again from Sir Joshua Reynolds, was a perfect illustra-tion of the logic of the ode. The fireworks that followed had been planned in three parts. The first began with a large line of rockets, each discharging three times, followed by twelve half-pound sky rockets and four "tourbillons," fireworks that rose and spun like a whirlwind. Next came four balloons, two vertical wheels, two cascades with loud reports, and one fire tree in "Chinese fire." The final section comprised two large pieces that underwent three transformations, from sun to porcupine quills and eight-pointed stars, two "pigeon wheels" with seven pigeons each, and two horizontal tables with six vertical wheels and illuminated globes. The bridge across the Avon had been rigged so that blazing serpents would appear along its span.

Unfortunately, for all the care Angelo had given his spectacle, he couldn't control the rain or stop the dark night from growing increasingly chill. Everything was so permeated with damp that not even the first round of fireworks would go off. "The rockets would not ascend for fear of catching cold," recalled his son, Henry, "and the surly crackers went out at a single pop." Meanwhile, the Avon continued to rise, submerging the meadow in inches of water. Of the many eyeing the rain with trepidation, only Hugo Meynell, the MP for Lymington, was wise enough to evacuate, arranging a relay of horses he offered to anyone who wished to leave before it was too late.

Having called off the pageant, Garrick refused to concede the ball, which he insisted would begin at eleven as advertised. The first to arrive was the industrialist Matthew Boulton, dressed in the character of a Turk wearing an outsized turban decorated with artificial jewels made by workers at his factory. He stood alone for a while, as it was another hour before the larger body of people began to drift in. This became a steady stream by midnight, among them Garrick, who came dressed only in the suit that had become his unofficial steward's uniform, lest the partygoers expect him to spend the whole night playing a role. He opened the ball with an

oration on the qualities of Shakespeare that amounted to a summary of eighteenth-century literary theory. After a long day of
speeches, it required every fiber of goodwill on the part of his audience to struggle through.

Of the
costumes at
the ball

Soon enough, the ball was "packed to extravagance,"
with various estimates placing the number of guests
between one and two thousand. Many of them were notable members of society, including three ladies dressed as
the weird sisters from *Macbeth* who also happened to be three of
the reigning beauties of the day—Lady Pembroke, Harriet Bouverie
(wife of the MP for Salisbury), and Mrs. Crewe. "The astonishing
contrast between the deformity of the feigned and the beauty of
the real appeared was every where observed," remarked one paper.
Beyond the Jubilee, Pembroke, Bouverie, and Crewe were also
known as members of the "anti-patriotic Coterie" for their loyalty
to the king and fierce opposition to John Wilkes.

The theatrical couple Mr. and Mrs. Yates came as a French fop
and a wagoner respectively. Lord Grosvenor, who had the same idea
as Matthew Boulton and came dressed as an eastern plenipotentiary
with a large turban and white feather, began immediately to tuck
into a plate of ham. The daughters of Sir Robert Ladbroke, the former mayor of London, came as a shepherdess and Dame Quickly
from *The Merry Wives of Windsor*, respectively, while other costumes
included a gentleman dressed as Lord Ogleby from *The Clandestine
Marriage* (a play by Garrick and George Colman), a jockey, a man
dressed to perform the "Dutch skipper" (a country dance), a trio of
female Quakers, a Wilksite patriot, a druid, several milkmaids, a
Chinese mandarin, two highlanders, Merlin, a fat Spanish courier,
and a man wearing only his regular clothes and a pair of cuckold's
horns. Also spotted in multiples were assorted sailors, Oxford dons
in scholarly gowns, conjurers, farmers, and harlequins. Many costumes consisted of mismatched garments or were simply confused.

Others put in no effort at all, the men either wearing dominos—the large, checkered, sacklike gowns traditionally worn at Venetian masquerades—or coming entirely unmasked. The problem was not demand but supply; the shocking profiteering in fancy dress was exposed by *Town and Country Magazine*, which revealed that "Dresses of the meanest sort were hired at four guineas each, and the person who carried them down from London made above four hundred on the occasion; those, however, who could not be accommodated to their minds or did not chuse to pay such a sum, were admitted with masques only, and there were many present even without masks." A rumor circulated that Samuel Foote was going to appear dressed as the Devil upon Two Sticks, the central character from one of his most successful productions, but Foote had already vacated Stratford in order to work on his Jubilee satire, complaining as he went that he had spent six guineas for nine hours' sleep. As always, a strand of erotic play ran through the night as classical goddesses passed through the crowd handing out favors: "An ear of wheat from a sweet Ceres, and a honey suckle from a beautiful Flora," wrote the correspondent from *The Gentleman's Magazine*, who "kissed each of their hands in testimony of my devotion."

As the Rotunda filled, a crowd of curious people hung by the entrance enjoying the costumes and hoping to peer in. Others sought entry despite arriving ticketless. One man from London, "made pot valiant with liquor," tried to push his way in, shouting, "Do you know who I am?" but failed in his attempt. Inside, the overall impression was that the event was not going very well. "So completely was the '*wet blanket*' spread over the masqueraders," wrote Henry Angelo, "that each, taking off the mask, appeared in true English character, verily grumblers." Nocturnal rheum had dulled the edge of wit. "It was remarked," wrote a correspondent for *The British Chronicle*, "that though so many of the *Belle Espirits* were present, very few attempts at wit were made during the evening, nor did our Correspondent recollect a single *Bon Mot* that was worth transmitting to us." One attempt at a joke was recorded on behalf of Cook, a clergyman of Powick in Worcestershire who had come dressed as a chimney sweep. Crying "Soot O! Soot O!" he was accosted by Lady Craven (then only nineteen years old but destined for a glamorous life as the Margravine of Anspach), who asked "Well, Mr. Sweep, why do you not come and sweep my chimney?" "Why, an' please your Ladyship," replied the Reverend Cook, "the last time I swept it, I burnt my Brush." Cook later found himself in an argument with a man dressed as a devil who had been making impertinent remarks to the ladies. The reverend struck him with his brush. The devil retaliated by punching Cook in the face.

Boswell makes his entrance

When Boswell entered, he came unmasked to represent, he said, "that the enemies to tyranny and oppression should wear no disguise." (It also helped, of course, to let people see who he was.) According to the anonymous account he would send to *The London Magazine,* he made quite the impression, writing that "one of the most remarkable masks upon this occasion was James Boswell Esq." He chatted first with Eva Garrick and then Lord Grosvenor, the two of them discussing the relative merits of the countries they represented "so opposite to each other—despotism and liberty," before reacquainting himself with the lovely Mrs. Sheldon and asking her to dance, confident that his pistols and dagger (items he prophylactically referred to as "armour") protected him. By this time, the swelling river that had previously confined itself to the meadow had begun to seep into the Rotunda, creeping across the dance floor and splashing over Boswell's shoes and splatterdashes as he danced. As the minuets concluded, the eight hundred guests who had purchased additional tickets sat down to an ingenious supper, served *in ambigu* in which "not one thing appeared as it really was." Once the tables were cleared, country

JAMES BOSWELL Esq.
In the Dress of an Armed Corsican Chief, as he appear'd at Shakespeare's Jubilee, at Stratford upon Avon September 1769.

James Boswell in his masquerade dress. Though hastily put together in London, it was striking enough to warrant a "fine Whole Length" in the September 1769 issue of *The London Magazine*.

dances began. At this point, William Kenrick, who had been waiting all night to make his entrance as the ghost of Shakespeare, came
in so wet and frozen that it rendered superfluous his white makeup.
He already looked like he'd died of exposure.

Boswell's poem   At two o'clock in the morning the small Scots boy
Boswell had entrusted with his verses arrived with a
single proof copy. Instead of distributing copies of this treasure as
originally planned, Boswell decided to recite it. Trying but failing
to capture the attention of all those within earshot, he managed at
least to collar Garrick, who stood patiently by as Boswell began to
rhapsodize in the voice of a Corsican patriot driven from his home to
soothe his soul "on *Avon's* sacred stream." Addressing Shakespeare's
global relevance, and lamenting that the bard was not alive to dra-
matize the Corsican struggles, he turned to heralding Garrick as
Shakespeare's heir "who Dame Nature's pencil stole, / Just where
Old *Shakespeare* drop it." Boswell's Corsican came, he insisted, not
to pity his country for their want of a Shakespeare or a Garrick but
merely to ask that a portion of the enthusiasm on display might used
to liberate his own island. "Let me plead for *Liberty* distrest," he read:

> And warm for her each sympathetick breast:
> Amidst the splendid honours which you bear,
> To save a sister island! be your care:
> With generous ardour make *us* also *free*,
> And give to *CORSICA, a noble* JUBILEE!

It was not a terrible effort given the time constraints, a thoroughly
Boswellian ode, professing a Boswellian logic that united Shakespeare, Garrick, and Corsica and placed Boswell at the center of it
all. And why not? This was exactly the kind of improvised meaning-
making that the open structure of the Jubilee, with its muddled

iconography and layered non sequiturs, encouraged. Garrick, listening patiently, noticed that the water was spilling into his shoes.

At five in the morning, with the water now up to the shins, a general call went up to abandon the Rotunda before the entire building floated away. "No delay could be admitted," wrote Joseph Cradock. Planks were laid across the meadow and used as ramps up to the steps of the carriages, the wheels of which were sunk as much as two feet deep in waterlogged grass. Men volunteered to carry women on their backs, including the impudent devil who gallantly took up a young woman only for a gust of wind to reveal a pair of leather breeches hidden beneath her skirts, at which point this man in drag was dumped unceremoniously into the water. Treacherous hidden ditches concealed themselves beneath the surface, as was discovered by "A Young Gentleman of London," according to *Berrow's Worcester Journal,* who slipped into "a very deep mirey Dyke, but fortunately being within Reach of a Stump, supported himself by it, and called out for Help." A rescuer went to his aid, "but in his hurry and eagerness likewise slipped in Lanthorn and all, and both of them must have been smother'd," had not others pulled them out. As the evacuees splashed away, the Rotunda creaked and groaned, loosening its hinges as its foundations imperceptibly rose and began to float.

Evacuation of the Rotunda

◀◦§

"We did not get home," wrote Boswell, recalling that sodden evening, "till past six in the morning." After three hours of shallow sleep, he rose and called again upon Richard Baldwin, with whom he ate breakfast. "The true nature of human life began now to appear," he said. "After the joy of the Jubilee came the uneasy reflection that I was in a little village in wet weather and know not how to get away."

Rain always depressed Boswell's spirits, an affliction Samuel Johnson had mocked him for, but on reflection, he was happy with what he felt he had achieved. "I pleased myself with a variety of ideas with regard to the Jubilee, peculiar to my own mind," he said. For him, the focus had not been on Shakespeare so much as the ways in which Shakespeare might be used as a means to draw together his own considerable talents for sociability, sensibility, sensuality, and self-promotion.

Stranded in Stratford   Like most in Stratford that Friday morning, Boswell's first thought was to flee, but with the rain continuing to fall for a third consecutive day, the few coaches and sedan chairs that clogged the muddy streets were all spoken for "I don't know how many times over, by different companies." John Payton prepared the usual public breakfast at the Town Hall knowing, as the agent and dispatcher for nearly all of the public conveyances within a fifty-mile radius, that many of his guests would have to stay on at an additional guinea a night. "We were like a crowd in a theatre," wrote Boswell. "It was impossible we could all go at a time." Escape was futile—"Five, nay Fifty Guineas were unable to attain it."

After several fruitless inquiries, Baldwin found Boswell a seat in a coach with an *"honest Scott"* that was due to leave the following morning. With nothing to do until that time, Boswell went to the White Lion and was introduced to two gentlemen from Lichfield who knew Johnson and Garrick and had heard of Boswell by repute—"It is fine to have such a character as I have," he mused. "I enjoy it much." After this, he went to Shakespeare's tomb, observing with pleasure that Shakespeare's wife, Anne Hathaway, had been older than him, just as Margaret was older than Boswell. While taking in the church, he began to have second thoughts about the carriage ride Baldwin had arranged for him, concerned that the "honest Scott" had a reputation for dissipation that might imperil the success he had had restraining himself so far. Instead, he sought out William Richardson and his friend Captain Johnston and persuaded them to give him a seat in their chaise.

With his money running low, Boswell next went to see Garrick and, presenting him with a packet of the previous night's verses, asked for a loan of five guineas. Garrick moodily dismissed the request with the claim that George had taken all his money. Boswell persisted. "Come, come, that won't do," he said to Garrick with curt familiarity. "Five guineas I must have, and you must find them for me." The exchange typified the way in which Boswell responded to Garrick's fame now that he had a taste of his own. Where he had once been awestruck, he was now competitive and almost insolent, as if he felt it was necessary to take Garrick down a peg or two in order to assert his own identity, or be subsumed by his friend's superior celebrity. But Garrick was exhausted and his mood was rapidly souring. With no patience to quarrel with Boswell, he called to Eva, who handed over her purse.

Garrick's sincerest wish was that he could leave too. When news filtered through that the continued *The Jubilee Cup* deluge meant that the pageant of characters had to be postponed again, and that the ruination of the Rotunda meant that it would be impossible to repeat the ode as had been requested, "the principal Part of the Company who had carriages of their own"—namely, aristocrats and wealthy businessmen—"went out of Town." Other events went ahead as planned, including the horse race scheduled for Friday afternoon set on a beautiful meadow in Shottery less than two miles out of town, largely at the urging of Lord Grosvenor. The Jubilee Cup, as the race was called, had only five entrants, all running up to their knees in water. The winner was the colt Whirligig and his rider, Mr. Pratt, who was presented with a silver trophy engraved with Shakespeare's arms and worth fifty pounds, before modestly declaring "his resolution never to part with it, though he honestly confessed—he knew very little about *Plays,* or Master SHAKESPEARE."

Those who remained had to fend for themselves. Some braved the waterlogged ruins to be entertained with a performance of clarinets and French horns, and by nine o'clock that evening the skies had dried enough for Angelo to give a truncated firework display, before packing up and moving on to the Lichfield races, where he had been given an offer to perform his show the following day. At eleven, the Town Hall hosted a final assembly led by Mrs. Garrick, who danced minuets and country dances until four in the morning.

Boswell gets away

Boswell finally escaped at dawn, struggling through streets that looked as if had been turned over by an advancing army with a full baggage train, only for his coach to break down in Oxford, where he was once more disturbed with thoughts of the sirenian Miss Reynolds. It was a difficult journey home, but Boswell reflected on it with stoicism. "Taking the whole of this jubilee, said I, is like eating an artichoke entire. We have some fine mouthfuls, but also swallow the leaves and the hair, which are confoundedly difficult of digestion." At least he made it home alive. Mr. James Henry Castle of St. Ives started sneezing and running a fever as a result of spending the night in damp sheets. He died, a martyr to the love of Shakespeare.

11

The comet loitered in the heavens, 16 degrees and 6 minutes from Betelgeuse in Orion's right shoulder. "It appears
remarkably well defined, and doth not seem to carry any thing with
it that may be destructive to any part of the planetary system," reas-
sured the *New Daily Advertiser.* Four days later it disappeared in the
direction of Venus at a rate calculated to be "five hundred times the
swiftness of a cannon ball." By this time, most visitors had managed
to find their way out of Stratford-upon-Avon. Some, like Boswell,
were delighted with their memories, especially when he saw that the
frontispiece of *The Gentleman's Magazine* for September was a full
portrait of himself in Corsican dress. Others made a more somber
reckoning with their pilgrimage. "That you may not think I complain without reason," wrote a correspondent to *Town and Country Magazine,* determined to enumerate exactly the reasons for his
complaint, "judge if my diversion was adequate to the following
expence":

	£. s. d.
Ticket	1 1 0
Post-chaise to Stratford, at 3s. per mile the last sixty miles —	11 0 0
Expences upon that road	1 11 6

Lodging	6 6 0
Board and other expences	4 12 0
Masquerade dress	5 5 0
Masquerade ticket	0 10 6
Occasional impositions to know the hour of the day, &c.	1 8 0
Chair hire	2 2 0
Servants	0 12 0
Post-chaise back	12 0 0
Expences upon the road	1 14 0
	49 2 0

Forty-nine pounds was enough to pay a coachman's wages for three years or Boswell's rent for two. One might purchase seven horses with that money, or enjoy fifty lavish nights at Ranelagh Gardens. The extravagance became a popular joke. One visitor, asking what to do if his carriage should be held up by highwaymen on the way home, was told, "Tell 'em you have been at the Jubilee and they won't suspect you have any money left."

Even more outrageous than the cost to individuals was the amount spent on staging the Jubilee "even in these times of *distress.*" Musidorus wrote, "What with travelling expences, and the money, circulated immediately in the town of Stratford, the Jubilee has cost fifty thousand pounds"—much of it wasted. "The Amphitheater, which is now above a foot deep in water, from the heavy rains, and its low situation on the border of the Avon, will be useless, as there is no expectation of ever seeing another Jubilee at the place." Even so, Musidorus was willing to aver that "after all the expence, fatigue, and disappointment" something special had taken place. "I candidly acknowledge that we were overpaid by the single recitation of the Ode," he wrote: "This part of the Jubilee was so thoroughly admirable, and gave so perfect a satisfaction, that I should not hesitate at another Stratford expedition, merely to hear it, and I am satisfied the majority of the company are entirely of my sentiments."

Such sentiments fueled a nationwide appetite to know more of this famous verse. The *Dedication Ode* was reprinted in newspapers and magazines, performed at Canterbury and Birmingham, and circulated among Garrick's broad and influential group of friends. Peter Garrick, David's once disapproving older brother, had it recited at his home in Lichfield. Even Voltaire had a copy. The supporters of John Wilkes, in an ongoing show of solidarity for their imprisoned hero and reiterating once again the parallels between their own models of expression and those of Garrick, held a "Patriot's Jubilee" outside Wilkes's prison cell. It included ribbons and favors, a song called "Middlesex" (based on "A Warwickshire Lad"), and a feast on a three-hundred-pound turtle.

Popular interest

Despite all the interest in his achievement, Garrick left Stratford in a stormy mood, retreating to the country to recover, telling his friend the clergyman Richard Kaye that "if the Heavens had favoured us—we should have returned to town in triumph—but it is over, and I am neither mad, or in a fever, both of which threatened me greatly." Predictably, Charles Dibdin took an opposing view, feeling that the rain was the best thing that could have possibly happened as it "served as a veil to cover what would otherwise have been a disgrace; everything succeeded even beyond his most sanguine wishes." This would indeed prove the case.

In mid-September, Garrick received a formal letter from the mayor, aldermen, and burgesses of Stratford, who "unanimously join in the general Voice of every Inhabitant of this place, in returning to you our most sincere and grateful Thanks," reserving special praise for those "Beautiful Ornaments" (referring to the Town Hall paintings and statue that had started it all) and for so "elegantly expressing your abhorrence

Relations with Stratford

in your most incomparable Ode, of that cruel Design, to destroy the Beauty of this Situation, by inclosing our open Fields." William Hunt, however, suspected that Garrick was not ready for such protestations of civic gratitude—"I expect you'll burn every Letter with a Stratford post mark, without opening it," he wrote in a note that accompanied the town's thanks. Lacy, meanwhile, continued to berate Garrick for the damage done to the Drury Lane wardrobe and properties, not to mention the expenses George had accrued over the summer, a quick calculation of which amounted to almost two thousand pounds. To make amends, Garrick instructed his brother to stay behind and salvage every last penny from the soggy aftermath, leaving George to run tours of the Rotunda at a shilling apiece before auctioning the whole thing off for timber. Having initially proposed a jubilee every seven years, Garrick was now adamant that there would never be another. Asked for advice on how to stage a successful jubilee, he offered an acerbic reply:

> Let 'em decorate ye Town (ye *happiest* and why not ye *handsomest* in England) let your streets be well pav'd, and kept clean, do something with ye delightful Meadow, allure every body to vist ye Holy Land; let it be well lighted, and clean under foot, and let it not be said for ye honour; and I hope for ye Interest that the Town, which gave Birth to the first Genius since the Creation, is the most dirty unseemly, ill pav'd, wretched-looking Town in all Britain.

Rival productions   While Garrick wanted nothing but to forget the whole ordeal, others seemed intent on litigating every detail, as a flood of pamphlets and Jubilee-related performances came out, with the first of them, George Saville Carey's "Shakespeare's Jubilee," appearing in print even before the Jubilee was over. Most of them poked fun at the rain and the expense but were careful to treat

Garrick with respect. Only Samuel Foote delivered the mockery he had promised, inserting into his performance of *The Devil upon Two Sticks* on September 13 this definition of "jubilee":

> A jubilee is a public invitation, urged by puffing, to go post without horses, to an obscure borough without representatives, governed by a mayor and aldermen who are no magistrates, to celebrate a great poet whose own works have made him immortal, by an ode without poetry, music without harmony, dinners without victuals, and lodgings without beds; a masquerade where half the people appeared barefaced, a horse race up to the knees in water, fireworks extinguished as soon as they were lighted, and a gingerbread amphitheatre, which, like a house of cards, tumbled to pieces as soon as it was finished.

The rumor persisted that a full-length piece was expected any day. Foote, it was said, was preparing to send out an actor wearing a brown velvet suit with a medallion, carrying a wand, and wearing white gloves. A ragamuffin was to address him with the lines from William Whitehead's address to Garrick—"A nation's taste depends on you / Perhaps a nation's virtue too"—to which "Garrick" was to respond by flapping his arms and crowing "cock a doodle doo." When news of this reached Garrick, he was so offended that he threatened dreadful retaliations until the Marquis of Stafford, a friend of both Garrick and Foote, stepped in to mediate; Foote then assured the manager of Drury Lane that he wouldn't let anyone appear onstage as him again. The agreement did not extend to puppets, however, and Foote let it be known that he was constructing a cast of Jubilee characters from papier-mâché. When asked if they were going to be life-size, Foote replied, "Oh no—not much above the size of Garrick."

As much as they irked him, Garrick knew that performances like these were an intractable part of a theatrical landscape that looked continually to capitalize on novelty and current affairs. He was no different, and in conversation with the painter Benjamin Wilson on the long drive from Stratford, hit upon a scheme to bring the Jubilee to London by opening the upcoming season with a rendition of his ode from the stage at Drury Lane. Delivered to the marble statue he had hauled up from his garden temple at Hampton, the performance played to a "cram'd house" and received "as much applause as his heart could desire." Aiming to build on this foundation, he was annoyed to hear that George Colman at Covent Garden was ready

Man and Wife | to mount a jubilee play of his own. Titled *Man and Wife; or the Stratford Jubilee*, it was, in the best traditions of theatrical exigency, an anglicized gutting of Philippe Destouches's farce *La Fausse Agnés*; it introduced the pageant of Shakespearean

Garrick reciting the *Dedication Ode* at Drury Lane. The statue that appeared with him at this time had been hauled up from the garden temple of his villa at Hampton. © *The Trustees of the British Museum*

characters at the end of Act 2, and a representation of the masked ball in Act 3. *Man and Wife* opened on October 7, 1769, but in spite of Covent Garden's reputation for superior pageantry, the haste with which Colman had mounted it let him down. The pageant "has no connection with the business of the play," wrote *Town and Country Magazine*, "and as it is represented, is an absolute dead march."

Colman reconsidered, and *Man and Wife* was temporarily retired as he looked to make improvements, by which time Garrick had readied a reply. Written in a day and a half, and titled simply *The Jubilee*, Garrick's play debuted at Drury Lane on October 14. *The Jubilee*, like Colman's play, began by erecting a precarious dramatic scaffold around what was essentially a costume parade. Consisting of the farcical comings and goings of a group of comic characters intended to represent the venal and superstitious locals, an Irish reveler forced to sleep in his coach (a caricature of Boswell's friend Thomas Sheridan, who hadn't even attended), and various guests who griped at the weather and struggled to obtain a hot meal, the scenes served to connect the songs from "Shakespeare's Garland" before introducing the abandoned pageant. The ringing of bells and the piping of fifes announced nineteen tableaux, beginning, as originally planned, with *As You Like It* and concluding with *Antony and Cleopatra*. The ode was omitted from this production, replaced by further comic business featuring the Stratford maids "Nancy," who had never left "this poor hole of a town," and "Sukey," her sophisticated friend who has been to Birmingham *and* Coventry and so understands "Shakespurs and the Jewbill" very well. Two large illuminated transparencies were then brought on stage "in which the capital characters of Shakespeare are exhibited at full length, with Shakespeare's statue in the middle crowned by Tragedy and Comedy, fairies and cupids surrounding him." Dancers and a troop of supernumeraries filled the stage, singing and wav-

Garrick's riposte

ing banners. As the swelling chorus came to a crescendo, guns were fired, bells were rung, and the Drury Lane chorus led the house in cheers of "Bravo Jubilee! Shakespeare forever!"

The Jubilee ran for ninety-one nights, a record for the London theatres of the eighteenth century, its success a result of the instincts Garrick had honed over three decades as a dramaturge. William Hopkins, the prompter at Drury Lane, believed it to be "the most Superb" performance "that ever was Exhibited," thanks to the variety of its dramatic textures "that gave so much pleasure to all Degrees Boxes pit and Gallery." On the one hand, it poked good-natured fun at the well-documented disaster (while being sure to attribute the grossest absurdities to foreigners and Stratfordians), while on the other, it delivered an ecstatically perfect version of the pageant and its beatification of the Bard in the controlled environment of Garrick's London theatre. In fact, the failure of the actual Jubilee became another means by which to measure Shakespeare's sublimity, a writer so transcendent that no attempt to praise him could ever match his excellence. The German traveler Johann Wilhelm von Archenholz enjoyed it so much he went to see it twenty-eight times. "This was a real *apotheosis*," von Archenholz wrote, "for it was not a literary fanaticism, but a just admiration of every thing that is truly great and sublime, which placed the statue of this immortal genius in the temple of immortality."

James Boswell, who had taken his seat on the opening night in the hopes of seeing his Corsican alter ego parade before him, was similarly impressed with Garrick's ability to turn mere entertainment into art. Since witnessing him commit the nation's soul so solemnly to Shakespeare's safekeeping, Boswell had reflected at length on the role actors played as intermediaries between the general public and the civilizing influences of the literary arts. Presenting his thoughts as a trio of short essays in *The London Magazine*, he argued that actors were "the real royalty of Great Britain," members of the intelligentsia who "should be ranked amongst the learned professions." No one had done more to elevate their status than David Garrick, said Boswell, by virtue of his principled coupling of aesthetic value to audience appeal, and by working studiously "not only to catch the immediate applause of the multitude, but to be the delight and admiration of the judicious, enlightened and philosophical spectators."

Boswell's belief in the nobility of actors was just one example of the heightened air of seriousness and solemnity that enveloped Shakespeare in the wake of the Jubilee. Writing in 1775, on the effect of Hamlet's "To be or not to be" speech on English audiences, another German visitor, Georg Christoph von Lichtenberg, noted, \

Solemnity

> A large part of the audience not only knows it by heart as well as they do a Lord's Prayer, but listens to it, so to speak, as if it were the Lord's Prayer, not indeed with the profound reflections which accompany our sacred prayer, but with a sense of solemnity and awe, of which some one who does not know England can have no conception. In this island Shakespeare is not only famous, but holy; his moral maxims are everywhere. . . . In this way his name is intertwined with the most solemn thoughts; people sing of him and from his works, and thus a large number of English children know him before they have learnt their A.B.C. and creed.

Such churchified reverence was the natural extension of Garrick's Stratford religiosity, not to mention a realization of the desire he had expressed twenty-five years earlier, when he had opened the Drury Lane season by pointing to the stage and announcing, "Sacred to Shakespeare was this spot design'd, / To pierce the heart

and humanize the mind." Through the final decades of the eighteenth century, this seriousness was further magnified by renewed
scholarly attention, as new editions of the collected works became
available, each seeking to outdo its rivals in exhaustiveness, erudition, and commitment to excavating the "real" Shakespeare. In
turn, these pages were scoured by new generations of writers and
critics, some of whom found in them a bodiless Shakespeare much
like the one conjured at the Jubilee. Samuel Taylor Coleridge, for
example, one of the first of the English Romantics to write extensively on Shakespeare, began to think of him primarily as a poet as
opposed to a dramatist, one whose words contained such untram-
meled imaginative force that they practically defied representation.
In a series of lectures delivered across London between 1808 and
1812, he argued that Shakespeare was a poet of the mind's eye, a
"closet" dramatist who never intended for his plays to be augmented
with scenery and the assorted trappings of theatricality, which
served only to highlight their artificiality.

This was a conviction shared by Coleridge's closest friend, the
essayist Charles Lamb, co-author, with his sister Mary, of *Tales from
Shakespeare,* an influential book of prose retellings of the plays that
brought Shakespeare into the schoolroom and nursery for numerous generations of young readers. Lamb went so far as to claim that
Shakespeare's plays were not fit to be performed, asserting instead
that they were "objects of meditation." Such extreme antitheatricality
was a reaction to the pragmatism of Garrick and the giants of former generations who had readily hacked and rewritten Shakespeare
to better serve their audiences, but it was also a sign of the degree to
which the Jubilee's rhetoric of veneration had taken hold, inspiring a
more private and internalized relationship with the works that cherished Shakespeare as somehow ineffable and too good for the world.
Of course, the theatrical tradition not only continued, it flourished.

Yet thanks to the Jubilee's diffuse and ethereal conception of who Shakespeare was and what he represented, the Bard had made the most profound and lasting transition of all, from stage to soul.

Meanwhile, back in the real Warwickshire, the Corporation of Stratford also experienced an afterglow. They were rather pleased with themselves, both for dodging any debt (due to their refusal to invest in the Jubilee) and for the notoriety that had allowed them to reap a series of rewards, including even some of the civilizing effects that William Hunt had initially hoped would accrue to the town. For example, three new magazines had opened, appealing to a genteel audience with an appetite for news and opinion that was far more fashionable and cosmopolitan than had been common for the Stratford press. A market for Shakespeare's works had also developed, serviced by Birmingham printers whose serialized editions improved with each new imprint.

But it was tourism that provided the most tangible bene- | *Tourism*
fits, as growing numbers of visitors came to town inspired by
lofty thoughts of literary pilgrimage. The birthplace—part of which had been rented out to a man named Thomas Hornby, who converted it into a butcher's shop—now sported a sign outside an upstairs window that proudly proclaimed, "The Immortal Shakspeare was born in this house." In time it would be purchased on behalf of the nation and restored, its transference into public ownership setting the stage for the larger heritage industry that was to come, illustrating once again how fully Shakespeare had fused with the national identity. In the immediate aftermath, however, commercialism bore a more primitive aspect, as evinced by the pragmatic spirit of Mrs. Hart, lessee of the birthplace in the wake of the Jubilee, who cheerfully welcomed visitors and happily helped them to a memento, including swatches of wood from the bedroom floor. Hosting the Hon. John Byng in 1781, she stopped before an eviscer-

ated chair identified as Shakespeare's favorite and, noting its dilapidated state, said that "it has been carefully handed down by our family but people never thought so much of it till after the Jubilee, and now see what pieces they have cut from it." Byng nodded and, without a second thought, Mrs. Hart kicked out the chair's bottom strut and sold it to him.

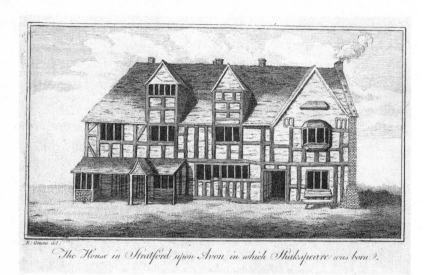

The birthplace. © *The Trustees of the British Museum*

Epilogue

The success of *The Jubilee* indemnified Garrick and mollified Lacy, bringing a fourfold return on every shilling they had ventured at Stratford. "It is no wonder that he should endeavour to make a God of Shakespear," grumbled Charles Macklin, "since he has usurped the office of his High-priest; and has already gained money enough by it, to make a golden calf." While cash flowed freely into Drury Lane, the Stratford "adventurers" who had put up their own money to support the Jubilee recorded a dismal loss. After initially being told by George Garrick that each man would receive a profit of £100, it became increasingly apparent that they would get nothing. Even John Payton, who was popularly assumed to have made a fortune from food, transport, and accommodation, had lost £200—thanks to the criminal dishonesty of the waiters he had hired from London, many of whom had palmed the guinea fee for the turtle feast and dropped it into their own pockets. Garrick promised that he would cover their losses and instructed his brother to see to it. But George was being evasive, not only about the money, but also about the condition in which he had left the College. The Reverend John Fullerton, the building's new owner, had repeatedly written to William Hunt with complaints of damage to the "Walls, Windows and Deficiencies in catalogue of goods etc. etc.," and of the litter of debris that George and his scene men had left behind.

As it became clear that the Garricks might not keep their word, relations between Stratford and Drury Lane deteriorated. "I am sorry that my Brother has such reason to complain of ill usage at Stratford," Garrick wrote sniffily to Hunt, "and particularly from Mr. Payton—I had ye greatest opinion of him, and his probity, and hope still I shall have no reason to change it." This was the prologue to a warning: "I will not suffer the least dirt to be thrown upon me, or my conduct, in an affair which I undertook for ye good of Stratford, and which has employ'd both my mind, body and purse." The letter closed with an invitation to Hunt to bring his wife up to London to see *The Jubilee*. George continued to promise restitution for a year, during which time the sole compensation Hunt received was a pile of wood worth £20 salvaged from the dismantled Rotunda.

"Dear Sir," Hunt wrote to Garrick in November 1770,

> I shou'd be sorry to hurry either you or him, yet I am persuaded you will both upon Reflection think that I have been too long out of my money.
>
> I do not in the least regret the Sums & the Time I have voluntarily expended, about what has proved so great an Honor and Advantage to some of my Neighbours, & to others.
>
> But it is too much that the only person in this place who was at any great trouble or Expence upon the Occasion, shou'd be *alone* capitally injured, & I am convinced *you will not suffer it*.

The letter made Garrick so furious that he had directed a servant to pen an immediate reply—he himself had injured his thumb and couldn't write. "Dear Sir," wrote Garrick's amanuensis, reminding Hunt what it meant to be a "volunteer Adventurer,"

> these words from you have hurt me much, from you who are ye Admirer of Shakespeare, a friend of Mine & was with me a Chief

promoter of ye Whole—what a different Spirit from that, which us'd to say with a liberal convivial Smile—*I don't mind spending a hundred or two of pounds in this Cause, & upon this Occasion!* indeed I did not expect you would have written to me in ye Manner you have after you Knew I intended to pay ye losses of ye Adventurers, & before I had settled ye Account—but I will not have Mr. Hunt ye *only capitally injur'd person,* & therefore (tho I flatter'd myself that I might have made a little more free with him that ye rest) I desire he will send his Acct. directly to be paid to his Order in Town, & if he means that ye *Capital Injury* may arise too from ye loss of Interest upon ye sum due to him wch. by his own Acct. is less that 80 pds. Mr. Garrick begs him to add that too, as he *will not suffer* (as Mr. Hunt expresses it) *one* he esteems so much *to be too long out of his Money.*

This was Garrick at his most pompous, coin-rubbing worst, but Hunt refused to be cowed. From "Mr G Garrick's Hints when I was last in Town," Hunt replied, "I must own I did understand that you had exprest some Intentions of reimbursing the Jubilee Loss." However,

no such assurance could I ever obtain till I received the favour of your angry Letter. I heard that other persons were satisfied, I found myself slighted, and refused an answer—I did not chose to *beg* the money—nor did I wish by the involuntary Loss of it, to bosome the ridicule of some about me, as a project Hunter or a fighter of windmills.

When Mr. G. Garrick soon after the Jubilee informed me that each adventurer wou'd profit 100£ or more, I was blamed by my *prudent* friends in looking out for an Eminence to erect a Pillar in Honor of Shakespear with ye Money—When he afterwards told me of my Reverse of fortune I think he will satisfy for me, that I neither repined or reflected upon myself or any men. My smiles have been as liberal since the Jubilee as before (*till lately*), and who can smile when you are pleased to frown?—and when I made ye Declaration you mention in the warmth of my Heart I spoke as I thought, and have always done so to you. —My stations in Life will not permit me to despise £20, I will not affect to do so, yet I think the Loss of such a sum will never hurt my Peace, nor wou'd I *now* accept the money, but to throw it into the Avon.

Having admitted to his hurt, Hunt went on to say that he defended Garrick at every opportunity, even to the extent of lying about the financial arrangements of the Jubilee. "The tongues of Envy and Slander in Warwickshire have been industrious to misrepresent your unbounded acts of Liberality at Stratford as proceeding from lucrative views," he wrote.

There is scarce a Gentleman's Table, or a publick meeting in that county, that will not witness for me, that I have stopp'd that Torrent of Scandal urging my personal Knowledge of the transactions, against every villainous hearsay—That a noble Statue, that a magnificent Picture, that the elegant Decorations of a publick Room, were the spontaneous acts of your Bounty long before a Jubilee either in Town or Country. —To prove your worthy and disinterested Principles beyond a Doubt, I have sworn a thousand Times (ye powers forgive me if it was a Crime) that the sums advanced by me and every Loser were generously returned by you immediately after the Jubilee, before it was possible to know that success wou'd crown it here; nor is there a person breathing (not even my wife) but believes it, unless you or your Brother have declared the Contrary—you may well laugh at my feeble Efforts to add the Smallest Ray to your Glory—but if I had not opened my Heart to you, it would have burst—It rejoices to hear that your early Intentions, have verified my Prediction.

Having thus given vent to his frustrations, Hunt concluded his letter with a litany of the ill effects that Jubilee had wrought upon him, including the anger of his friend,

> for pressing him to cut down his Willows—The anger of Mr. Fullerton for giving up the College to *your Friend and Mine.* —The abuse of my Neighbours of the Lower sort for endeavouring to prevent their extortion—The Sneers of the witty—The Pity of the [pious] and Solemn—Thanks from no person living that I know of. —This I cou'd have laughed at, all this I cou'd have despised, and have Set down happily with a Balance so amply in my favour; for the greatest Genius of the age, had condescended to call me his Friend. —I now, alas find that felicity vanished also, and my Credit Side, become a total Blank. —Experience the surest Guide of human affairs remains indeed sagely to advise me; so to form my future Conduct, as never to meddle with what I do not understand—nor aim at Friendships, beyond the Reach of my abilities, to presume.

With that, William Hunt of Stratford remained unpaid, a warning to provincial clerks everywhere to tread carefully when dealing with London celebrities intent on worshipping their idols.

David Garrick acted less and less, taking instead the role of theatrical innovator and bringing to the stage more refinements and visual spectacles, before making an emotional series of farewell performances in the spring of 1776. He and Eva retired into the newly built Adelphi town houses backing on to the Thames at what used to be Durham Yard, the wharf of warehouses where he and his brother Peter had begun as wine wholesalers almost forty years before. Some of his friends urged him to become a member of Parliament, but his health was not up to it. When he died of kidney failure in 1779, a funeral cortege of thirty-three coaches worthy of a head of state carried him to Westminster Abbey and laid him to rest at the foot of the monument to Shakespeare. Three months later, George made his way to a grave of his own. When someone in the greenroom at Drury Lane noted what an extraordinary coincidence it was that George Garrick had died so soon after his brother, the old actor John Bannister said, "Not at all. DAVID wanted him."

For the rest of his life, James Boswell continued to carry with him a reverence for Shakespeare and the artistry of the theatre. By most reckonings, that life might be considered to have been a happy and accomplished one. He and Margaret had five children, among them James Boswell the Younger, who would himself support Shakespeare's legacy by working alongside Edmund Malone, the most significant Shakespeare scholar of his age, and helping to shepherd his 1821 variorum edition of Shakespeare to press after Malone's death. The elder Boswell attained the estates of Auchinleck and role of laird following the death of his father, while his literary celebrity and talent for clubbability meant that he was always traveling and spending time with Johnson and other close friends.

However, to a mind as restless and self-questioning as his own, it fell short of what, as a younger man, he felt his life had promised. Disconsolate that he had not attained wealth by means of the law and greatness through some significant public office, he mithered to his friends and drank with the recklessness of a man half his age, falling often into the familiar pattern of embarrassing himself and deepening his disappointments. When Margaret died after twenty years of marriage, he was riddled with guilt at his chronic infidelities and the significant amount of time he had spent away from her and their children. The success of his *Life of Samuel Johnson. LL.D.,* published in 1791, a work that would ensure his literary immortality by giving form and structure to modern biography, afforded episodic boosts of cheer, but it was a depressed and waning James Boswell who entered his final years. Perhaps this dullness of spirit is why, in 1795, he was so ready to be moved when, having finished a tumbler of warm brandy, he got down on his knees in an attic room in the London home of Samuel Ireland and bowed before a trunk filled with brittle parchments tattooed with scratchy ink-work. In the discovery of the century, Ireland's son, William Henry, had found some unknown manuscripts of Shakespeare's in an old chest, including a letter the poet had written to Anne Hathaway, some additions to *King Lear* and *Hamlet,* and a note of thanks from Elizabeth I. Bringing them to his lips, Boswell kissed the documents again and again. "I now kiss the invaluable relics of our bard," he wrote, "and thanks to God that I have lived to see them!" It was a formulation remarkably Garrick-like in its admixture of Shakespeare worship and scriptural allusion, echoing as it did Luke 2:29–30—"Lord, now lettest thou my servant depart in peace, according to thy word: For mine eyes have seen thy salvation."

Boswell did not live long enough to learn it, but William Henry Ireland was a fraud and his relics were a fake. Shakespeare remained elusive still.

Garrick's Ode[1]

To what blest genius of the isle,
      Shall Gratitude her tribute pay,
      Decree the festive day,
Erect the statue, and devote the pile?

Do not your sympathetic hearts accord,
      To own the "bosom's lord?"[2]
'Tis he! 'tis he! —that demi-god!
Who Avon's flow'ry margin trod,
      While sportive *Fancy* round him flew,
Where *Nature* led him by the hand,
      Instructed him in all she knew,
And gave him absolute command!
      'Tis he! 'tis he!
"The god of our idolatry!"[3]

---

[1] *An Ode upon Dedicating a Building, and Erecting a Statue, to Shakespeare, at Stratford upon Avon. By D.G.* (London: printed for T. Becket and P. A. De Hondt, 1769). Copy texts: Beinecke Rare Book and Manuscript Library, Yale University, Misc. Poems 48; and British Library (hereafter BL), English Short Title Catalogue number T42012.

[2] From *Romeo and Juliet*, 5.1.3—"My bosom's lord sits lightly in his throne."

[3] This phrase, used by Garrick and by others to describe Garrick's relationship to Shakespeare, derives from a line in *Romeo and Juliet:* "Do not swear at all. / Or, if thou wilt, swear by thy gracious self, / Which is the god of my idolatry" (2.2.118–20). As Garrick wrote to Jean Suard, a French journalist, in 1765, "I will not despair of seeing you in my temple of Shakespeare, confessing your infidelity, and bowing your head to the *god of my idolatry*, as he himself well expresses it." See David Garrick, *The Letters of David Garrick,* ed. David M. Little and George M. Kahrl (London: Oxford University Press, 1963), 2:463.

To him the song, the Edifice we raise,
He merits all our wonder, all our praise!
Yet ere impatient joy break forth,
In sounds that lift the soul from earth;
And to our spell-bound minds impart
Some faint idea of his magic art;
Let awful silence still the air!
From the dark cloud, the hidden light
Bursts tenfold bright!
Prepare! prepare! prepare!
Now swell the choral song,[4]
Roll the full tide of harmony along;
Let Rapture sweep the trembling strings,
And Fame expanding all her wings,
With all her trumpet-tongues proclaim,[5]
The lov'd, rever'd, immortal name!
SHAKESPEARE! SHAKESPEARE! SHAKESPEARE!
Let th'inchanting sound,
From Avon's shores rebound:
Thro' the Air,
Let it bear,
The precious freight the envious nations round!

---

[4] The BL copy text contains numerous handwritten marginal notes by an unknown author, composed primarily of attributions and rewritten lines, the latter reflecting the personal preferences of a private reader or perhaps the notes of an audience member marking alterations to the printed text made by Garrick in performance. Here, the line has been revised to read "Now swell *at once* the choral song," a revision that, through the addition of two syllables, makes the line conform to the octameter that constitutes much of this verse.

[5] Adapted from *Macbeth*, 1.7.19–20—"Will plead like angels, trumpet-tongued, against / The deep damnation of his taking-off."

CHORUS

Swell the choral song,
Roll the tide of harmony along,
Let Rapture sweep the strings,
Fame expand her wings,
With her trumpet-tongues proclaim,
The lov'd, rever'd, immortal name!
SHAKESPEARE! SHAKESPEARE! SHAKESPEARE!

AIR[6]

I

Sweetest bard that ever *sung,*
Nature's *glory,* Fancy's *child;*
Never sure did witching tongue,
Warble forth such wood-notes wild![7]

II

Come each Muse, *and sister* Grace,
Loves *and* Pleasures *hither come;*
Well you know this happy place,
Avon's *banks were once your home.*

III

Bring the laurel, bring the flow'rs,
Songs of triumph to him raise;[8]

---

[6] Marginal note in BL copy text reads "Mr. Baddely." Robert Baddeley (1733–1794) was a longstanding member of the Drury Lane company.

[7] An appropriation from John Milton's *L'Allegro* (published 1645): "Or sweetest Shakespeare, Fancy's child / Warble his native wood-notes wild."

[8] Much of this Air bears similarity to the third part of Handel's *Judas Macca-*

He united all your pow'rs,
All uniting, sing his praise!

Tho' *Philip's* fam'd unconqur'd son,[9]
Had ev'ry blood-stain'd laurel won;
He sigh'd—that his creative word,
    (Like that which rules the skies,)
Could not bid other nations rise,
To glut his yet unsated sword:

But when our SHAKESPEARE'S matchless pen,
Like *Alexander's* sword, had done with men;
    He heav'd no sigh, he made no moan,
      Not limited to human kind,
      He sir'd his wonder-teeming mind,
Rais'd other worlds, and beings of his own![10]

---

beus (1746)—"See, the Conqu'ring Hero Comes"—libretto by Thomas Morell, including lines such as "Myrtle wreaths and roses twine / to deck the hero's brow divine"; "Songs of triumph to him sing!"; "The laurel bring."

[9] A reference to Alexander the Great (356–323 BC). His father was Philip II of Macedon.

[10] In October 1769, Charles Macklin wrote to Garrick to critique the ode and raise numerous poetical quibbles, including a long passage on this verse in which Macklin objected to the phrase "wonder-teeming mind" and argued (according to Garrick) that he had "heard of *raising Cabbages,* etc but never *of worlds* before." In answer, Garrick quoted *Hamlet,* 5.1.269–70, "Conjures the wand'ring stars and makes them stand / Like wonder-wounded hearers?" as well as Milton's *Paradise Lost,* book 12, lines 547–50: "Raise / From the conflagrant mass, purg'd and refin'd / New Heav'ns, new Earth, Ages of endless date / Founded in righteousness and peace and love." "These are not Cabbages or cucumbers," wrote Garrick (*Letters,* 2:672).

AIR[11]

When Nature, smiling, hail'd his birth,
To him unbounded pow'r was given;
The whirlwind's wing to sweep the sky,
"The frenzy-rowling eye,
To glance from heav'n to earth,
From earth to heaven!"[12]

O from his muse of fire[13]

Could but one spark be caught,

Then might these humble strains aspire[14]

To tell the wonders he has wrought,

To tell, —how sitting on his magic throne,

Unaided and alone,

In dreadful state,

The subject passions round him wait;

Who tho' unchain'd, and raging there,

He checks, inflames, or turns their mad career;

With that superior skill,

Which winds the fiery steed at will,

He gives the aweful word—

And they, all foaming, trembling, own him for their Lord.[15]

---

[11] A marginal annotation to the BL copy text reads "Vernon." Joseph Vernon (1731?–1782) was an actor, singer, and composer.

[12] A reworking of Theseus's lines in *A Midsummer Night's Dream:* "The poet's eye, in a fine frenzy rolling, / Doth glance from heaven to Earth, from Earth to heaven" (5.1.12–13).

[13] This invokes the opening lines of the prologue to *Henry V*: "O, for a muse of fire that would ascend / The brightest heaven of invention!"

[14] A handwritten note in the BL copy text revises this line to read: "That might the strains inspire," seemingly with the purpose of making the line conform to the hexameter of the previous two lines.

[15] BL copy text revises this line to read "'Tis done; they pause; and own him for their Lord."

With these his slaves he can control,
Or charm the soul;
So realized are all his golden dreams,
Of terror, pity, love, and grief,
Tho' conscious that the vision only seems,
The woe-struck mind finds no relief:
Ingratitude would drop the tear,
Cold-blooded age take fire,
To see the thankless children of old *Lear,*
Spurn at their king, and sire!
With *his* our reason grows wild!
What nature hath disjoin'd,
The poet's pow'r combined,
Madness and *age, ingratitude* and *child.*

Ye guilty, lawless tribe,
Escap'd from punishment, by art or bribe,
At *Shakespeare's* bar appear!
No bribing, shuffling there—
His genius, like a rushing flood,
Cannot be withstood,
Out bursts the penitential tear![16]
The look appall'd, the crime reveals,
The marble-hearted monster feels,[17]
Whose hand is stain'd with blood.

---

[16] This echoes *Two Gentlemen of Verona*, 2.4.135–36—"With bitter fasts, with penitential groans, / With nightly tears and daily heart-sore sighs."

[17] This echoes *King Lear*, 1.4.270—"Ingratitude, thou marble-hearted fiend / More hideous when thou show'st thee in a child."

SEMI-CHORUS

When law is weak, and justice fails,
The poet holds the sword and scales.

AIR[18]

Though crimes from death and torture fly,
The swifter muse,
Their flight pursues,
Guilty mortals more than die!
They live indeed, but live to feel
The scourge and wheel,
"On the torture of the mind they lie;"[19]
Should harrass'd nature sink to rest,
The Poet wakes the scorpion in the breast,
Guilty mortals more than die!

When our *Magician*, more inspired,
By charms, and spells, and incantations fir'd,
Exerts his most tremendous pow'r;
The thunder growls, the heavens low'r,
And to his darken'd throne repair,
The *Demons* of the deep, and *Spirits* of the air!

But soon those horrors pass away,
Thro' storms and night breaks forth the day:
He smiles, —they vanish into air!

---

[18] Marginalia in BL copy text reads "Champness." Samuel Thomas Champness (d. 1803) was an actor and singer.

[19] This echoes *Macbeth*, 3.2.22–25: "Better be with the dead, / Whom we, to gain our peace, have sent to peace, / Than on the torture of the mind to lie / In restless ecstasy."

The buskin'd warriors disappear!
Mute the trumpets, mute the drums,
The scene is chang'd—*Thalia* comes,
Leading the nymph *Euphrosyne*,[20]
Goddess of joy and liberty!
She and her sisters, hand in hand,
Link'd to a num'rous frolick band,
With roses and with myrtle crown'd,
O'er the green velvet lightly bound,
Circling the Monarch of th'inchanted land!

AIR[21]

I

Wild, frantick with pleasure,
They trip it in measure,
To bring him their treasure,
The treasure of joy.

---

[20] In classical Greek mythology, Thalia is the muse of Comedy; Euphrosyne (also known as Euthymia) was one of the three Graces associated with mirth and joy. The passage appears to borrow from Milton's *L'Allegro*, lines 12–18: "But com thou Goddes fair and free / in Heav'n ycleap's *Euphrosyne*, / And by men, heart-easing Mirth, / Whom lovely *Venus* at a birth / With two sister Graces more / To Ivy-crowned *Bacchus* bore; / Or whether (as som Sager sing) / The frolick Wind that breathes the Spring."

[21] Marginalia in BL copy text reads "Miss Radley." Eleanor Radley (later Fitzgerald, d. 1772) was a singer and actress. This song, "The Treasure of Joy," bears similarities to one of the choruses from John Dryden's poem "Alexander's Feast or the Power of Music; An Ode in Honour of St. Cecilia's Day" (1697), an ode originally set to music: "Bacchus' blessings are a treasure, / Drinking is the soldier's pleasure; / Rich the treasure, / Sweet the pleasure, / Sweet is pleasure after pain."

II

How gay is the measure,
How sweet is the pleasure,
How great is the treasure,
　　The treasure of joy.

III

Like roses fresh blowing,
Their dimpled-cheeks glowing,
His mind is overflowing;
　　A treasure of joy!

IV

His rapture perceiving,
They smile while they're giving,
He smiles at receiving,
　　A treasure of joy.

　　With kindling cheeks, and sparkling eyes,
Surrounded thus, the Bard in transport dies;
　　　　The little *Loves*, like bees,
　　Clust'ring and climbing up his knees,
　　　　　　His brows with roses bind;
　　While *Fancy, Wit,* and *Humour* spread
　　Their wings, and hover round his head,
　　　　　　Impregnating his mind.
Which teeming soon, as soon brought forth,
　　　　Not a tiny spurious birth,
　　　　　　But out a mountain came,
　　　　A mountain of delight!
LAUGHTER roar'd out to see the sight,

And FALSTAFF was his name!
With sword and shield he, puffing, strides;
The joyous revel-rout
Receive him with a shout,
And modest *Nature* holds her sides:[22]
No single pow'r the deed had done,
But great and small,
Wit, *Fancy*, *Humour*, *Whim*, and *Jest*,
The huge, misshapen heap impress'd;
And lo—SIR JOHN!
A compound of 'em all,
A comic world in ONE.

AIR[23]

A world where all pleasures abound,
So fruitful the earth,
So quick to bring forth,
And the world too is wicked and round.

As the well-teeming earth,
With rivers and show'rs,
Will smiling bring forth
Her fruits and her flow'rs;
So FALSTAFF *will never decline;*
Still fruitful and gay,
He moistens his clay,
And his rain and his rivers are wine;
Of the world he has all, but its care;

---

[22] This is suggestive of Milton's *L'Allegro*, line 32—"And Laughter holding both his sides."

[23] Marginalia in the BL copy text reads "Mr. Vernon." See note 11, above.

No load, but of flesh, will he bear;
    He laughs off his pack,
    Takes a cup of old sack,
And away with all sorrow and care.

Like the rich rainbow's various dyes,
Whose circle sweeps o'er earth and skies,
    The heav'n-born muse appears;
Now in the brightest colors gay,
Now quench'd in show'rs, she fades away,
    Now blends her smiles and tears.

Sweet *Swan of Avon*! ever may thy stream
Of tuneful numbers be the darling theme;
Not *Thames* himself, who in his silver course
    Triumphant rolls along,
    Britannia's riches and her force,
    Shall more harmonious flow in song.

O had those bards, who charm the list'ning shore
Of Cam and Isis, tun'd their classic lays,[24]

---

[24] Cam and Isis: rivers running through the university towns of Cambridge and Oxford, respectively. Garrick had initially sought a university poet to pen the ode, but finding no takers, had adopted the task himself. "Longinus," the anonymous author of a series of scathing critiques of the ode published in October and November 1769 (who was possibly Macklin), doubts that Garrick was truly sincere in his search for an author other than himself: "Let him say what reward was offered to any others, out of the immense sums which he gained by Shakespeare, for the best Ode that should be produced on the occasion of this Jubilee. Had this been done without success, he might have had some excuse for undertaking it himself. But he well knows he did not mean to share with any one, any part of the expected glory which was to arise from this memorable project. He would share nothing but the loss upon the ill-judged expence attending the execution of it, which he liberally allowed some of the

And from their full and precious store,
Vouchsaf'd to fairy-haunted *Avon* praise!
    (Like to that kind bounteous hand,[25]
Which lately gave the ravish'd eyes
        Of Stratford swains
        A rich command,
Of widen'd river, lengthen'd plains,
        And opening skies)
Nor *Greek*, nor *Roman* streams would flow along,
More sweetly clear, or more sublimely strong,
Nor thus a shepherd's feeble notes reveal,
At one the weakest numbers, and the warmest zeal.

AIR

I

Thou soft-flowing Avon, *by thy silver stream,*
Of things more than mortal, sweet Shakespear *would dream,*
The fairies by moonlight dance round his green bed,
For hallow'd the turf is which pillow'd his head.

II

The love-stricken maiden, the soft-sighing swain,
Here rove without danger, and sigh without pain,

---

unfortunate artisans, concerned in the undertaking, to divide amongst them" (Anon., *Anti-Midas: A Jubilee Preservative From Unclassical, Ignorant, False, and Invidious Criticism.* [London, 1769], 33).

[25] An asterisk appears in the copy texts directing the reader to a footnote that reads: "The D—— of D——, with the concurrence of Mr. B——y, most generously ordered a great number of Trees to be cut down, to open the river *Avon* for the Jubilee." The men referred to are the Duke of Dorset and Dionysus Bradley; see chapter 3, page 49.

The sweet bud of beauty, no blight shall here dread,
For hallow'd the turf is which pillow'd his head.

III

Here youth shall be fam'd, for their love, and their truth,
And chearful old age, feel the spirit of youth;
For the raptures of fancy here poets shall tread,
For hallow'd the turf is that pillow'd his head.

IV

Flow on, silver Avon, in song ever flow,
Be the swans on thy bosom still whiter than snow,
Ever full be thy stream, like his fame may it spread,
And the turf ever hallow'd which pillow'd his head.

Tho' bards with envy-aching eyes,
Behold a tow'ring eagle rise,
    And would his flight retard;
Yet each to *Shakespeare*'s genius bows,
Each weaves a garland for his brows
    To crown th' heaven-distinguish'd Bard.
Nature had form'd him on her noblest plan,
    And to the genius join'd the feeling man.
What tho' with more than mortal art,
    Like *Neptune* he directs the storm,
Lets loose like winds the passions of the heart,
    To wreck the human form;
Tho' from his mind rush forth, the Demons to destroy,
His heart ne'er knew but love, and gentleness, and joy.

AIR[26]

More gentle than the southern gale,
Which softly fans the blossom'd vale,
And gathers on its balmy wing,
The fragrant treasures of the spring,
Breathing delight on all it meets,
"And giving, as it steals, the sweets."

Look down blest SPIRIT from above,
With all thy wonted gentleness and love;
And as the wonders of thy pen,
By heav'n inspir'd,
To virtue sir'd,
The charm'd, astonish'd, sons of men!
With no reproach, even now, thou view'st thy work,
To nature sacred as to truth,
Where no alluring mischiefs lurk,
To taint the mind of youth.
Still to thy native spot thy smiles extend,
And as thou gav'st it fame, that fame defend;
And may no sacrilegious hand
Near *Avon's* banks be found,
To dare to parcel out the land,
And limit Shakespear's hallow'd ground.[27]
For ages free, still be it unconfin'd,
As broad, and general, as thy boundless mind.

---

[26] Marginalia in the BL copy text reads "Mr. Baddely." See note 6, above.

[27] An asterisk appears in the copy texts directing the reader to a footnote that reads: "This alludes to a design of inclosing a large common field at *Stratford*."

Can *British* gratitude delay,
To him the glory of this isle,
To give the festive day
The song, the statue, and devoted pile?
To him the first of poets, best of men?
"We ne'er shall look upon his like again!"[28]

DUETT

Shall the hero laurels gain,
For ravag'd fields, and thousands slain?
And shall his brows no laurels bind,
Who charms to virtue humankind?

CHORUS

We will, —his brows with laurel bind,
Who charms to virtue human kind:
Raise the pile, the statue raise,
Sing immortal *Shakespeare's* praise!
The song will cease, the stone decay,
But his Name,
And undiminish'd fame,
Shall never, never pass away.

---

[28] An echo of *Hamlet*, 1.2.195–96—"He was a man. Take him for all in all. / I shall not look upon his like again"—as well as the inscription on the Jubilee medals.

Notes

Prologue

xv **"Was there ever such stuff"**: Frances Burney, *Journals and Letters,* ed. Peter Sabor and Lars E. Troide (Harmondsworth, Eng.: Penguin, 2001), 228.

xvi **"fitt"**: See Gunnar Sorelius, "The Rights of the Restoration Theatrical Companies in the Older Drama," *Studie Neophilologica* 37 (1967): 176.

xvii **archaic and tortuous to the Restoration ear:** A brief example of D'Avenant's smoothing of Shakespeare's language for a contemporary audience may help to illustrate. In Shakespeare's *Macbeth,* the description of Macbeth battling the rebel Macdonwald appears as follows (1.2.18–25):

> For Brave Macbeth (well he deserves that name),
> Disdaining Fortune, with his brandished steel,
> Which smoked with bloody execution,
> Like Valor's minion carved out his passage
> Till he faced the slave;
> Which ne'er shook hands, nor bade farewell to him,
> Till he unseamed him from the nave to th' chops,
> And fix'd his head upon our battlements.

D'Avenant's version has:

> But brave *Macbeth* (who well deserves that name)
> Did with his frowns put all her smiles to fright:
> And Cut his passage to the Rebels person:
> Then having Conquer'd him with single force,
> He fixt his Head upon out Battlements.

The result is a less ferocious Macbeth, no longer in the midst of gory hand-to-hand evisceration, his enemy's bowels ribboning at his feet. Consider also the murder of Duncan. In the mouth of D'Avenant's Macbeth,

If it were well when done; then it were well
It were done quickly; if his Death might be
Without the Death of nature in my self,
And killing my own rest; it wou'd suffice;
But deeds of this complexion still return
To plague the doer, and destroy his peace.
Yet let me think; he's here in double trust.

In Shakespeare, his thoughts are far less linear:

If it were done, when 'tis done, then 'twere well
It were done quickly. If th' assassination
Could trammel up the consequence, and catch
With his surcease, success; that but this blow
Might be the be-all and the end-all here,
But here, upon this bank and shoal of time,
We'd jump the life to come. But in these cases
We still have judgment here, that we but teach
Bloody instructions, which, being taught, return
To plague th' inventor. This even-handed justice
Commends th' ingredient of our poison'd chalice
To our own lips. He's here in double trust. (1.7.1–12)

D'Avenant's reworking retains the sense in summary but lacks entirely Shakespeare's cosmic scale. In the original, Macbeth fixes the crime within the competing temporalities of fate and free will, the one focused on an isolated moment—"here, / But here"—while the other is aware of its relationship to all time. The contending mind is caught in looping syntax and hopscotch words that shift between eternity and the "bank and shoal of time," before ultimately resigning itself to the logic of tragedy—that those who kill must in turn be killed—which is also, to some degree, an admission that he himself is a fiction.

xviii **"Decency and good Manners"**: Quoted in Michael Dobson, *The Making of the National Poet: Shakespeare, Adaptation and Authorship, 1660–1769* (Oxford: Clarendon, 2001), 157. The Shakespeare Ladies Club was responsible for reviving a number of plays at Covent Garden that had otherwise fallen out of the repertoire, including *Richard II*, the second part of *Henry IV*, and the comedies *Twelfth Night*, *As You Like It*, and *The Merchant of Venice*, all of which were supported by the excellence of the actors who played their strong female leads. See Arthur H. Scouten, *The London Stage, 1729–1747: A Critical Introduction* (Carbondale: Southern Illinois University Press/Ferrer and Simons, 1968), l.

xviii **"natural, free and easy"**: *London Evening Post*, January 29–31, 1741.

xviii **"Perhaps a nation's virtue too"**: William Whitehead, *Poems on Several Occasions, with the Roman Father, a Tragedy* (London, 1754), 105.

xviii **"whether Shakespeare owes more to Garrick"**: James Granger, *A Biographical History of England, from Egbert the Great to the Revolution* (London, 1769), 2:288.

xviii *"the house of William Shakespeare"*: David Garrick, *The Letters of David Garrick*, ed. David M. Little and George M. Kahrl (London: Oxford University Press, 1963), 1:172.

 xix **"Quietness and Devotion"**: Joseph Pittard, *Observations on Mr. Garrick's Acting; in a Letter to the Right Hon. the Earl of Chesterfield* (London, 1758), 22.

 xix **"assisted the deficiencies"**: *The London Magazine*, 1769, 407.

 xix **"an elegant and truly classical"**: *Public Advertiser,* September 16, 1769. Nicola J. Watson has usefully described the Jubilee as "a theatricalization of the biographical within topography"; see her "Shakespeare on the Tourist Trail," in *Shakespeare and Popular Culture*, ed. Robert Shaughnessy (Cambridge: Cambridge University Press, 2007), 205.

  xx **"hand in hand with Shakespeare"**: Antijubileana, Saunders Papers (1769), ER1/83/4, n.p., Shakespeare Birthplace Trust.

 xxi **"like a Frenchman at an ordinary"**: James Boswell, *Boswell in Search of a Wife: 1766–1769*, ed. Frank Brady and Frederick A. Pottle (New York: McGraw-Hill, 1956), 283.

Chapter 1

 1 **"ye Bed of Death"**: David Garrick, *The Letters of David Garrick*, ed. David M. Little and George M. Kahrl (London: Oxford University Press, 1963), 2:640.

 1 **born with only a single kidney**: See Michael Caines, *Shakespeare and the Eighteenth Century* (Oxford: Oxford University Press, 2013), 92.

 2 **"The freedom of your town"**: Garrick, *Letters*, 1:345.

 3 **"the Trojan Horse"**: *Public Advertiser,* July 1, 1769.

 4 **"to be kept up every seventh Year"**: *Public Advertiser,* May 15 and May 11, 1769.

 7 **"the scars of his scrophula"**: James Boswell, *Life of Johnson* (Oxford: Oxford World's Classics, 2008), 68.

 8 **"signalized, for many years, as the emporium of wit"**: Anon., *Memoirs of the Bedford Coffee-House. By a Genius* (London 1763), 1.

 8 **"the English are the Frenchman's Apes"**: Francis Gorse, *A Provincial Glossary, with a Collection of Local Proverbs, and Popular Superstitions* (London, 1787), n.p.

 9 **face a fifty-pound fine**: See Julia Swindells, "The Political Context of the 1737 Licensing Act," in *The Oxford Handbook of Georgian Theatre*, ed. Julia Swindells and David Francis Taylor (Oxford: Oxford University Press, 2014), 110.

 9 **required that patrons purchase a pint**: See Arthur H. Scouten, *The London*

Stage 1729–1747: A Critical Introduction (Carbondale: Southern Illinois University Press/Ferrer and Simons, 1968), li–lvii.

11 **"loud and reiterated applause"**: Thomas Davies, *Memoirs of the Life of David Garrick* (London, 1784), 1:40.

11 **"a complete master of his art"**: Arthur Murphy, *The Life of David Garrick, Esq.* (Dublin, 1801), 18.

11 **"the splendour of St. James's"**: Davies, *Garrick*, 1:41.

11 **"ye best Actor"**: Garrick, *Letters*, 1:31.

11 **"(as You must know) has always been"**: Ibid., 1:28.

12 **"Sir John Brute all day"**: David Williams, *A letter to David Garrick, Esq. On His Conduct as Principal Manager and Actor at Drury-Lane* (London, 1778), 17.

13 **To prepare for this new interpretation:** See Robert Shaughnessy, "Shakespeare and the London Stage," in *Shakespeare in the Eighteenth Century*, ed. Fiona Richie and Peter Sabor (Cambridge: Cambridge University Press, 2012), 177.

13 **"subtle, selfish, fawning"**: James Thomas Kirkman, *Memoirs of the Life of Charles Macklin, Esq, Compiled from his Own Papers and Memorandums* (London, 1799), 1:260.

13 **"This is the Jew"**: Quoted in ibid., 1:264. I use the word "allegedly" because no verification of Pope's endorsement exists beyond Kirkman's biography. See Fiona Ritchie, "Shakespeare and the Eighteenth Century Actress," *Borrowers and Lenders: The Journal of Shakespeare Appropriation* 11, no. 2 (2006): 9.

13 **"save by costume and outbursts of fury"**: Quoted in George Winchester Stone Jr. and George M. Kahrl, *David Garrick: A Critical Biography* (Carbondale: Southern Illinois University Press/Feffer and Simons, 1979), 29.

13 **"to intrap applause"**: Davies, *Garrick*, 1:40.

14 **"Declamation roared"**: Murphy, *Garrick*, 12.

14 **"heaving up his words"**: Davies, *Garrick*, 1:40. See also Celestine Woo, *Romantic Actors and Bardolatry: Performing Shakespeare from Garrick to Kean* (New York: Peter Lang, 2008), 21.

14 **"the fixed glare of tragic expression"**: Joseph Haslewood, *The Secret History of the Green Room* (London, 1795), 1:68.

14 **Macklin's unnecessary fidgeting:** William Cooke, *Memoirs of Charles Macklin, Comedian, With the Dramatic Characters, Manners, Anecdotes etc. of the Age in Which He Lived.* 2nd ed. (London, 1806), 99.

15 **"I believe my eyeball"**: Kirkman, *Memoirs of Charles Macklin*, 1:202.

15 **He died the following day:** Ibid., 1:197.

15 **"he dropped it"**: Murphy, *Garrick*, 20.

15 **"I learned to imitate madness"**: Ibid., 21.

16 **"*great Excellency in Characters*"**: David Garrick, *An Essay on Acting* (London, 1744), 9–10.

16 **"When Garrick entered the scene"**: Murphy, *Garrick*, 30.

16 **"He was so natural"**: Quoted in Jocelyn Powell, "Dance and Drama in the Eighteenth Century: David Garrick and Jean Georges Noverre," *Word & Image* 4, no. 3–4 (1988): 679.

16 **"Parts so *naturally*"**: *The Gentleman's Magazine*, May 1743, 254.

16 **"seniority was considered"**: Anon., *The Life of James Quin, Comedian, With the History of the Stage From His Commencing Actor to His Retreat to Bath* (London, 1887), 17.

17 **"as if a whole century"**: Richard Cumberland, *Memoirs of Richard Cumberland, Written By Himself*, ed. Henry Flanders (Philadelphia, 1856), 47.

Chapter 2

18 **"I used to adore and look upon"**: James Boswell, *Boswell's London Journal: 1762–1763*, ed. Frederick A. Pottle (New York: McGraw-Hill, 1950), 161.

19 **"so much *yes* and *no*"**: James Boswell, *Boswell in Search of a Wife: 1766–1769*, ed. Frank Brady and Frederick A. Pottle (New York: McGraw-Hill, 1956), 213.

19 **"Her most desirable person"**: Ibid.

19 **"I am exceedingly in love"**: James Boswell, *The Correspondence of James Boswell and William Johnson Temple, 1756–1795*, ed, Thomas Crawford (Edinburgh/New Haven: Edinburgh University Press/Yale University Press, 1997), 1:246.

19 **"newspaper fame"**: Boswell, *Boswell in Search of a Wife*, 272.

20 **"I liked to see the effect"**: Ibid., 268.

20 **"I am really the *Great Man* now"**: Boswell, *Correspondence of Boswell and Temple*, 1:236.

22 **philosopher named John Williamson**: See Alexander Alladyce, ed., *Scotland and Scotsmen in the Eighteenth Century* (Edinburgh: William Blackwood, 1888) 2:327.

23 **"yielding to received opinions"**: James Boswell, "Sketch of the Early Life of James Boswell, Written by Himself for Jean Jacques Rousseau, 5 December 1764," in Frederick A. Pottle, *James Boswell: The Earlier Years, 1740–1769* (New York: McGraw-Hill, 1966), 4.

24 **"with a mixture of narrow-minded horror"**: Boswell, *London Journal*, 85.

24 **"The impression he made upon"**: James Boswell, *The Correspondence of James Boswell with David Garrick, Edmund Burke, Edmond Malone*, ed. George M. Kahrl, Rachel McClellan, Thomas W. Copeland, James M. Osborn, and Peter S. Baker (London: Heinemann, 1986), 77.

24 **"She has the finest Person"**: [James Boswell], *A View of the Edinburgh Theatre During the Summer Season, 1759* (London, 1760), 11.

25 **become a Catholic priest**: See Robert Zaretsky, *Boswell's Enlightenment* (Cambridge, Mass.: Harvard University Press, 2015), 40.

26 **"for your particular kindness"**: James Boswell, *Ode to Tragedy, by a Gentleman of Scotland* (Edinburgh, 1761), dedication.

26 **"Thou greatest of men"**: Boswell, *London Journal*, 161.

26 **"so very high"**: Ibid., 256–57.

27 **"who lurk about the house avenues":** *Theatrical Monitor,* December 19, 1767.

27 **"plain, sober Tradesmen":** Ralph James, *The Taste of the Town: Or, A Guide to All Publick Diversions* (London, 1731), 139.

27 **"*Encore* the cow!":** Samuel Johnson and James Boswell, *A Journey to the Western Islands of Scotland* and *The Journal of a Tour to the Hebrides,* ed. Peter Levi (London: Penguin, 1984), 406n.

27 **"*confine* myself to the cow":** Ibid.

28 **"hush men":** James Boaden, *The Memoirs of Mrs. Siddons, Interspersed with Anecdotes of Authors and Actors* (Philadelphia, 1837), 374.

29 **"generous contemplative mind":** James Boswell, *The Correspondence of James Boswell and John Johnston of Grange,* ed. Ralph S. Walker (New York: McGraw-Hill, 1966), 17.

Chapter 3

30 **"considered himself as under the necessity":** James Northcote, *The Memoirs of Joshua Reynolds* (Philadelphia, 1817), 120.

30 **They began at the birthplace:** See Christian Deelman, *The Great Shakespeare Jubilee* (New York: Viking, 1964), 103.

30 **"every body will be there":** David Garrick, *The Letters of David Garrick,* ed. David M. Little and George M. Kahrl (London: Oxford University Press, 1963), 2:651.

30 **"There is much talk":** Garrick, *Letters,* 2:647.

31 **Its size and character:** Levi Fox, *The Borough Town of Stratford upon Avon* (Stratford: Corporation of Stratford upon Avon, 1953), 48.

31 **"with such violence as to deprive":** *The Gentleman's Magazine,* 1769, 269.

32 **"the wretchedest old town":** Horace Walpole, *The Letters of Horace Walpole, Fourth Earl of Oxford,* ed. Paget Toynbee (Oxford: Clarendon, 1904), 3:65.

32 **the famous mulberry tree:** See Samuel Schoenbaum, *Shakespeare's Lives,* new ed. (Oxford: Clarendon, 1991), 125.

32 **These intrusions so aggrieved Gastrell:** See Martha Winburn England, *Garrick and Stratford* (New York: New York Public Library, 1962), 8–9.

33 **had the entire building demolished:** Robert Bell Wheler, *History and Antiquities of Stratford-upon-Avon* (London, [1806?]), 37–38.

33 **"Trinkets, Seals, Tweezer and Tooth Pick cases":** Quoted in Jenny Uglow, *The Lunar Men: Five Friends Whose Curiosity Changed the World* (New York: Farrar, Straus and Giroux, 2002), 17.

33 **Toy work employed over twenty thousand people:** See Donald Read, *The English Provinces, c. 1760–1960* (New York: St. Martin's, 1964), 18; Uglow, *Lunar Men,* 64.

34 **"The West-Indies":** William Hutton, *An History of Birmingham, to the End of the Year 1780* (Birmingham, 1781), 70.

34 **"Surrounded with impassable roads":** Ibid., 64.

35 **"sixty feet long":** Articles for Erecting Stratford Town Hall, 1767, BRU 21/10, Shakespeare Birthplace Trust.

35 **open colonnade to house the corn market:** Ibid.

36 **"as hearty, as sensible, and as polite a being":** "Letter from the Place of Shakespeare's Nativity," *The British Magazine*, 1762, 301–2.

37 **"In order to flatter Mr Garrick":** Jubilee Correspondence, Saunders Papers, ER1/83/1, Shakespeare Birthplace Trust.

37 **"I am Certain Mr Garrick":** Autograph Letter Signed [hereafter ALS], George Alexander Stevens to John Payton, December 28, 1767, Borough of Stratford, The New Town Hall, ER1/37, Shakespeare Birthplace Trust.

38 **"never failed to enjoy adulation":** Charles Dibdin, *The Professional Life of Mr. Dibdin* (London, 1803), 1:97.

38 **"The Corporation of Stratford":** British Library Jubilee Scrapbook, General Reference Collection, C.61.e.2, pp. 127–28, British Library.

38 **"He told me he thought himself obliged":** ALS, George Alexander Stevens to John Payton, December 30, 1767, Borough of Stratford, The New Town Hall, ER1/37, Shakespeare Birthplace Trust.

39 **"grateful temple to Shakespeare":** Quoted in Ian McIntyre, *Garrick* (Harmondsworth, Eng.: Penguin, 1999), 233.

39 **"A most noble statue":** Quoted in George Winchester Stone Jr. and George M. Kahrl, *David Garrick: A Critical Biography* (Carbondale: Southern Illinois University Press/Feffer and Simons, 1979), 429.

39 **"SHAKESPEARE revives!":** Richard Rolt, "Poetical Epistle from Shakespeare in Elysium, to Mr. Garrick, at Drury-Lane Theatre" (London, 1752), 6.

40 **had the empty page inscribed:** See Michael Dobson, *The Making of the National Poet: Shakespeare, Adaptation and Authorship, 1660–1769* (Oxford: Clarendon, 2001), 141–46.

42 **Dealing with celebrities:** These transactions are detailed at length in Deelman, *Great Shakespeare Jubilee*, 66–72.

43 **"entirely laid out in the Honor of Shakespeare":** Garrick, *Letters*, 3:1353.

43 **"the stately Palace of some Duke":** Quoted in Peter M. Jones, "'I had L[or]ds and Ladys to wait on yesterday . . . ': Visitors to the Soho Manufactory," in *Matthew Boulton: Selling What All the World Desires*, ed. Shena Mason (Birmingham: Birmingham City Council/Yale University Press, 2009), 71.

43 **"All well regulated states":** Quoted in John Money, *Experience and Identity: Birmingham and the West Midlands, 1760–1800* (Manchester: Manchester University Press, 1977), 90.

44 **"determinate and final answer":** Garrick, *Letters*, 3:1353.

44 **encouraging Hunt to put up:** See Deelman, *Great Stratford Jubilee*, 105.

44 **"The money which this Jubilee":** *Whitehall Evening Post*, September 2–5, 1769.

45 **"large family, in which there are":** Garrick, *Letters*, 1:370.

45 **"Tartar":** Ibid., 2:741.

45 **"had so many admirable traits":** Dibdin, *Professional Life*, 1:97n.

45 **"particularly bebitched":** Garrick, *Letters*, 2:496.

46 **"capacious, handsome, and strong":** Wheler, *History and Antiquities*, 91.

46 **"Being addicted to inebriety"**: R. B. Wheler, Jubilee Album, ER1/14, p. 88
    verso, Shakespeare Birthplace Trust.
46 **"was always in anxiety, lest in his absence"**: Dibdin, *Professional Life*, 1:98n.
47 **"2 barges and Fishing Boat"**: Garrick, *Letters*, 3:1354.
47 **"We shall want 8, 10, or a dozen"**: Ibid., 3:360.
48 **"fine imperial tea"**: Jerry White, *A Great and Monstrous Thing: London in the
    Eighteenth Century* (Cambridge, Mass.: Harvard University Press, 2013),
    322; see also Tobias Smollet, *The Expedition of Humphrey Clinker*, ed. Lewis
    M. Knapp (Oxford: Oxford World's Classics, 1992), 92.
48 **"a vast amphitheatre"**: Quoted in Hannah Grieg, *The Beau Monde: Fashion-
    able Society in Georgian London* (Oxford: Oxford University Press, 2013), 68.
49 **a lawyer named Dionysus Bradley**: See *The Gentleman's Magazine*, July
    1769, 364.
49 **As the landlord of the White Lion**: See Garrick, *Letters*, 3:1354.
49 **"Jubilee chicken"**: *The Gentleman's Magazine*, September 1769, 422.
49 **"either pursuing their occupations"**: Ibid., 421.
50 **"The low People of Stratford"**: *St. James Chronicle*, October 10, 1769.
50 **"riddotoes [sic] alternately"**: *Town and Country Magazine*, July 1769, 344.
50 **"an intellectual feast"**: *The Gentleman's Magazine*, August 1769, 375.
51 **"desolate appearance"**: Joseph Cradock, *Literary and Miscellaneous Memoirs*
    (London, 1828), 1:213.
51 **"If that great and striking object"**: Garrick, *Letters*, 2:662.
51 **"We never were so uncomfortably circumstanced"**: Cradock, *Literary and
    Miscellaneous Memoirs*, 1:213.
51 **"have all their plate stolen"**: Ibid., 1:214.
52 **"There will be no Jubilee"**: Ibid., 1:212.

Chapter 4
53 **"I have seen, within a year"**: Benjamin Franklin, *The Memoirs of Benjamin
    Franklin* (Philadelphia: McCarty and Davis, 1834), 2:514.
54 **"the people are taxed"**: *The Gentleman's Magazine*, March 1769, 167.
54 **the price of bread had doubled**: See George Rudé, *Wilkes and Liberty: A
    Social Study of 1763–1774* (Oxford: Clarendon, 1963), 90.
54 **"The papers are filled"**: Quoted in ibid, 11.
55 **"a tessellated pavement"**: Quoted in Anon., *Authentic Memoirs of the Right
    Honourable the Late Earl of Chatham* (London, 1778), 97.
55 **"The laws are despoiled"**: Edmund Burke, *Thoughts on the Cause of the Pres-
    ent Discontents* (London, 1770), 2–3.
56 **"poignant acrimony"**: James Boswell, *Boswell's London Journal: 1762–1763*,
    ed. Frederick A. Pottle (New York: McGraw-Hill, 1950), 187.
56 **"honorable to the crown"**: Thomas Smart Hughes, *The History of England
    from the Accession of George III to the Accession of Queen Victoria* (London,
    1846), 1:311.

57 **"I am in doubt"**: John Wilkes et al., *The North Briton From No. I. to No. Xlvi. Inclusive* (London, 1763), 2:231.

58 **"Authors, Printers and Publishers"**: Quoted in Jerry White, *A Great and Monstrous Thing: London in the Eighteenth Century* (Cambridge, Mass.: Harvard University Press), 516–17.

58 **Boswell joined the crowd**: Boswell, *London Journal*, 261.

58 **"solely as the reward"**: James Boswell, *Life of Johnson* (Oxford: Oxford World's Classics, 2008), 264.

59 **"isthmus between arbitrary power and anarchy"**: Quoted in John Brewer, *Party Ideology and Popular Politics at the Accession of George II* (Cambridge: Cambridge University Press, 1976), 245.

59 **"the middling and inferior set"**: Quoted in White, *Great and Monstrous Thing*, 517.

59 **"This hero is as bad"**: Horace Walpole, *The Letters of Horace Walpole, Fourth Earl of Oxford*, ed. Paget Toynbee (Oxford: Clarendon, 1904), 5:315.

60 **"rough, blunt fellow"**: Boswell, *London Journal*, 266.

60 **"the phoenix of convivial felicity"**: Boswell, *Life of Johnson*, 862.

60 **"an enemy to the true old British"**: James Boswell, *Boswell on the Grand Tour: Italy, Corsica, and France, 1765–1766*, ed. Frank Brady and Frederick A. Pottle (New York: McGraw-Hill, 1955), 69.

60 **"Never think on futurity"**: Ibid., 55.

60 **"Go home by Holland"**: Ibid., 57.

60 **"three or four whores"**: Ibid., 54.

60 **"to many she gives not"**: Ibid., 56. Wilkes had been a member of the Medmenham Monks, a group of twelve men who would convene among the old elms at Buckinghamshire's Medmenham Abbey for parties that included drinking, masquerades, sex games, and travesties of Catholic ritual hosted in an old church accessed through a door that had been fashioned to resemble a vagina. All who entered had to swear not to reveal the secrets within. Images of Harpocrates and Angerona, the god and goddess of silence, reminded them of their oath, while their abbot, the dissolute Sir Francis Dashwood, poured votive libations onto a goddess without eyes. During the initial phase of the *North Briton* affair, Wilkes had asked his printer to make up twelve copies of a pornographic poem he had written titled *The Essay on Women* in emulation of Alexander Pope's *Essay on Man*, to share with his fellow monks. When a copy of this graphic and misogynistic work reached Lord Sandwich, himself a Medmenham Monk, but also a political opponent of Wilkes, Sandwich chose loyalty to his king over loyalty to his faux monastic order and read several lines aloud in the House of Lords as evidence of the full extent of Wilkes's depravity. A chorus of shouts went up as Sandwich read lines such as "since life can little more supply / Than just a few good Fucks and then we die." Some voices called for him to stop, others for him to carry on. See Augustus Henry Fitzroy, Duke of Grafton, *Let-*

ters Between the Duke of Grafton and John Wilkes, esq. (London, 1769), 1:46; White, *Great and Monstrous Thing*, 519.

61 **"Be Spaniard: girl every day"**: Boswell, *Grand Tour: Italy, Corsica, and France*, 51.

61 **"champions of liberty will in time"**: Ibid., 73.

61 **"the confusion and the noise"**: James Boswell, *Boswell in Search of a Wife: 1766–1769*, ed. Frank Brady and Frederick A. Pottle (New York: McGraw-Hill, 1956), 142.

62 **When he recounted this tale to Samuel Johnson**: Ibid., 148.

63 **free beer to the mob**: See Rudé, *Wilkes and Liberty*, 43.

63 **"very sink of vice"**: Boswell, *Boswell in Search of a Wife*, 158–59.

63 **escape a party to attend a prison**: See *The Gentleman's Magazine*, 1769, 109.

63 **twenty thousand in the afternoon**: See Rudé, *Wilkes and Liberty*, 50.

63 **"Wilkes and Liberty"**: Quoted in ibid.

64 **"object of persecution"**: Burke, *Thoughts on the Cause of the Present Discontents*, 40.

65 **Fifteen county petitions**: See Peter D. G. Thomas, *John Wilkes: A Friend to Liberty* (Oxford: Clarendon, 1996), 104; Rudé, *Wilkes and Liberty*, 132–33.

65 **"the restless offspring"**: Quoted in John Money, *Experience and Identity: Birmingham and the West Midlands, 1760–1800* (Manchester: Manchester University Press, 1977), 172, 69.

65 **Garrick's mulberry box**: See Hugh Tait, "Garrick, Shakespeare and Wilkes," *The British Museum Quarterly* 24, no. 3–4 (1961): 106.

65 **"The people of England"**: An Account of the Jubilee Celebrated at Stratford-upon-Avon in Honour of Shakspeare, 1769 . . . Collected and Arranged from Different Authorities, Saunders Papers, ER1/82, Shakespeare Birthplace Trust.

66 **"purify my blood"**: Boswell, *Boswell in Search of a Wife*, 269.

66 **"When I left Scotland"**: Ibid.

66 **"it belonged to the chapter"**: Ibid., 272.

66 **gifted statue as "terrible"**: Boswell, *Life of Johnson*, 402.

67 **"envious malignity or superstitious veneration"**: Samuel Johnson, *Mr. Johnson's Preface to His Edition of Shakespear's Plays* (London, 1765), 22.

67 **"a blind indiscriminate admiration"**: Boswell, *Life of Johnson*, 350.

67 **"Shakespear never has six lines together"**: Ibid., 863, 418, 412.

68 **"partake in the festival of genius"**: Ibid., 469, 402.

68 **"that *Davy Garrick*, who was"**: James Boswell, *Boswell for the Defence, 1769–1774*, ed. William K. Wimsatt Jr. and Frederick A. Pottle (New York: McGraw-Hill, 1959), 119.

68 **consult with Dr. Kennedy**: Boswell, *Boswell in Search of a Wife*, 278.

68 **"a very handsome vine"**: Ibid., 274.

Chapter 5

69 **"in general, much dissatisfied"**: Benjamin Victor, *The History of the Theatres of London from the Year 1760 to the Present Times* (London, 1771), 231–32.

69 **"I heard yesterday to my Surprise"**: David Garrick, *The Letters of David Garrick*, ed. David M. Little and George M. Kahrl (London: Oxford University Press, 1963), 2:660.

70 **Back kitchens, landings, outhouses**: See John Solas Dodd, *Essays and Poems, Satirical, Moral, Political, and Entertaining* (Cork, 1770), 250.

70 **"no hovel almost remained"**: An Account of the Jubilee Celebrated at Stratford-upon-Avon in Honour of Shakspeare, 1769 . . . Collected and Arranged from Different Authorities, Saunders Papers, ER1/82, Shakespeare Birthplace Trust.

70 **"the exorbitant price that some"**: Garrick, *Letters*, 2:661.

70 **"The Fame of Shakespeare"**: *Public Advertiser,* July 29, 1769.

71 **"Come brothers of Stratford"**: Quoted in Dodd, *Essays and Poems*, 263–64.

72 **"a dreadful example to those"**: British Library Jubilee Scrapbook, General Reference Collection, C.61.e.2, p. 43, British Library.

72 **"an epistle in verse to Monsieur de Voltaire"**: *St. James Chronicle*, June 1, 1769; *Public Advertiser,* June 6, 1769.

72 **"Because you have no taste"**: James Boswell, *Boswell on the Grand Tour: Germany and Switzerland, 1764*, ed. Frederick A. Pottle (New York: McGraw-Hill, 1953), 299.

73 **"French Plunderer"**: *Public Advertiser,* June 8, 1769.

73 **"beauteous Nature fills"**: George Keate, *Ferney: An Epistle to Monsr. De Voltaire* (London, 1768), 2.

73 **"Above Controul, above each classic Rule"**: Ibid., 13.

73 **"Your present to Keate"**: David Garrick to William Hunt, July 14, 1769, Jubilee Correspondence, Saunders Papers, ER1/83/1, Shakespeare Birthplace Trust.

73 **"*asthmatic* and *intermittent* nibblers"**: Anon., *Anti-Midas: A Jubilee Preservative from Unclassical, Ignorant, False, and Invidious Criticism* (London, 1769), 3.

73 **"little critics that shall carp"**: James Boaden, ed., *The Private Correspondence of David Garrick* (London, 1831), 1:263.

73 **"Was the Roman Conqueror"**: Isaac Bickerstaff, *Judith, A Sacred Drama: As Performed in the Church of Stratford upon Avon, on Occasion of the Jubilee Held There, September 6, 1769, in Honour of the Memory of Shakespeare* (London, 1769), ii.

74 **Doge's palace in Venice**: Johann Wilhelm von Archenholz, *A Picture of England: Containing a Description of the Laws, Customs, and Manners of England* (Dublin, 1791), 40.

74 **"the contemptible and indecent attacks"**: *Lloyd's Evening Post,* August 16, 1769.

74 **"At length, as sunk in":** *Public Advertiser,* August 5, 1769.

75 *"was fun to vex":* Garrick, *Letters,* 2:679.

75 **manufactured the controversy:** David Williams, *A letter to David Garrick, Esq. On His Conduct as Principal Manager and Actor at Drury-Lane* (London, 1778), 3–4.

75 **"I am so busy":** David Garrick to William Hunt, August 27, 1769, Jubilee Correspondence, Saunders Papers, ER1/83/1, Shakespeare Birthplace Trust.

75 **"the precipitancy of his temper":** Thomas Davies, *Memoirs of the Life of David Garrick* (London, 1784), 1:77–78.

76 **"Why should not there be taken":** David Garrick to William Hunt, August 15, 1769, Jubilee Correspondence, Saunders Papers, ER1/83/1, Shakespeare Birthplace Trust.

76 **"I am unable to learn how Oratorios":** *Public Advertiser,* August 23, 1769.

76 **"If I come off with only a fever":** Garrick to Hunt, August 27, 1769.

76 **"works like a dragon":** Garrick, *Letters,* 2:651.

76 **"met with much approbation":** Garrick to Hunt, August 27, 1769.

78 **"marking genius":** *Theatrical Monitor,* October 24, 1767.

79 **"Your mouth has no sweetness":** Williams, *Letter to David Garrick,* 26.

79 *"whispering gallery":* William Cooke, *Memoirs of Charles Macklin, Comedian. With the Dramatic Characters, Manners, Anecdotes etc. of the Age in Which He Lived,* 2nd ed. (London, 1806), 140.

79 **"more affected by any pleasantry":** Archenholz, *Picture of England,* 169. See also Samuel Johnson and James Boswell, *A Journey to the Western Islands of Scotland* and *The Journal of a Tour to the Hebrides,* ed. Peter Levi (London: Penguin, 1984), 325.

79 **"Another man has his dram and is satisfied":** James Boswell, *The Correspondence of James Boswell with David Garrick, Edmund Burke, Edmond Malone,* ed. George M. Kahrl, Rachel McClellan, Thomas W. Copeland, James M. Osborn, and Peter S. Baker (London: Heinemann, 1986), 11.

80 **"Admittance, is frequently more difficult":** Theophilus Cibber, *Cibber's Two Dissertations on the Theatres, with an Appendix, in Three Parts* (London, [1757?]), 29.

80 **"privilege reserved only for the happy few":** Oliver Goldsmith, *An Enquiry into the Present State of Polite Learning in Europe* (London, 1759), 173.

80 **"on the rack of ridicule":** Williams, *Letter to David Garrick,* 9.

80 **happened to be tall:** See Cibber, *Two Dissertations,* 38; Joseph Haslewood, *The Secret History of the Green Room* (London, 1795), 1:66.

80 **"is fond of sidling up to me":** Quoted in Ian McIntyre, *Garrick* (Harmondsworth, Eng.: Penguin, 1999), 304.

80 **"the most *insignificant* person":** Cooke, *Memoirs of Charles Macklin,* 246.

80 **"anxiety for his fame":** Arthur Murphy, *The Life of David Garrick, Esq.* (Dublin, 1801), 214.

81 **"the revival of expiring":** Cooke, *Memoirs of Charles Macklin,* 244; see also

James Boaden, *The Memoirs of Mrs. Siddons, Interspersed with Anecdotes of Authors and Actors* (Philadelphia, 1837), 374; see also Thaddeus Fitzpatrick, *An Enquiry into the Real Merit of a Certain Popular Performer* (London, 1760).

81   **the custom of taking half-price admissions:** See Gillian Russell, "'Keeping Place': Servants, Theater and Sociability in Mid-Eighteenth Century Britain," *Eighteenth Century: Theory and Interpretation* 42, no. 1 (Spring 2001): 1–18.

81   **"Whatever notions modern performers":** Thaddeus Fitzpatrick, *A Dialogue in the Green-Room upon a Disturbance in the Pit* (London, 1763), 6.

82   **"As Englishmen, it is our duty":** Ibid., 1.

82   **"In less than an hour":** Giacomo Casanova, *The Memoirs of Jacques Casanova de Seingalt, the Prince of Adventurers* (London: Chapman and Hall, 1902), 2:156–57.

82   **"Knees, knees!":** Anon., *An Historical and Succinct Account of the Late Riots at the Theatres of Drury Lane and Covent Garden* (London, 1763), 19.

83   **"Fitzp——k was my foe":** "Garrick's Epitaph Written by Himself in a Fit of Sickness at Munich in Bavaria," Folger Digital Image Collection, Y.d.120 (26). See also Garrick, *Letters*, 2:425.

83   **"Knight of ye Woefull Countenance":** Garrick, *Letters*, 2:425.

83   **Garrick lost a significant amount:** See ibid., 2:429.

83   **"I have at present lost all taste":** Ibid., 2:430.

83   **"to the world the uprightness":** *Theatrical Monitor,* December, 19, 1767.

84   **"If we weigh his merits":** Ibid., November 7, 1767.

84   **"GARRICK, attend!":** Ibid., February 6, 1768.

84   **An average season at Drury Lane:** See George Winchester Stone Jr. and George M. Kahrl, *David Garrick: A Critical Biography* (Carbondale: Southern Illinois University Press/Feffer and Simons, 1979), 659–60.

84   **"We know that each Apartment":** *Public Advertiser,* August 23, 1769.

Chapter 6

87   **thirty-two pounders:** Robert Bell Wheler, *History and Antiquities of Stratford-upon-Avon* (London, [1806?]), 168.

88   **"The Britannic artist":** Philip H. Highfill, Kalman A. Burnim, and Edward A. Langhans, eds., *A Biographical Dictionary of Actors, Actresses, Musicians, Dancers, Managers and Other Stage Personnel in London, 1660–1800* (Carbondale: Southern Illinois University Press, 1973), 3:338–41.

89   **the drunken African servant Mungo:** See Julie A. Carlson, "New Lows in Eighteenth-Century Theater: The Rise of Mungo," *European Romantic Review* 18, no. 2 (2007): 139–47.

89   **around £1500 each:** Charles Dibdin, *The Professional Life of Mr. Dibdin* (London, 1803), 1:71.

89   **"The circumstance followed me":** Ibid., 1:72.

89   **"pecuniary obligations":** Ibid., 1:78.

89 **"The ostensible motive"**: Ibid., 1:74.

90 **"and to the astonishment of GARRICK"**: Ibid., 1:80.

91 **"Let Beauty with the sun arise"**: David Garrick, "The Morning Address to the Ladies," in *Shakespeare's Garland, Being a Collection of New Songs, Ballads, Roundelays, Catches, Glees, Comic-Serenatas, etc., Performed at the Jubilee at Stratford upon Avon* (London, 1769), 1.

91 **"I knew what credit to give"**: Dibdin, *Professional Life*, 1:81.

91 **Duchess of Devonshire**: See *St. James Chronicle*, September 9, 1769.

91 **"Ye *Warwickshire* lads"**: David Garrick, "Warwickshire: A Song," in *Shakespeare's Garland*, 2–4.

94 **"an instrument of Nature"**: Alexander Pope, "The Preface of the Editor," in William Shakespeare, *The Works of Shakespear in Six Volumes, Collated and Corrected by the Former Editions, By Mr. Pope*, ed. Alexander Pope, (London, 1725), 1:ii.

94 **They beat a reveille**: *Public Advertiser,* September 2, 1769.

94 **"you, who have done the memory"**: Wheler, *History and Antiquities*, 170–71.

96 **the cannon fired**: Ibid., 171.

96 **"When Learning's Triumph o'er her barb'rous Foes"**: Samuel Johnson, *Prologue and Epilogue, Spoken at the Opening of the Theatre in Drury-Lane 1747* (London, 1747), 2–3.

97 **"the whimsical advertisement"**: James Boswell, *Life of Johnson* (Oxford: Oxford World's Classics, 2008), 402.

97 **Shrewsbury races**: David Garrick, *The Letters of David Garrick*, ed. David M. Little and George M. Kahrl (London: Oxford University Press, 1963), 3:1355.

97 **"all the inns and roads"**: British Library Jubilee Scrapbook, General Reference Collection, C.61.e.2, p. 37, British Library.

98 **"Shakespeare's Road"**: *Public Advertiser,* August 18, 1769.

98 **no room for mooring**: Christian Deelman, *The Great Shakespeare Jubilee* (New York: Viking, 1964), 170.

99 **"no more shall be taken"**: Garrick, *Letters*, 3:1353.

99 **"An innkeeper . . . was kind enough"**: R. B. Wheler, Jubilee Album, ER1/14, p. 61, Shakespeare Birthplace Trust.

100 **"Neglected by the waiters"**: *Whitehall Evening Post*, September 7–9, 1769.

100 **"for parlour, for kitchen, for hall"**: *London Evening Post,* September 16, 1769.

100 **"the then appearance of the company"**: British Library Jubilee Scrapbook, p. 13, verso.

100 **"the Ruins of St. Giles"**: *Whitehall Evening Post*, September 7–9, 1769.

101 **"Smart beaux"**: Francis Gentleman, *Scrub's Trip to the Jubilee: A New Comedy of Two Acts* (London, 1769), 5.

101 **"a new Species of Bacchanalian Revelling"**: Anon., *Garrick's Vagary:*

Or, England Run Mad. With Particulars of the Stratford Jubilee (London, 1769), 7.

101   **"a plot of the Jews and Papishes"**: David Garrick, *The Jubilee*, in *The Plays of David Garrick: A Complete Collection of the Social Satires, French Adaptations, Pantomimes, Christmas and Musical Plays, Preludes, Interludes, and Burlesques*, ed. Harry William Pedicord and Fredrick Louis Bergmann (Carbondale: Southern Illinois University Press, 1980), 2:104.

101   **The bill had been so unpopular**: See Paul Langford, *A Polite and Commercial People: England, 1727–1783* (Oxford: Clarendon, 1989), 224–25.

102   **"the resurrection of Shakespeare"**: *The Gentleman's Magazine*, 1769, 422.

103   **"Why to drive all us poor folks"**: Garrick, *The Jubilee*, 2:104.

103   **"the enormous increase of Papists and Popery"**: *Gazetteer and New Daily Advertiser*, September, 28, 1769.

Chapter 7

104   **"its name was Boswell"**: Quoted in Frederick A. Pottle, *James Boswell: The Earlier Years, 1740–1769* (New York: McGraw-Hill, 1985), 121.

105   **"you labored hard . . . before fair lady"**: James Boswell, *Boswell in Holland, 1763–1764*, ed. Frederick A. Pottle (New York: McGraw-Hill, 1952), 39, 32, 38, 44.

105   **the best kinds of breeches**: Ibid., 59.

105   **"too foolishly and too freely"**: Ibid., 56.

105   **"to be read over frequently"**: Ibid., 387.

105   **"Your great loss is too much"**: Ibid., 389.

106   **"O great philosopher"**: James Boswell, *Boswell on the Grand Tour: Germany and Switzerland, 1764*, ed. Frederick A. Pottle (New York: McGraw-Hill, 1953), 251.

106   **"Your great difficulty"**: Ibid., 252–53.

107   **"gently along her yellow locks"**: James Boswell, *Boswell in Search of a Wife: 1766–1769*, ed. Frank Brady and Frederick A. Pottle (New York: McGraw-Hill, 1956), 276.

107   **"Such crowds had passed"**: Ibid., 279.

108   **"partly by threatenings"**: Ibid., 280.

108   **"a tolerable old-fashioned room"**: Ibid.

108   **"a clergyman in disguise"**: Ibid.

109   **"drawing from its sheath"**: Isaac Bickerstaff, *Judith, A Sacred Drama: As Performed in the Church of Stratford upon Avon, on occasion of the Jubilee Held There, September 6, 1769, in Honour of the Memory of Shakespeare* (London, 1769).

109   **with whom Garrick had a difficult relationship**: David Garrick, *The Letters of David Garrick*, ed. David M. Little and George M. Kahrl (London: Oxford University Press, 1963), 1:369.

110   **"so young and so blooming"**: Ibid., 1:361.

110 **"some parts of it were exceedingly fine"**: John Wesley, *The Journal of the Rev. John Wesley* (London, 1827), 3:155.

110 **"The choruses were almost as meagre"**: Joseph Cradock, *Literary and Miscellaneous Memoirs* (London, 1828), 216.

110 **"that prayers had not been read"**: *Public Advertiser*, September 16, 1769.

111 **Garrick led the guests out through**: Robert Bell Wheler, *History and Antiquities of Stratford-upon-Avon* (London, [1806?]), 172.

111 **"From whom all care, and sorrow fly"**: David Garrick, "Chorus from the Church," in *Shakespeare's Garland, Being a Collection of New Songs, Ballads, Roundelays, Catches, Glees, Comic-Serenatas, etc., Performed at the Jubilee at Stratford upon Avon* (London, 1769), 14.

111 **"the Joy and the Satisfaction"**: *Public Advertiser*, September 16, 1769.

112 **Garrick's rotunda was only twenty feet**: Wheler, *History and Antiquities*, 167n.

112 **"It would make a lover"**: Ibid., 168.

113 **Mrs. Love was at least twenty years**: Pottle, *Boswell: The Earlier Years*, 77.

113 **"a most agreeable little woman"**: Boswell, *Boswell in Search of a Wife*, 281.

113 **"Wenches!"**: British Library Jubilee Scrapbook, General Reference Collection, C.61.e.2, p. 37, British Library.

114 **"all ye Beauties at ye Jubilee"**: Garrick, *Letters*, 3:658.

114 **"last Night, the fat Landlady"**: *Public Advertiser*, September 2, 1769.

114 **"very good young Lady"**: Richard Peters to William Hunt, September 3, 1769, Jubilee Correspondence, Saunders Papers, ER1/83/1, Shakespeare Birthplace Trust.

114 **"Miss Tripsy expecting that Stratford will prove"**: Francis Gentleman, *Scrub's Trip to the Jubilee: A New Comedy of Two Acts* (London, 1769), 6.

115 **"one admired her person"**: Joseph Haslewood, *The Secret History of the Green Room* (London, 1795), 1:205.

115 **"Yet of such gifts"**: Hugh Kelly, *Thespis: Or, a Critical Examination into the Merits of all the Principal Performers Belonging to Drury-Lane Theatre* (London, 1766), 32.

116 **"committed an act that deterred her"**: Elizabeth Steele, *The Memoirs of Mrs. Sophia Baddeley, Late of Drury Lane Theatre* (London, 1787), 1:10.

117 **"GARRICK the body"**: Anon, *Anti-Thespis: or, A Vindication of the Principal Performers at Drury-Lane Theatre* (London, 1767), 4.

118 **"Behold this fair goblet"**: Garrick, *Shakespeare's Garland*, 7.

118 **"a good person, moderate beauty"**: Horace Walpole, *Memoirs of the Reign of King George the Third*, 4 vols. (London, 1845), 4:164.

119 **"steadfastly at that beautiful, insinuating creature"**: Boswell, *Boswell in Search of a Wife*, 281.

119 **"What I feared was love"**: Ibid.

120 **"I recollected my former inconstancy"**: Ibid., 281–82.

120 **"Already in climbing trees"**: Quoted in Pottle, *Boswell: The Earlier Years*, 30.

121 **"In my mind, there cannot be higher felicity"**: James Boswell, *Boswell's*

London Journal: 1762–1763, ed. Frederick A. Pottle (New York: McGraw-Hill, 1950), 84.

121 **"humane, polite, generous"**: Boswell, *Boswell in Search of a Wife*, 121.

121 **"curious young pretty"**: Pottle, *Boswell: The Earlier Years*, 76.

121 **"rogered Φ forenoon, and P afternoon"**: Ibid., 85.

121 **died at the age of fifteen months**: James Boswell, *The Correspondence of James Boswell and John Johnston of Grange*, ed. Ralph S. Walker (New York: McGraw-Hill, 1966), 103.

122 **"This is a damned difficult case"**: Boswell, *London Journal*, 178.

122 **infection free for the next three years**: See James Boswell, *The Correspondence of James Boswell and William Johnson Temple, 1756–1795*, ed. Thomas Crawford (Edinburgh/New Haven: Edinburgh University Press/Yale University Press, 1997), 168.

122 **"from the splendid Madam"**: Boswell, *London Journal*, 84.

122 **sex with Nanny Baker**: Ibid., 236–37.

122 **"a little girl into a court"**: Ibid., 240–41.

122 **"a little heat in the members"**: Ibid., 149.

122 **"gleet"**: Ibid., 178.

122 **"Thus ended my intrigue"**: Ibid., 161.

123 **he lost the wager**: Boswell, *Correspondence of Boswell and Temple*, 168.

123 **The book was not sufficient**: Boswell, *London Journal*, 165.

123 **"implements of safety"**: Dan Cruickshank, *The Secret History of London: How the Wages of Sin Shaped the Capital* (London: Random House, 2009), 212.

123 **"a fresh, agreeable young girl"**: Boswell, *London Journal*, 262.

123 **"Since my being honored"**: Ibid., 305 and 305n3.

124 **"I should like to have thirty women"**: Boswell, *Grand Tour: Germany and Switzerland*, 253–54.

124 **"If you want to be a wolf"**: Ibid., 253.

124 **"a hardy and vigorous lover"**: Ibid., 278.

124 **"like a bad rider galloping downhill"**: Ibid.

Chapter 8

125 **"testifying their reverence for the great Father"**: British Library Jubilee Scrapbook, General Reference Collection, C.61.e.2, p.13, recto, British Library.

126 **"a fungus attached to an oak"**: William Kenrick, *A Review of Doctor Johnson's New Edition of Shakespeare, in Which the Ignorance, or Inattention of That Editor is Exposed* (London, 1765), v.

126 **lodged at the Bear Inn**: See Christian Deelman, *The Great Shakespeare Jubilee* (New York: Viking, 1964), 178–79.

126 **"The whole art of acting"**: James Thomas Kirkman, *Memoirs of the Life of Charles Macklin, Esq, Compiled from his Own Papers and Memorandums* (London, 1799), 1:248–49.

126 **Garrick had conspired to have him fired:** Joseph Haslewood, *The Secret History of the Green Room* (London, 1795), 1:62.

126 **"intractable, unreasonable Obstinacy":** Charles Macklin, *Mr. Macklin's Reply to Mr. Garrick's Answer: To which are Prefix'd, All the Papers, Which Have Publickly Appeared, in Regard to this Important Dispute* (London, 1743), 12.

126 **"banditti":** Haslewood, *Secret History*, 1:64.

126 **"bitterest enemy":** William Cooke, *Memoirs of Charles Macklin, Comedian, With the Dramatic Characters, Manners, Anecdotes etc. of the Age in Which He Lived*, 2nd ed. (London, 1806), 97.

127 **"extraordinary powers of entertainment":** Samuel Johnson and James Boswell, *A Journey to the Western Islands of Scotland* and *The Journal of a Tour of the Hebrides*, ed. Peter Levi (London: Penguin, 1984), 403.

127 **employing life-size puppets:** Arthur H. Scouten, *The London Stage, 1729–1947: A Critical Introduction* (Carbondale: Southern Illinois University Press/Ferrer and Simons, 1968), lvii–lix.

127 **amputated above the knee:** See Ian Kelly, *Mr. Foote's Other Leg: Comedy, Tragedy and Murder in Georgian London* (London: Picador, 2012), 222–33.

128 **"It has cost me above fourteen pounds":** *Whitehall Evening Post*, September 7–9, 1769.

129 **"for nothing more than having it":** British Library Jubilee Scrapbook, p. 24.

129 **"I'll give you a crown":** British Library Jubilee Scrapbook, p. 13.

129 **"Long life to your honour":** *Whitehall Evening Post*, September 7–9, 1769.

129 **"instance of conscience":** British Library Jubilee Scrapbook, p. 24, verso.

130 **"of Stand-dishes, Tea-chests":** Benjamin Victor, *The History of the Theatres of London from the Year 1760 to the Present Times* (London, 1771), 203.

131 **"ten or a dozen skulls, at least":** Henry Angelo, *The Reminiscences of Henry Angelo* (New York: Benjamin Blom, 1969), 1:34. So profitable and well stocked was the mulberry market that any relic eventually became suspicious, to the extent that Thomas Sharp had to defend the integrity of his business on his deathbed, signing an affidavit attesting to the authenticity of his mulberry products in 1799. See Deelman, *Great Shakespeare Jubilee*, 52.

132 **"Had the keepers of my dungeon":** John Solas Dodd, *Essays and Poems, Satirical, Moral, Political, and Entertaining* (Cork, 1770), 255.

132 **"a very summary Account":** *Public Advertiser*, July 12, 1769.

133 **"the withered Mulberry began to move":** Ibid., July 7, 1769.

134 **"among mice-gnawn records":** Dodd, *Essays and Poems*, 252.

134 **a religious jubilee for all Catholics:** See Anon., *Instructions for Gaining the Jubilee Granted by His Holiness Pope Clement XIV. Soon after his election, which was on the 4th of June, 1769* (Dublin, 1770).

134 **"Saint Mulberry's Priest":** Anon., *An Essay on the Jubilee at Stratford-Upon-Avon* (London, [1769]), 8.

135 **"the low Circumstances of *Shakespeare*":** Victor, *History of the Theatres*, 207.

136 **"could not part with them":** Quoted in Melanie Doderer-Winkler, *Mag-*

nificent Entertainments: Temporary Architecture for Georgian Festivals (New Haven: Yale University Press, 2013), 33.

136 **"It was fairyland":** Charles Dibdin, *The Professional Life of Mr. Dibdin* (London, 1803), 1:76–77.

136 **"All is Joy and Festivity here":** *St. James Chronicle*, September 5–7, 1769.

137 **"Notwithstanding the prodigious benefit":** British Library Jubilee Scrapbook, p. 24, recto.

137 **"I told her that perhaps":** James Boswell, *Boswell in Search of a Wife, 1766– 1769*, ed. Frank Brady and Frederick A. Pottle (New York: McGraw-Hill, 1956), 282.

Chapter 9

138 **"What an absurd climate!":** Henry Angelo, *The Reminiscences of Henry Angelo* (New York: Benjamin Blom, 1969), 1:36.

138 **"a super-abundance of water":** Ibid., 1:48.

138 **"the greatest Plenty of Apples":** *St. James Chronicle*, June 1, 1769.

139 **"'tis God's revenge against Vanity!":** Antijubileana, Saunders Papers (1769), ER1/83/4, n.p., Shakespeare Birthplace Trust.

139 **"some capital part of it in Action":** David Garrick, *The Jubilee*, in *The Plays of David Garrick: A Complete Collection of the Social Satires, French Adaptations, Pantomines, Christmas and Music Plays, Preludes, Interludes, and Burlesques*, ed. Harry William Pedicord and Fredrick Louis Bergmann (Carbondale: Southern Illinois University Press, 1980), 2:116n.

140 **Fluellen forcing Pistol to eat a leek:** Ibid., 2:119n63.

140 **"who the devil, Davy":** Angelo, *Reminiscences*, 1:48.

140 **"the deepest of all politicians":** David Garrick, *The Letters of David Garrick*, ed. David M. Little and George M. Kahrl (London: Oxford University Press, 1963), 1:172, 146.

140 **"There is a rank viciousness":** Ibid., 2:427, 618, 622. Garrick also forwent his own benefit nights, the end-of-season evenings where established members of the company would pocket the entirety of the takings on the door.

141 **"I am quite Sick of his Conduct":** Ibid., 1:189.

141 **"never forgive my being the means":** Ibid., 2:449.

142 **"from the corner of his mouth":** Joseph Cradock, *Literary and Miscellaneous Memoirs* (London, 1828), 1:217.

142 **"remains of our famous relation":** Garrick, *Letters*, 1:353.

143 **"confused or intimidated":** *Warwickshire Journal*, September 14, 1769.

144 **"Pious ears were offended":** *Lloyd's Evening Post*, September 15–18, 1769.

145 **"the dullest part of Musick":** Garrick, *Letters*, 2:653.

145 **"had so great Effect":** Benjamin Victor, *The History of the Theatres of London from the Year 1760 to the Present Times* (London, 1771), 216.

145 **"His eyes sparkled":** [James Boswell], *The London Magazine*, September 1769, 452.

145 **"Powers and Tone of Voice":** *Warwickshire Journal*, September 14, 1769.

147 **"Such is ye Power of Shakespeare":** Garrick, *Letters*, 2:671.

149 **"deserved the thunder of applause":** *Lloyd's Evening Post*, September 15–18, 1769.

149 **"for which after the Performance":** Garrick, *Letters*, 2:651.

150 **"Mr. Garrick that he had affected":** *Public Advertiser*, September 16, 1769.

150 **"When I saw the Statue of *Shakespeare*":** *Lloyd's Evening Post*, September 15–18, 1769.

150 **"The whole audience were fixed":** [James Boswell], *Public Advertiser*, September 16, 1769.

151 **distill the substance of Shakespeare:** See Vanessa Cunningham, *Shakespeare and Garrick* (Cambridge: Cambridge University Press, 2008), 107–9.

152 **"I must say that his ode":** [Boswell], *Public Advertiser*, September 16, 1769.

152 **"What the critics may say":** Ibid.

152 **"the Ode in itself will not bear reading":** *Warwickshire Journal*, September 14, 1769.

152 **"I have blushed":** Horace Walpole, *The Letters of Horace Walpole, Fourth Earl of Oxford*, ed. Paget Toynbee (Oxford: Clarendon, 1904), 7:325.

153 **"foolish business against a very foolish man":** Garrick, *Letters*, 2:673.

153 **"My indignation is at length":** Anon., *Anti-Midas: A Jubilee Preservative From Unclassical, Ignorant, False and Invidious Criticism* (London, 1769), 33.

153 **"superior to Criticism":** *Lloyd's Evening Post*, September 15–18, 1769.

153 **"not only without sense or poetry":** *The London Museum*, 1770, 48.

153 **"I would not pay them so ill":** Quoted in Victor, *History of the Theatres*, 219.

154 **"*for* or *against* Shakespeare":** Ibid., 219–20.

154 **"to be moved at nothing":** Ibid., 221.

155 **"a Trap laid on Purpose":** [Boswell], *Public Advertiser*, September 16, 1769.

155 **"I could wish that that part":** *Lloyd's Evening Post*, September 15–18, 1769.

155 **"If GARRICK felt all this extacy":** Charles Dibdin, *The Professional Life of Mr. Dibdin* (London, 1803), 1:77.

Chapter 10

156 **"an entertainment at least as good":** James Boaden, ed., *The Private Correspondence of David Garrick* (London, 1831), 1:332.

156 **Three separate dishes could be made:** "This is the most proper method of dressing this fish in any part of the Indies, or in England, approved by the best and most experienced cooks who undertake to dress them." Anon., *The British Jewel; or Complete Housewife's Best Companion* (London, [1785?]), 116–17.

157 **"to gratify ostentatious pride":** *Lloyd's Evening Post*, September 15–18, 1769.

157 **"a war-like appearance":** *The London Magazine*, September 1769, 455.

158 **"When I looked at myself":** James Boswell, *Boswell in Search of a Wife: 1766–1769*, ed. Frank Brady and Frederick A. Pottle (New York: McGraw-Hill, 1956), 278.

159 **"The rockets would not ascend"**: Henry Angelo, *The Reminiscences of Henry Angelo* (New York: Benjamin Blom, 1969), 1:37.

160 **"The astonishing contrast"**: British Library Jubilee Scrapbook, General Reference Collection, C.61.e.2, p. 24, British Library.

160 **"anti-patriotic Coterie"**: *Lloyd's Evening Post*, May 18–21, 1770.

161 **"Dresses of the meanest sort"**: British Library Jubilee Scrapbook, p. 24, recto.

161 **"An ear of wheat"**: *The Gentleman's Magazine*, September 1769, 423.

161 **One man from London**: John Solas Dodd, *Essays and Poems, Satirical, Moral, Political, and Entertaining* (Cork, 1770), 276.

161 **"So completely was the *'wet blanket'* spread"**: Angelo, *Reminiscences*, 1:37.

161 **"many of the *Belle Espirits* were present"**: R. B. Wheler, *Jubilee Album*, Shakespeare Birthplace Trust, ER1/14, p. 102 recto.

162 **"why do you not come and sweep my chimney"**: Ibid.

162 **"that the enemies to tyranny"**: Dodd, *Essays and Poems*, 275.

162 **"one of the most remarkable masks"**: [James Boswell], *The London Magazine*, September 1769, 455.

162 **"not one thing appeared as it really was"**: Dodd, *Essays and Poems*, 276.

164 **"Let me plead for *Liberty* distrest"**: *The London Magazine*, September 1769, 455.

165 **"No delay could be admitted"**: Joseph Cradock, *Literary and Miscellaneous Memoirs* (London, 1828), 1:218.

165 **"a very deep mirey Dyke"**: Quoted in Christian Deelman, *The Great Shakespeare Jubilee* (New York: Viking, 1964), 252.

165 **"We did not get home"**: Boswell, *Boswell in Search of a Wife*, 283.

166 **"I pleased myself with a variety"**: Ibid.

166 **"I don't know how many times over"**: Ibid.

166 **"We were like a crowd in a theatre"**: [James Boswell], *St. James Chronicle*, September 9–12, 1769.

166 **"It is fine to have such a character"**: Boswell, *Boswell in Search of a Wife*, 284.

167 **"Come, come, that won't do"**: Ibid.

167 **"the principal Part of the Company"**: *St. James Chronicle*, September 9–12, 1769.

168 **"he knew very little about *Plays*"**: Quoted in Deelman, *Great Shakespeare Jubilee*, 256.

168 **"Taking the whole of this jubilee"**: *The London Magazine*, September 1769, 454.

Chapter 11

169 **"It appears remarkably well defined"**: *Gazetteer and New Daily Advertiser*, September 12, 1769.

169 **"swiftness of a cannon ball"**: *London Chronicle*, September 19–21, 1769.

169 **"That you may not think I complain without reason"**: *Town and Country Magazine*, September 1769, 477.

170 **"Tell 'em you have been at the Jubilee":** *Lloyd's Evening Post*, September 11–13, 1769.

170 **"even in these times of *distress*":** British Library Jubilee Scrapbook, General Reference Collection, C.61.e.2, p. 24, British Library.

171 **The *Dedication Ode* was reprinted:** Vanessa Cunningham, *Shakespeare and Garrick* (Cambridge: Cambridge University Press, 2008), 195n16.

171 **The supporters of John Wilkes:** Anon., *The Patriot's Jubilee, Being Songs Proper to be Sung on Wednesday, the 18th of April, 1770* (n.p., 1770).

171 **"we should have returned to town":** Quoted in George Winchester Stone Jr. and George M. Kahrl, *David Garrick: A Critical Biography* (Carbondale: Southern Illinois University Press/Feffer and Simons, 1979), 583.

171 **"served as a veil to cover":** Charles Dibdin, *The Professional Life of Mr. Dibdin* (London, 1803), 1:74.

171 **"our most sincere and grateful Thanks":** ALS, William Hunt to David Garrick, September 26, 1769, Jubilee Correspondence, Saunders Papers, ER1/83/1, Shakespeare Birthplace Trust.

172 **"Let 'em decorate ye Town":** David Garrick to William Hunt, Friday [?] 8, 1769, Jubilee Correspondence, Saunders Papers, ER1/83/1, Shakespeare Birthplace Trust.

173 **"A jubilee is a public invitation":** *Town and Country Magazine*, September 1769, 477.

173 **"cock a doodle doo":** William Cooke, *Memoirs of Samuel Foote, Esq, with a Collection of His Bon-Mots, Anecdotes, Opinions, Etc., Mostly Original, and Three of His Dramatic Pieces Not Published in His Works* (London, 1805), 1:166.

173 **dreadful retaliations:** Ibid., 1:169.

173 **"Oh no—not much above the size of Garrick":** Ibid., 2:58.

174 **"as much applause as his heart could desire":** David Garrick, *The Letters of David Garrick*, ed. David M. Little and George M. Kahrl (London: Oxford University Press, 1963), 2:666; see also Philip H. Highfill, Kalman A. Burnim, and Edward A. Langhans, eds., *A Biographical Dictionary of Actors, Actresses, Musicians, Dancers, Managers and Other Stage Personnel in London, 1660–1800* (Carbondale: Southern Illinois University Press, 1973), pt. 4, 3:1425.

175 **"an absolute dead march":** *Town and Country Magazine*, October 1769, 547.

176 **"the most Superb" performance:** Quoted in Ian McIntyre, *Garrick* (Harmondsworth, Eng.: Penguin, 1999), 439.

176 **"This was a real *apotheosis*":** Johann Wilhelm von Archenholz, *A Picture of England: Containing a Description of the Laws, Customs and Manners of England* (Dublin, 1791), 238.

177 **"the real royalty":** James Boswell, "On the Profession of a Player," essay I, *The London Magazine*, August 1770, 397.

177 **"enlightened and philosophical spectators":** Ibid.

177 **"A large part of the audience":** Quoted in Joseph Roach, "Celebrity Culture and the Problem of Biography," *Shakespeare Quarterly* 65, no. 4 (Winter 2014): 471–72.

177 **"Sacred to Shakespeare was this spot":** Quoted in Cunningham, *Shakespeare and Garrick*, 5.

178 **"objects of meditation":** Charles Lamb, "On the Tragedies of Shakespeare, Considered with Reference to Their Fitness for Stage Representation," in *English Critical Essays: Nineteenth Century*, ed. Edmund D. Jones (London: Oxford University Press, 1921), 2:109.

179 **three new magazines had opened:** John Money, *Experience and Identity: Birmingham and the West Midlands, 1760–1800* (Manchester: Manchester University Press, 1977), 123.

180 **"it has been carefully handed down":** See Nicola J. Watson, *The Literary Tourist* (Basingstoke, Eng.: Palgrave, 2006), 62.

Epilogue

181 **"It is no wonder that he should endeavour":** Anon., *Anti-Midas: A Jubilee Preservative From Unclassical, Ignorant, False, and Invidious Criticism* (London, 1769), 24.

181 **"Walls, Windows and Deficiencies":** Rev. John Fullerton to William Hunt, November 10, 1769, Jubilee Correspondence, Saunders Papers, ER1/83/1, Shakespeare Birthplace Trust.

182 **"I am sorry that my Brother":** David Garrick, *The Letters of David Garrick*, ed. David M. Little and George M. Kahrl (London: Oxford University Press, 1963), 2:667.

182 **"I shou'd be sorry to hurry":** ALS, William Hunt to Garrick, November 8, 1770, Jubilee Correspondence, Saunders Papers, ER1/83/1, Shakespeare Birthplace Trust.

182 **"these words from you have hurt me":** Garrick, *Letters*, 2:721–22.

183 **"Mr G Garrick's Hints":** ALS, William Hunt to David Garrick, November 21, 1770, Jubilee Correspondence, Saunders Papers, ER1/83/1, Shakespeare Birthplace Trust.

186 **"Not at all. DAVID wanted him":** Charles Dibdin, *The Professional Life of Mr. Dibdin* (London, 1803), 1:98n.

187 **"I now kiss the invaluable relics":** William Henry Ireland, *Confessions* (London, 1805), 96.

Bibliography

Manuscript Sources

An Account of the Jubilee Celebrated at Stratford-upon-Avon in Honour of Shakspeare, 1769 . . . Collected and Arranged from Different Authorities. Saunders Papers, ER1/82. Shakespeare Birthplace Trust, Stratford-upon-Avon.

Antijubileana. Saunders Papers, ER1/83/4. Shakespeare Birthplace Trust, Stratford-upon-Avon.

Articles for Erecting Stratford Town Hall, 1767. BRU 21/10, Shakespeare Birthplace Trust, Stratford-upon-Avon.

Borough of Stratford, The New Town Hall. ER1/37. Shakespeare Birthplace Trust, Stratford-upon-Avon.

British Library Jubilee Scrapbook. General Reference Collection, C.61.e.2, British Library, London.

Jubilee Correspondence. Saunders Papers, ER1/83/1, Shakespeare Birthplace Trust, Stratford-upon-Avon.

R. B. Wheler, Jubilee Album. ER1/14. Shakespeare Birthplace Trust, Stratford-upon-Avon.

R. B. Wheler, History and Antiquities of Stratford upon Avon (Extra Illustrated). ER1/27. Shakespeare Birthplace Trust, Stratford-upon-Avon.

Periodicals

The Annual Register, or View of the History, Politics, and Literature for the Year 1761
Gazetteer and New Daily Advertiser
The Gentleman's Magazine
Lloyd's Evening Post
London Evening Post
The London Magazine; or, Gentleman's Monthly Intelligencer
The London Museum
Public Advertiser
The Rambler
St. James Chronicle, or the British Evening Post

Theatrical Monitor or Stage Management and Green Room Laid Open
Warwickshire Journal
Whitehall Evening Post or London Intelligencer

Printed Sources

Alladyce, Alexander, ed. *Scotland and Scotsmen in the Eighteenth Century.* 2 vols. Edinburgh: William Blackwood, 1888.

Angelo, Henry. *The Reminiscences of Henry Angelo.* 2 vols. New York: Benjamin Blom, 1969.

Anon. *Anti-Midas: A Jubilee Preservative From Unclassical, Ignorant, False, and Invidious Criticism.* London, 1769.

———. *Anti-Thespis: or, A Vindication of the Principal Performers at Drury-Lane Theatre.* London, 1767.

———. *Authentic Memoirs of the Right Honourable the Late Earl of Chatham.* London, 1778.

———. *The British Jewel; or Complete Housewife's Best Companion.* London, [1785?].

———. *An Essay on the Jubilee at Stratford-upon-Avon.* London, [1769].

———. *Garrick's Vagary: Or, England Run Mad. With Particulars of the Stratford Jubilee.* London, 1769.

———. *An Historical and Succinct Account of the Late Riots at the Theatres of Drury Lane and Covent Garden.* London, 1763.

———. *Instructions for Gaining the Jubilee Granted by His Holiness Pope Clement XIV. Soon after his election, which was on the 4th of June, 1769.* Dublin, 1770.

———. "Letter from the Place of Shakespeare's Nativity," in *The British Magazine; or, Monthly Repository for Gentlemen and Ladies* (1762): 301–2.

———. *The Life of James Quin, Comedian, With the History of the Stage From His Commencing Actor to His Retreat to Bath.* London, 1887.

———. *Memoirs of the Bedford Coffee-House. By a Genius.* London 1763.

———. *Observations on the Importance and Use of Theatres; Their Present Regulation and Possible Improvements.* London, 1759.

———. *The Patriot's Jubilee, Being Songs Proper to be Sung on Wednesday, the 18th of April, 1770.* N.p., 1770.

———. *Theatrical Biography: or, Memoirs of the Principal Performers of the Three Theatres.* 2 vols. Dublin, 1772.

———. *The Usefulness of the Stage to Religion, and to Government: Shewing the Advantage of the Drama in all Nations Since Its First Institution.* London, 1738.

Archenholz, Johann Wilhelm von. *A Picture of England: Containing a Description of the Laws, Customs, and Manners of England.* Dublin, 1791.

Avery, Emmett L. *The London Stage 1700–1729: A Critical Introduction.* Carbondale: Southern Illinois University Press, 1968.

Bickerstaff, Isaac. *Judith, A Sacred Drama: As Performed in the Church of Stratford upon Avon, on Occasion of the Jubilee Held There, September 6, 1769, in Honour of the Memory of Shakespeare.* London, 1769.

Boaden, James, ed. *The Private Correspondence of David Garrick.* 2 vols. London, 1831.

Boaden, James. *The Memoirs of Mrs. Siddons, Interspersed with Anecdotes of Authors and Actors.* Philadelphia, 1837.

Boswell, James. *Boswell for the Defence, 1769–1774.* Edited by William K. Wimsatt Jr. and Frederick A. Pottle. New York: McGraw-Hill, 1959.

———. *Boswell in Holland, 1763–1764.* Edited by Frederick A. Pottle. New York: McGraw-Hill, 1952.

———. *Boswell in Search of a Wife: 1766–1769.* Edited by Frank Brady and Frederick A. Pottle. New York: McGraw-Hill, 1956.

———. *Boswell's London Journal: 1762–1763.* Edited by Frederick A. Pottle. New York: McGraw-Hill, 1950.

———. *Boswell on the Grand Tour: Germany and Switzerland, 1764.* Edited by Frederick A. Pottle. New York: McGraw-Hill, 1953.

———. *Boswell on the Grand Tour: Italy, Corsica, and France, 1765–1766.* Edited by Frank Brady and Frederick A. Pottle. New York: McGraw-Hill, 1955.

———. *The Correspondence of James Boswell and John Johnston of Grange.* Edited by Ralph S. Walker. Vol. 1 of *The Yale Editions of the Private Papers of James Boswell, Research Edition, Correspondence.* New York: McGraw-Hill, 1966.

———. *The Correspondence of James Boswell and William Johnson Temple, 1756–1795.* Edited by Thomas Crawford. Edinburgh/New Haven: Edinburgh University Press/Yale University Press, 1997.

———. *The Correspondence of James Boswell with David Garrick, Edmund Burke, Edmond Malone.* Edited by George M. Kahrl, Rachel McClellan, Thomas W. Copeland, James M. Osborn, and Peter S. Baker. London: Heinemann, 1986.

———. *Facts and Inventions: Selections from the Journalism of James Boswell.* Edited by Paul Tankard. New Haven: Yale University Press, 2014.

———. *Life of Johnson.* Oxford: Oxford World's Classics, 2008.

———. *Ode to Tragedy, by a Gentleman of Scotland.* Edinburgh, 1761.

———. "On the Profession of a Player" (three essays). *The London Magazine,* August, September, and October 1770.

———. "Sketch of the Early Life of James Boswell, Written by Himself for Jean Jacques Rousseau, 5 December 1764." In *James Boswell: The Earlier Years, 1740–1769* Frederick A. Pottle, 1–6. New York: McGraw-Hill, 1966.

[Boswell, James]. *A View of the Edinburgh Theatre During the Summer Season, 1759.* London, 1760.

Brewer, John. *Party Ideology and Popular Politics at the Accession of George II.* Cambridge: Cambridge University Press, 1976.

Burke, Edmund. *Thoughts on the Cause of the Present Discontents.* London, 1770.

———, ed. *The Annual Register, or A View of the History, Politicks, and Literature, of the Year 1758.* London, 1759.

Burney, Frances. *Journals and Letters*. Edited by Peter Sabor and Lars E. Troide. Harmondsworth, Eng.: Penguin, 2001.

Burnim, Kalman A. *David Garrick, Director*. Pittsburgh: University of Pittsburgh Press, 1961.

Caines, Michael. *Shakespeare and the Eighteenth Century*. Oxford: Oxford University Press, 2013.

Camões, Luís de. *The Lusiad; or, the Discovery of India*. Translated by William Julius Mickle. London, 1776.

Candido, Joseph. "Prefatory Matter(s) in the Shakespeare Editions of Nicholas Rowe and Alexander Pope." *Studies in Philology* 97, no. 2 (2000): 210–28.

Carlson, Julie A. "New Lows in Eighteenth-Century Theater: The Rise of Mungo." *European Romantic Review* 18, no. 2 (2007): 139–47.

Casanova, Giacomo. *The Memoirs of Jacques Casanova de Seingalt, the Prince of Adventurers*. 2 vols. London: Chapman and Hall, 1902.

Cibber, Colley. *Plays written by Mr. Cibber. In two volumes. Containing, Love's Last Shift; or, The Fool in Fashion. The Tragical History of King Richard the Third. Love makes a Man; or, The Fop's Fortune. She would, and she would not; or, The Kind Impostor. The Careless Husband*. 2 vols. London, 1721.

Cibber, Theophilus. *Cibber's Two Dissertations on the Theatres, with an Appendix, in Three Parts*. London, [1757?].

———. *An Epistle from Mr. Theophilus Cibber, to David Garrick, Esq; To Which Are Prefixed, Some Occasional Verses, Petitions, &c*. London, 1755.

Cooke, William. *Memoirs of Charles Macklin, Comedian, With the Dramatic Characters, Manners, Anecdotes etc. of the Age in Which He Lived*. 2nd ed. London, 1806.

———. *Memoirs of Samuel Foote, Esq, with a Collection of His Bon-Mots, Anecdotes, Opinions, Etc., Mostly Original, and Three of His Dramatic Pieces Not Published in His Works*. 3 vols. London, 1805.

Cradock, Joseph. *Literary and Miscellaneous Memoirs*. 4 vols. London, 1828.

Cruickshank, Dan. *The Secret History of London: How the Wages of Sin Shaped the Capital*. London: Random House, 2009.

Cumberland, Richard. *Memoirs of Richard Cumberland, Written By Himself*. Edited by Henry Flanders. Philadelphia, 1856.

Cunningham, Vanessa. *Shakespeare and Garrick*. Cambridge: Cambridge University Press, 2008.

D'Avenant, Sir William. *Macbeth, a Tragedy: With all the Alterations, Amendments, Additions and New Songs*. London, 1674.

———. *A Proposition for Advancement of Moralities by a New Way of Entertainment of the People*. London, 1654.

———, and John Dryden. *The Tempest; or, The Enchanted Island, A Comedy*. London, 1670.

Davies, Thomas. *Memoirs of the Life of David Garrick*. 2 vols. London, 1784.

Deelman, Christian. *The Great Shakespeare Jubilee*. New York: Viking, 1964.

Dibdin, Charles. *The Professional Life of Mr. Dibdin*. 4. vols. London, 1803.

Dobson, Michael. *The Making of the National Poet: Shakespeare, Adaptation and Authorship, 1660–1769.* Oxford: Clarendon, 2001.

Dodd, John Solas. *Essays and Poems, Satirical, Moral, Political, and Entertaining.* Cork, 1770.

Doderer-Winkler, Melanie. *Magnificent Entertainments: Temporary Architecture for Georgian Festivals.* New Haven: Yale University Press, 2013.

Downes, John. *Roscius Anglicanus, or an Historical Review of the Stage.* London, 1708.

Dryden, Sir John. *The Comedies, Tragedies and Operas Written by John Dryden, Esq.* 2 vols. London, 1701.

Dugas, Don-John. *Marketing the Bard: Shakespeare in Performance and Print.* Columbia: University of Missouri Press, 2006.

England, Martha Winburn. *Garrick and Stratford.* New York: New York Public Library, 1962.

Fitzpatrick, Thaddeus. *A Dialogue in the Green-Room upon a Disturbance in the Pit.* London, 1763.

———. *An Enquiry into the Real Merit of a Certain Popular Performer.* London, 1760.

Fox, Levi. *The Borough Town of Stratford upon Avon.* Stratford: Corporation of Stratford upon Avon, 1953.

Franklin, Benjamin. *The Memoirs of Benjamin Franklin.* 2 vols. Philadelphia: McCarty and Davis, 1834.

Garrick, David. *The Dedication Ode.* London, 1769.

———. *An Essay on Acting.* London, 1744.

———. "Garrick's Epitaph Written by Himself in a Fit of Sickness at Munich in Bavaria," Folger Digital Image Collection, Y.d.120 (26).

———. *The Letters of David Garrick.* Edited by David M. Little and George M. Kahrl. 3 vols. London: Oxford University Press, 1963.

———. *The Plays of David Garrick: A Complete Collection of the Social Satires, French Adaptations, Pantomimes, Christmas and Musical Plays, Preludes, Interludes, and Burlesques.* Edited by Harry William Pedicord and Fredrick Louis Bergmann. 7 vols. Carbondale: Southern Illinois University Press, 1980.

———. *Shakespeare's Garland, Being a Collection of New Songs, Ballads, Roundelays, Catches, Glees, Comic-Serenatas, etc., Performed at the Jubilee at Stratford upon Avon.* London, 1769.

Gentleman, Francis. *Scrub's Trip to the Jubilee: A New Comedy of Two Acts.* London, 1769.

Goldsmith, Oliver. *An Enquiry into the Present State of Polite Learning in Europe.* London, 1759.

Gorse, Francis. *A Provincial Glossary, with a Collection of Local Proverbs, and Popular Superstitions.* London, 1787.

Grafton, Augustus Henry Fitzroy, Duke of, *Letters Between the Duke of Grafton and John Wilkes, esq.* 2 vols. London, 1769.

Granger, James. *A Biographical History of England, from Egbert the Great to the Revolution.* 4 vols. London, 1769.

Grieg, Hannah. *The Beau Monde: Fashionable Society in Georgian London.* Oxford: Oxford University Press, 2013.

Haslewood, Joseph. *The Secret History of the Green Room.* 2 vols. London, 1795.

Highfill, Philip H., Kalman A. Burnim, and Edward A. Langhans, eds. *A Biographical Dictionary of Actors, Actresses, Musicians, Dancers, Managers and Other Stage Personnel in London, 1660–1800.* 16 vols. Carbondale: Southern Illinois University Press, 1973.

Hughes, Thomas Smart. *The History of England from the Accession of George III to the Accession of Queen Victoria.* 7 vols. London, 1846.

Hume, Robert D. "Before the Bard: 'Shakespeare' in Early Eighteenth-Century London." *ELH* 64 no. 1 (1997): 41–75.

Hutton, William. *An History of Birmingham, to the End of the Year 1780.* Birmingham, 1781.

Ireland, William Henry. *Confessions.* London, 1805.

James, Ralph. *The Taste of the Town: Or, A Guide to All Publick Diversions.* London, 1731.

Jarvis, Simon. "Alexander Pope." In *Dryden, Pope, Johnson, Malone,* ed. Claude Rawson, 66–114. Vol. 1 of *Great Shakespeareans.* London: Continuum, 2010.

Johnson, Samuel. *Mr. Johnson's Preface to His Edition of Shakespear's Plays.* London, 1765.

——. *Prologue and Epilogue, Spoken at the Opening of the Theatre in Drury-Lane 1747.* London, 1747.

——, and James Boswell. *A Journey to the Western Islands of Scotland* and *The Journal of a Tour to the Hebrides.* Edited by Peter Levi. London: Penguin, 1984.

Keate, George. *Ferney: An Epistle to Monsr. De Voltaire.* London, 1768.

Kelly, Hugh. *Thespis: Or, A Critical Examination into the Merits of all the Principal Performers Belonging to Drury-Lane Theatre.* London, 1766.

Kelly, Ian. *Mr. Foote's Other Leg: Comedy, Tragedy and Murder in Georgian London.* London: Picador, 2012.

Kenrick, William. *A Review of Doctor Johnson's New Edition of Shakespeare, in Which the Ignorance, or Inattention of That Editor is Exposed.* London, 1765.

Kirkman, James Thomas. *Memoirs of the Life of Charles Macklin, Esq, Compiled from his Own Papers and Memorandums.* 2 vols. London, 1799.

Lamb, Charles. "On the Tragedies of Shakespeare, Considered with Reference to Their Fitness for Stage Representation." In *English Critical Essays: Nineteenth Century,* ed. Edmund D. Jones, 95–119 of vol. 2. London: Oxford University Press, 1921.

Langford, Paul. *A Polite and Commercial People: England, 1727–1783.* Oxford: Clarendon, 1989.

Macklin, Charles. *Mr. Macklin's Reply to Mr. Garrick's Answer: To which are*

Prefix'd, All the Papers, Which Have Publickly Appeared, in Regard to this Important Dispute. London, 1743.

Mason, Shena, ed. *Matthew Boulton: Selling What All the World Desires.* Birmingham: Birmingham City Council/Yale University Press, 2009.

McIntyre, Ian. *Garrick.* Harmondsworth, Eng.: Penguin, 1999.

Money, John. *Experience and Identity: Birmingham and the West Midlands, 1760–1800.* Manchester: Manchester University Press, 1977.

Murphy, Arthur. *The Life of David Garrick, Esq.* Dublin, 1801.

Northcote, James. *The Memoirs of Joshua Reynolds.* Philadelphia, 1817.

Pittard, Joseph. *Observations on Mr. Garrick's Acting; in a Letter to the Right Hon. the Earl of Chesterfield.* London, 1758.

Porter, Roy. *Enlightenment: Britain and the Creation of the Modern World.* London: Allen Lane, 2000.

Pottle, Frederick A. *James Boswell: The Earlier Years, 1740–1769.* New York: McGraw-Hill, 1966.

Powell, Jocelyn. "Dance and Drama in the Eighteenth Century: David Garrick and Jean Georges Noverre." *Word & Image* 4, no. 3–4 (1988): 678–91.

Read, Donald. *The English Provinces, c. 1760–1960.* New York: St. Martin's, 1964.

Roach, Joseph. "Celebrity Culture and the Problem of Biography." *Shakespeare Quarterly* 65, no. 4 (Winter 2014): 470–81.

Rolt, Richard. "Poetical Epistle from Shakespeare in Elysium, to Mr. Garrick, at Drury-Lane Theatre." London, 1752.

Ritchie, Fiona. "Shakespeare and the Eighteenth Century Actress." *Borrowers and Lenders: The Journal of Shakespeare Appropriation* 11, no. 2 (2006): 1–12.

———. *Women and Shakespeare in the Eighteenth Century.* Cambridge: Cambridge University Press, 2014.

Rudé, George. *Wilkes and Liberty: A Social Study of 1763–1774.* Oxford: Clarendon, 1963.

Russell, Gillian. "'Keeping Place': Servants, Theater and Sociability in Mid-Eighteenth Century Britain." *Eighteenth Century: Theory and Interpretation* 42, no. 1 (Spring 2001): 1–18.

———. *Women, Sociability and Theater in Georgian London.* Cambridge: Cambridge University Press, 2010.

Rymer, Thomas. *A Short View of Tragedy.* Menston, Eng.: Scolar Press, 1970.

Schoenbaum, Samuel. *Shakespeare's Lives.* New ed. Oxford: Clarendon, 1991.

Scouten, Arthur H. *The London Stage, 1729–1747: A Critical Introduction.* Carbondale: Southern Illinois University Press/Ferrer and Simons, 1968.

Shakespeare, William. *Romeo and Juliet. By Shakespear. With Alterations, and an Additional Scene: As It Is Performed at the Theatre-Royal in Drury-Lane.* London, 1752.

———. *The Works of Mr. William Shakespear; in Six Volumes.* Edited by Nicholas Rowe. 6 vols. London, 1709.

———. *The Works of Shakespeare: in Seven Volumes. Collated with the Oldest Copies, and Corrected; with Notes, Explanatory, and Critical: by Mr. Theobald.* Edited by Lewis Theobald. 7 vols. London, 1733.

———. *The Works of Shakespear in Six Volumes, Collated and Corrected by the Former Editions, By Mr. Pope.* Edited by Alexander Pope. 6 vols. London, 1725.

Shaughnessy, Robert. "Shakespeare and the London Stage." In *Shakespeare in the Eighteenth Century,* ed. Fiona Richie and Peter Sabor, 161–84. Cambridge: Cambridge University Press, 2012.

Smollet, Tobias. *The Expedition of Humphrey Clinker.* Edited by Lewis M. Knapp. Oxford: Oxford World's Classics, 1992.

Sorelius, Gunnar. "The Rights of the Restoration Theatrical Companies in the Older Drama." *Studie Neophilologica* 37 (1967): 174–89.

Steele, Elizabeth. *The Memoirs of Mrs. Sophia Baddeley, Late of Drury Lane Theatre.* 6 vols. London, 1787.

Stockdale, John Joseph, ed. *Covent Garden Journal.* London, 1810.

Stone, George Winchester, Jr. *The London Stage, 1747–1776: A Critical Introduction.* Carbondale: Southern Illinois University Press/Ferrer and Simons, 1968.

———, and George M. Kahrl. *David Garrick: A Critical Biography.* Carbondale: Southern Illinois University Press/Feffer and Simons, 1979.

Swindells, Julia. "The Political Context of the 1737 Licensing Act." In *The Oxford Handbook of Georgian Theatre,* ed. Julia Swindells and David Francis Taylor, 107–22. Oxford: Oxford University Press, 2014.

Tait, Hugh. "Garrick, Shakespeare and Wilkes." *The British Museum Quarterly* 24, no. 3–4 (1961): 100–107.

Thomas, Peter D. G. *John Wilkes: A Friend to Liberty.* Oxford: Clarendon, 1996.

Uglow, Jenny. *The Lunar Men: Five Friends Whose Curiosity Changed the World.* New York: Farrar, Straus and Giroux, 2002.

Vickers, Brian, ed. *Shakespeare: The Critical Heritage.* 6 vols. London: Routledge, 1974.

Victor, Benjamin. *The History of the Theatres of London from the Year 1760 to the Present Times.* London, 1771.

Voltaire. "On Tragedy." In *Philosophical Letters: Or, Letters Regarding the English Nation,* ed. John Leigh, trans. Prudence L. Steiner. Indianapolis: Hackett, 2007.

Walpole, Horace. *Memoirs of the Reign of King George the Third.* 4 vols. London: 1845.

———. *The Letters of Horace Walpole, Fourth Earl of Oxford.* Edited by Paget Toynbee. 16 vols. Oxford: Clarendon, 1904.

Walsh, Marcus. "Editing and Publishing Shakespeare." In *Shakespeare in the Eighteenth Century,* ed. Fiona Ritchie and Peter Sabor, 21–40. Cambridge: Cambridge University Press, 2012.

Watson, Nicola J. *The Literary Tourist.* Basingstoke, Eng.: Palgrave, 2006.

———. "Shakespeare on the Tourist Trail." In *Shakespeare and Popular Culture,* ed. Robert Shaughnessy, 199–226. Cambridge: Cambridge University Press, 2007.

Webster, Mary. *Johan Zoffany, 1733–1810.* New Haven: Yale University Press, 2012.

Wesley, John. *The Journal of the Rev. John Wesley.* 4 vols. London, 1827.

Wheler, Robert Bell. *A Guide to Stratford upon Avon.* Stratford-upon-Avon, 1814.

———. *History and Antiquities of Stratford-upon-Avon.* London, [1806].

White, Jerry. *A Great and Monstrous Thing: London in the Eighteenth Century.* Cambridge, Mass.: Harvard University Press, 2013.

Whitehead, William. *Poems on Several Occasions, with the Roman Father, a Tragedy.* London, 1754.

Wilkes, John, et al. *The North Briton From No. I. to No. Xlvi. Inclusive.* 3 vols. London, 1763.

Williams, David. *A letter to David Garrick, Esq. On His Conduct as Principal Manager and Actor at Drury-Lane.* London, 1778.

Williems, Michèle. "Voltaire." In *Voltaire, Goethe, Schlegel, Coleridge,* ed. Roger Paulin, 5-43. Vol. 3 of *Great Shakespeareans.* London: Continuum, 2010.

Woo, Celestine. *Romantic Actors and Bardolatry: Performing Shakespeare from Garrick to Kean.* New York: Peter Lang, 2008.

Young, Edward. *Conjectures on Original Composition in a Letter to the Author of Sir Charles Grandison.* London, 1759.

Zaretsky, Robert. *Boswell's Enlightenment.* Cambridge, Mass.: Harvard University Press, 2015.

Index

Page numbers in *italics* indicate figures.